ARNOLD GESELL—THEMES OF HIS WORK

Dr. Arnold Gesell (1880–1961)

ARNOLD GESELL—THEMES OF HIS WORK

Louise Bates Ames, Ph.D.
Gesell Institute of Human Development
New Haven, Connecticut

 **HUMAN SCIENCES PRESS, INC.**

Copyright © 1989 by Human Sciences Press, Inc.
A Subsidiary of Plenum Publishing Corporation
233 Spring Street, New York, N.Y. 10013

Printed in the United States of America

Library of Congress Cataloging in Publication Data

Ames, Louise Bates.
    Arnold Gesell: themes of his work / by Louise Bates Ames.
        p.   cm.
    Bibliography: p.
    ISBN 0-089885-421-0
    1. Child psychology.   2. Gesell, Arnold, 1880–1961.   I. Title.
    BF721.A578   1988   87-33416
    155.4′092′4—dc19   CIP

CONTENTS

INTRODUCTION

Dr. Arnold Gesell's professional life was characterized by several factors which made him, at the peak of his career, possibly the best known child specialist in the world. The first of these was his prodigious productivity. By the time of his death his bibliography numbered over 400 items, including over 20 major books, many translated into numerous foreign languages.

A second factor that made his work outstanding was the unusual variety of his scientific interests and the number of fields of behavior to which he not only contributed, but outstandingly.

A third factor responsible for the strong influence he had on his chosen area of science was that not only did he begin his career at a relatively early age, but many of his outstanding themes first expressed themselves very early. Thus of the 21 themes chosen as worthy of being included in this summary of his life's work, five first appeared in print as early as 1912, very shortly after he began his career at Yale, and 14 more were first mentioned before 1930.

A fourth factor that contributed to his rather remarkable success was, added to his total dedication to his work, the steadfastness with which he maintained his philosophical position in the face of often very strong criticism, Dr. Gesell was in no way a politician, nor was his work in any way influenced by a wish to be popular with colleagues or public policy. He was remarkably unswayed by arguments

of those who disagreed with him, or by the winds of change that
swept psychology during his lifetime. With single minded persis-
tence he pursued his course in the face of Watsonian behaviorism
and the arguments of the many other schools of environmentalism,
and of the entire psychoanalytic movement.

An early start, wide interests, unbelievably hard work, a supportive academic setting in which to work—all these were important
factors. The times were not always favorable—the 1940s were not
particularly friendly to a maturational point of view. Also, the entire
Freudian movement, which all too often blamed parents for such
childhood problems as autism or schizophrenia (or even left-hand-
edness) cast a dark cloud over the efforts of those who, like Dr.
Gesell, insisted that, to a very large extent, behavior was a function
of structure and that in major respects the answer to child behavior
problems lay in the organism.

But in one major respect the historical setting in which he worked
was highly favorable. The entire field of child behavior was in its
infancy at the time he began his studies. It is obviously easier to be a
pioneer in a new field. Dr. Gesell, in my opinion, would have made a
major contribution at any time in history. That his work was pioneering in both concept and methodology, and lay in a largely uncharted area, made it all the more outstanding.

Though in many circles, not only with professional people but
especially with parents, Dr. Gesell's work was vastly admired and
respected, he had many critics. The field of human behavior seems
to be especially sensitive. One of the many and lasting divisions of
opinion in this field has to do with the relative contributions of
heredity and environment. In the 1930s and 1940s this disagreement
divided individual investigators and groups of investigators into
armed camps. Questions as specific as "What percentage does heredity contribute to human behavior and what percentage is contributed by the environment?" were asked. Also, the more claims made
by environmentalists, the more the hereditarians dug in their heels.
This sometimes pushed each group to extremes.

Though in the late 1980s we like to believe that we are being
more realistic and less emotional in our approach to the problem,
probably most investigators, parents, and educators do tend to be
more sympathetic to one of these factors than to the other, more (or
less) convinced that what one *does* to or with a child substantially
changes his behavior.

At any rate, probably the major criticism of Dr. Gesell's work was that he did not pay enough attention to the environment. This criticism, like the second major objection, that he thought all children were alike and did not pay enough attention to individual differences, suggests a lack of familiarity with his writings.

The Gesell position—though not all of his publications emphasize it—was, as Chapter 18 on Heredity and Environment points out, that environmental factors modulate and inflect, but do not *determine* the progressions of development. Also that, as he put it, since *interaction* is the crux of the matter, too much emphasis should not be put on *either* extreme.

As to the similarity of one child to another, as discussed in Chapter 8 on Individuality, though Dr. Gesell believed that nearly all children develop through more or less identical stages, each does so at his own pace and in his own way. As he so consistently put it, "Infants are individuals."

Thus, though certainly any scientist will attract followers and others who are helped or impressed by what he or she has to say, and others who object, it seems quite possible that many took exception to Dr. Gesell's writings as a result of misunderstanding rather than validly disagreeing with his position.

Certainly, for example, those who have said, "We don't go along with Dr. Gesell, we follow Piaget because Piaget 'believes' in interaction and Dr. Gesell doesn't," cannot have been aware that both Gesell and Piaget "believed" that behavior develops through patterned and largely predictable stages, but that all behavior results from an interaction of environmental and hereditary forces.

Though it is not practical to attempt to reproduce the thousands of pages written by Dr. Gesell during his professional lifetime, the present volume attempts to offer to readers the main themes of his writings and interests. We present here the 20 or so chief areas which he researched and wrote about, tracing each from the time when it was first introduced to its completion. Thus readers will no longer need to rely on hearsay or on evaluations by others, but can judge and evaluate for themselves his contributions and his attitudes toward vital issues in the general field of developing human behavior.

Of these areas of interest the one that probably most influences people today is the very first—School Readiness. Dr. Gesell's interest in education was solid. Before coming to Yale he taught school at Stevens Point, Wisconsin, served as the principal at Chippewa Falls, Wisconsin, then taught at the Los Angeles State Normal School. In

1915 the Connecticut State Board of Education appointed him to be the first "school psychologist" in the United States.

Shortly thereafter, in 1919, he first suggested that the amount of school failure in this country could be vastly reduced if children were started in school on the basis of their developmental level, or behavior readiness, rather than their age in years. This concept is now at the basis of current work, by Gesell staff, in schools throughout the nation. We now train annually several thousand individuals —teachers, administrators, psychologists—in the implementation of this concept.

Throughout the years, however, the work for which Dr. Gesell has been most universally known is his norms of development, covering behavior from 4 weeks through 6 years of age. He not only introduced the concept that human behavior develops in a patterned way and that such norms thus are feasible, but provided the norms themselves. These were first published in 1925, and have gone through a series of revisions. They have provided not only the basis for much of Gesell's later work but also the basis for many other scales of behavior, such as the Denver Developmental Scale, which is almost identical, item for item, with the Gesell Developmental from which it was derived.

A third major area of Dr. Gesell's interest, and one which in actual practice has by no means come to full fruition, was his substantial effort to encourage pediatricians to understand and respect maturity, or immaturity, of behavior. His slogan was that "Development as well as disease lies in the province of clinical pediatrics." Though development is now taught in some medical schools, real respect for maturity (or immaturity) of behavior is still sadly lacking in the offices of many practicing pediatricians.

One group of studies for which Dr. Gesell and his staff were very well-known was the work with identical twins. Contributing strongly to his theoretical position that even vigorous efforts on the part of the environment can speed up behavior only very minimally, his studies with twins used one of a pair of identical twins as a control, and made substantial efforts to *train* the other twin in such behaviors as stair climbing, block building, and language. All studies in the series demonstrated that even when one twin had been successfully trained in a behavior, *added age alone* very shortly brought the untrained twin up to a level of performance equal to that of the one who had received training. His conclusion was that though outside intervention can in some instances temporarily speed up or improve some behaviors, it has no substantial or lasting results.

Another of Dr. Gesell's substantial contributions which began early and lasted late, was his use of films to record and investigate the intricacies of infant and child behavior. At the time of his retirement from Yale, the Yale Films of Child Development were in all likelihood the largest collection of child behavior films in the world.

Though he was at all times respectful of individual differences among infants and children—his way of phrasing it was "Infants are individuals"—Dr. Gesell did not develop a systematic method of evaluating individuality. With colleagues, however, he did develop one of his outstanding and best-known contributions in the field of individuality. That is, he proposed that not only is each human being an individual, but that each *age* has its own individuality, and that ages of inwardized behavior alternated with those of outwardized behavior, ages of equilibrium with ages of disequilibrium.

His position had always been that it was the responsibility of the child development specialist to inform parents as well as scientists, and of all his publications probably the best known, most widely distributed, and most often translated was his so-called *Trilogy: Infant and Child in the Culture of Today, The Child From Five to Ten,* and *Youth: The Years from Ten to Sixteen.*

This summary by no means includes all of Dr. Gesell's important contributions, but in our estimation it covers those which were most important to him.

Chapter 1

DR. GESELL AND SCHOOL READINESS

Dr. Gesell's earliest substantial comments about school readiness and proper school placement appeared in 1919, as follows:

> If there is indeed such a thing as human engineering, nothing could be more unscientific than the unceremonious, indiscriminating, wholesale method with which we admit children into our greatest social institution, the public school. (1, p. 64).
>
> I will outline certain possibilities which seem to me workable if we really believe that mental hygiene should be introduced into the public schools . . . I suggest a psycho-physical entrance examination of every school beginner. This examination should be comprehensive, thorough-going and in close cooperation with parent or guardian.[1] (p. 5)

Though we now speak of "developmental examination" instead of "psycho-physical examination," this statement represents current Gesell Institute thinking. It is thus perhaps a little surprising to note that both of these statements were written by Dr. Arnold Gesell in 1919.

Two years later, in 1921, he had this to say:

> No feature of public school administration is apparently under less control than that of school entrance. There are laws

13

which state the age when compulsory education shall begin and often a statute which requires vaccination, but beyond these there are few regulations except as to attendance and promotion.

The excessive repetition in Grade I (about one out of four first-graders fails of promotion) is itself a sad commentary. We virtually place a premium upon failure by insisting so speedily on academic standards of promotion. In other words, we annually recruit three millions of school children into our great educational camp without meeting the hygienic responsibilities and opportunities involved.

The whole matter of school entrance is in the last analysis one of hygiene. It should be conditioned primarily by standards of health and development; it should be regulated by a policy of medical oversight and educational observation.

Instead of unceremoniously and haphazardly admitting three million of children and failing one-fourth of our first-graders at the end of the first year, we should gradually reorganize the kindergarten and the primary school in such a way that the school beginner will be under systematic, purposeful observation. This means a gradual relaxation of our present zeal to "teach" him the three Rs, and the substitution of a much more wholesome solicitude, namely one to safeguard his health and to understand his psychology[2] (p. 563).

In 1923, Dr. Gesell recommended that at the beginning of school:

> . . . there should be an induction period, with a system of record-keeping and *classification of pupils to determine their immediate educational treatment in the grades. . . . Let us permit full emphasis on the basic developmental needs of the child, rather than on reading, spelling and arithmetic.*
>
> All that has been said in regard to examination and supervision of physical development applies with equal force to mental development. It is important to discover the individual differences and the psychological excellencies and weaknesses of the school entrant.
>
> Through careful observation of each individual child we can discover the superior, the balanced, the inadequate, the unstable, the infantile, and all the exceptional children who need a specialized educational hygiene and a readjustment of procedure as to school entrance.
>
> From the standpoint of school entrance it is both desirable and practical that we should have in our possession a brief,

cumulative biographic record which will summarize the child's previous development. . . . Hygiene and education cannot do their best for the child unless his developmental history is known. The further back we push this observation the better.

We must take into account the developmental maturity of the children, a factor which is at present so much ignored that approximately one pupil out of every four fails of promotion at the end of the first year.[3] (pp. 70, 74, 77, 81)

Gesell continues, in 1924:

> School entrance constitutes our permanent recruiting problem. Every year we draft some 3,000,000 young children into our vast public-school army. We do it rather unceremoniously and haphazardly.
>
> Although our great system of popular education is a splendid achievement which accomplishes untold good to the greatest number, *it must be confessed that the administration of school entrance is still extremely faulty. More unresolved problems of mental and educational hygiene are heaped up at the threshold of our public school system than elsewhere.*
>
> Fundamentally this situation grows out of the fact that we have been slow in appreciating the medical and developmental significance of the early years of childhood.[4] (p. 6)

Actually several comments *before* 1919 (the year when Gesell made first mention of the importance of giving "a psycho-physical entrance examination to every school beginner"), though they did not mention *school entrance* specifically, imply that he was, as early as 1912, concerned with the matter of school readiness.

Thus he makes the comment:

> The primary teacher is not allowed to determine whether the 6-year-old child is ready to master the technicalities of the printed page. She is instructed to proceed with the course of study without discussion of its merits, and her problem is solely one of method. . . . The difficulties of mastering the printed page are so great as any ever offered by the elementary school and yet we complacently present them to the child of six.[5] (p. 194)

On a later page of the same volume he adds:

> It is time to have a reckoning, to realize before it is too late
> the futility of pushing nature.[5] (p. 308)

And in the following year, 1913, he emphasized the problem of overplacement. In discussing the "typical" first grade he notes that it is a "motley assembly," and adds:

> There are frequently a few children still in the baby stages
> . . . who should for sound hygienic reasons be detained in the
> kindergarten. . . . It will be the task of the child hygienist, with
> the assistance of the primary teacher, to pass opinion as to
> whether a child shall be detained, and, further, as to what kind
> of treatment he may specially need in his subsequent school
> career.[6] (p. 3)

In view of this early and rather specifically expressed interest in the dangers of overplacement and the importance of evaluating readiness (or nonreadiness) for school entrance, it is rather interesting to note that Gesell appears to have dropped this subject entirely, at least from his writings, after 1924. (This in contrast to his continuing interest in such a subject as twinning, a topic to which he returned again and again in the years 1922 to 1952, there being 12 articles, three book reviews, and two films on twins in his bibliography.)

It is even more surprising that when the whole matter of school readiness was taken up vigorously by other members of his staff (Drs. Ilg and Ames, whose first publication on the subject, *School Readiness* (7) appeared in 1964), neither Gesell, Ilg, nor Ames seemed aware of the fact of his earlier interest in the subject, which by 1980 was involving much of the time and effort of nearly the entire staff of the Developmental Department of the Gesell Institute.

Chapter 2

DR. GESELL'S LIFETIME INTEREST
IN DEFECT AND DEVIATION

Dr. Gesell's contributions to the field of retardation, mental defects, and handicaps in general was, in the early decades of this century, rather tremendous, though it seems quite likely that many working in this field today may be unaware of this fact.

Problems of mental defects and handicaps were for him an early and very strong concern. He was firmly intent on bringing these problems to the attention of both the public and the profession and, more than that, he was concerned that something be done about them.

Twenty-three of the 64 publications which he authored between 1913 and 1926 dealt with these topics. After 1926 he published 17 more such articles, though after 1926 many dealt more specifically with such problems as mongolianism, cretinism, and cerebral palsy, and less with retardation in general. (In addition to topics covered in the present survey are further studies on both blindness and deafness.)

Dr. Gesell's major thesis was that it is the responsibility of the public to help with the care and education of those with less than normal endowment. His concern about the welfare of handicapped children involved considerably more than his frequent publications. He lectured; he gave courses; he served on commissions. His was a genuine concern to increase public interest in these problems and to encourage official provisions for classes for the exceptional child and for supervised work opportunities for them once they had finished school.

According to Dr. Walter Miles, in his *Bibliographical Memoir* of Dr. Gesell:

> In 1918 Dr. Gesell undertook a mental survey of the elementary schools of the city of New Haven and, having brought this to a conclusion, wrote a report entitled *Exceptional Children and Pulic School Policy*, which was published in 1921 by the Yale University Press. No doubt this had much to do with the development of an excellent system of special classes in New Haven which had been placed under the direction of Dr. Norma Cutts. Dr. Gesell had already prepared a manual entitled *What Can the Teacher Do for the Deficient Child?* The Governor of Connecticut in 1919 set up a Commission on Child Welfare. Dr. Gesell was a member of this group and prepared portions of a two-volume report dealing with the status of handicapped children and advancing formulations for legislative consideration. This weighty report was influential in creating sentiment for the subsequent formation of a Division for Exceptional Children under the Connecticut Board of Education. These community and state activities in which Dr. Gesell participated as a leader, and which required a great deal of time and effort, exemplify his devotion to human welfare.[1] (pp. 63–64)

We may also assume that it was at least in part due to his efforts that in 1921 Connecticut passed a law empowering the State Board of Education to make regulations requiring enumeration and reporting of all educationally exceptional children.

Actually, Dr. Gesell's first mention of defect and retardation appeared in 1913[2] in an article titled "The Village of a Thousand Souls." Here he reported the results of a survey made by him of all 200 families which included "one thousand souls." His observations covered a period of 33 years, and included members of three generations.

Feeblemindedness was found in 37 of the 220 families, some including one, two, three, or even four individuals. This was equal to 16 percent of the entire population. Dr. Gesell stressed the probable hereditary basis of much of this retardation and also noted that in a village situation many can survive more comfortably than would be possible in the more demanding life of a city.

A second 1913 article,[3] "The University in Relation to the Problems of Mental Deficiency and Child Hygiene," is missing from our files, but in 1918, as School Psychologist for the State Board of Education, he produced a substantial manual for teachers titled, *What Can the Teachers do for the Deficient Child?* In this he makes the point that "a special class, small in numbers, with a special teacher, and a special program and equipment all adapted to laggard minds, is the ideal arrangement for subnormal children, since we cannot expect too much of the regular teacher"[4] (p. 5).

However, "Since we do not have the legal machinery or the public opinion to make it all practical to exclude all mentally deficient children from the public school"[4] (p. 5), this booklet was written "to help the regular teacher meet her responsibilities to these children."

This book contains, in addition to a lucid discussion of the causes and problems of retardation, an entire section of "Practical Suggestions for a Special Program for the Deficient Child."

A second 1918 publication[5] reports the number of feeble-minded children in the Country Home Schools of Connecticut. Its recommendation was that since defective children need special educational consideration, intelligence tests of all dependent children should be carried out in order to make the best possible plans for them.

The year 1919 was marked by three publications and an increasing interest in the topic of mental defect. "A Follow-Up Study of One Hundred Mentally Deficient School Children"[6] was authored by Arnold Gesell, who identified himself as School Psychologist. The encouraging part of this report is that 34 of these individuals were reported as "working," as in a factory or on a farm. As Dr. Gesell notes, "These figures confirm the impression that many high-grade feeble-minded pupils succeed after a fashion on leaving school. Sometimes no doubt their vocational success is much more marked than their school success."

A second 1919 publication,[7] also undertaken by Dr. Gesell in his role of school psychologist, was a survey of "mental conditions" in the rural and city schools of Connecticut and was published under the title *Special Provisions for Exceptional School Children: A Guidebook on the Public School Care of Mentally Deficient and Otherwise Exceptional Pupils, with Special Reference to Conditions and Possibilities in Connecticut.* The aim of this handbook was "to further a complete system of care and registration of feebleminded children in our state."

This study reports 134 special classes for exceptional children in the state, though 32 of 50 communities surveyed had no special class provisions. This report discusses at length the organization of a special class, equipment needed, qualifications of the teacher, its program and functions. It is to be noted that one of the collaborators on this publication was Dr. Norma Cutts, who from then on was frequently involved in Dr. Gesell's work with the retarded.

A third publication in this same year is the *Announcement of a One Month Course for the Training of Teachers of Backward and Deficient Children*,[8] this course to be given from April 28 to May 24, 1919. The title is self-explanatory and here again Norma Cutts is mentioned, as one of the several instructors along with Dr. Gesell.

The following year, 1920, also is marked by three further, though minor, publications. A chapter titled "Mental Diagnosis" is found in the pamphlet "Educational Congress—Albany, New York".[9] A very brief report on "The Problem of Mental Subnormality" appears in the *Bulletin of Child Welfare*.[10] The third reference to defect in this year is a review of Dr. H. H. Goddard's book *Psychology of the Normal and Subnormal*. The review appeared in the *Psychological Bulletin* for April 1920.[11]

An extremely prolific year was 1921, so far as writing about the topic of mental defects was concerned. "Vocational Probation for Subnormal Youth"[12] proposes that:

> Just as the special class has proved that by a differential type of treatment it is possible to maintain defectives in a public school, so it is now clear that by a similar approach we can solve the problem of community control of wage-earning defectives.[12] (p. 320)

Gesell elaborates:

> Not many years ago institutional segregation was regarded as *the* solution for the problem of feeblemindedness. In discussions of the subject it was gratuitously assumed that a feebleminded person is one who really ought to be in an institution. We are gradually coming to a more reasonable and a more humane point of view. The excessive expense of wholesale segregation has had a deterrent effect; so has the potential economic value of the high-grade defective. The instinctive affection of the brothers, sisters, and parents of the feebleminded has also resisted undue institutional segregation.

> Accumulating evidence that the Moron, and even the high-
> grade imbecile, do not completely fail in ordinary life under
> favorable conditions has suggested the possibility of creating
> these conditions outside of institutions.[12] (p. 321)

He proposes a court-supervised "vocational probation" which
would allow defective individuals, once out of school, to work at
simple tasks under supervision. As he put it:

> We appreciate that all of these requirements cannot be sud-
> denly created even by an enlarged system of juvenile probation.
> We believe, however, that it is sound policy to unite the func-
> tions of moral and vocational probation and to coordinate them
> with the school system on the one hand and a juvenile court on
> the other.[12] (p. 326)

"Public School Provision for Exceptional Children," a chapter in
The Annals of the American Academy of Political and Social Science for
November, 1921[13] elaborates his basic thesis that although a generation earlier the exceptional child was not considered to be a legitimate public-school problem, society is gradually taking over responsibility for the teaching of boys and girls with special problems. In
this chapter he discusses the various kinds of special children who
exist, and ways they can be helped and best served by the public
schools either in regular or special classes.

*Exceptional Children and Public School Policy, Including a Mental
Survey of the New Haven Elementary Schools* updates and elaborates Dr.
Gesell's earlier 1921 publication on the subject. As he comments:

> This brief volume is based on a study of actual conditions. It
> aims not only to report the facts, but to give them a general
> interpretation from the standpoint of public policy.[14] (p. 5)

This paper, as Dr. Gesell notes, was read as part of a symposium
on mental hygiene and education at the annual meeting of the
Massachusetts Society for Mental Hygiene in Boston, January 16,
1919. It reports the results of a survey of some 24,000 New Haven
elementary school children. As had become the custom, those children with superior endowment as well as those who were defective
are included in the category "exceptional."

It was generally believed that this report had much to do with
the development of a fine system of special classes in New Haven, a
system under the supervision of Norma Cutts.

A further example of Dr. Gesell's public activity in behalf of the handicapped is another 1921 publication, "Report of the Commission on Child Welfare to the Governor: Handicapped Children in School and Court by Dr. Arnold Gesell, Chairman of the Commission."[15] This report, according to the author:

> . . . sketches in brief outline a state-wide system of welfare for defective and handicapped children, which will bring into articulation and co-operation existing institutions, a group of children's courts, and the elementary schools.

Also in 1921 appears the first of a number of special studies which, instead of discussing retardation and defect in general, consider a special type of handicap. "Hemihypertrophy and Mental Defect"[16] emphasizes the fact that anomalies of anatomical development and mental defect are often found in close association. It gives detailed information about the behavior of a single hemihypertrophic subject who is feebleminded. It also provides a comprehensive tabulation of all known cases to date, showing a total of 40 cases recorded in medical literature.

Combining his concern for preschoolers with his concern for the handicapped, Dr. Gesell contributed an article titled "The Preschool Hygiene of Handicapped Children" to the September 1922 issue of *The Pedagogical Seminary*. In this paper he discusses the significance of the pre-school years for each of the eight major classes of handicap found among young children: blindness, deafness, crippling, other physical defects, mental abnormality, delinquency, special defect, and mental defect.

He suggests that:

> A consecutive health and development supervision of preschool children, the hygienic regulation of school entrance, and a special adaptation of nursery and kindergarten methods in behalf of exceptional children, educational social workers in the field of infant welfare and special mobile teachers for home visitation and home training—these are some of the possibilities which a public mental hygiene of the future may have in store.[17] (p. 246)

A single title in 1923, "Feeblemindedness—State Policy of Control," proposes that:

> The feebleminded present a complex but practical problem. The ground-work for control has been laid by pre-vocational training in the public schools. Auxiliary centers for specific training, followed by placement and supervision can gradually be developed as part of a state system of control. We cannot at a stroke wipe out feeblemindedness, but we can cope with it, and defeat its most harmful manifestation.[18] (p. 1)

He points out, rather quaintly, that even a girl with a mental age of six years can earn as much as nine dollars a week in a factory under special, adapted conditions. He notes that, according to available figures, there are well over 3,000 juvenile mental defectives in Connecticut.

Another year of marked concern on the part of Dr. Gesell for these general problems is 1925, with five publications—one a major book—which discuss retardation. "The Exceptional Child"[19] is just a talk piece and does not add greatly to what has already been said. Other writings that year are more substantial.

"The Early Diagnosis of Mental Deficiency" stresses the point so often emphasized by Dr. Gesell in the years to come that mental defect can and should be identified in infancy or certainly in the preschool years. As he points out, "The pediatrist ought to be in a position to discover the condition long before the school physician reports it."[20] (p. 194)

In "Developmental Diagnosis in Infancy," describing his methods of developmental diagnosis in general, Dr. Gesell makes the point that:

> The most obvious field of application for the normative data and diagnostic procedures above outlined lies in the early recognition of mental deficiency. Although nearly all cases of mental deficiency are still beyond medical relief, we must go on the assumption that early diagnosis will lead at least to better educational management. Even in the field of mental defect and deficiency we must place a medical premium upon early diagnosis.[21] (p. 5)

Next, also in 1925, comes a major contribution, a book entitled *The Retarded Child and How to Help Him.*[22] This is a revision and update of his earlier manual.[4] Its four comprehensive chapters cover the topics: "The Nature and Signs of Mental Deficiency,"

"Illustrative Cases of Exceptional Children," "How to Make a Special Program for the Defective Pupil," and "Where Teacher and Pupil Can Get Further Help."

In the same year Dr. Gesell devoted one chapter of his *Mental Growth of the Preschool Child*[23] to the topic of "Retardation and Inferiority." Among the points especially emphasized in this chapter, which is amply illustrated with photographs of retarded infants responding to our Gesell infant examination situations, is the fact that when a retarded child is given a series of examinations over a period of time there is considerable consistency in the ratio between the chronological age and developmental status ascertained at each examination.

This series of articles, supplemented with an occasional book, especially those which clustered in the years 1918–1925, constituted Dr. Gesell's rather massive attack on the problems of retardation and what might be done by schools, government, and professional people to face the problem and to help children so affected. (It is interesting to note that his strong emphasis on the setting up of special classes for the retarded is in sharp contrast to the current notion that retarded children should *not* be serviced in special classes but should be mainstreamed.)

After 1925, though general discussion of problems of retardation and what psychologist and physician might do about them continued (as will be indicated below) much of his writing about handicap was made up of discussion of specific kinds of handicap.

A special and somewhat unusual kind of handicap or deviation from the normal about which Dr. Gesell wrote fairly frequently was puberty praecox. That his interest in the topic was genuine is suggested by the fact that at least six of the items in his bibliography (references 24 to 29) all dealt with this subject. Actually most of these references deal chiefly with a single subject, a girl who, most unusually, first menstruated at the age of 3 years and 7 months.

The chief question which he raised was—is "mental" and other behavior accelerated along with accelerated puberty? Some, like Margaret Mead (in personal conversation) have maintained that it might be more effective to relate behavior and behavior age to the time of menstruation rather than to chronological age. That is, she would expect a ten-year-old who was already menstruating to behave more like a twelve or thirteen-year-old than like other ten-year-olds.

That this does not seem to work out in cases of precocious

puberty does not necessarily mean that Dr. Mead was wrong. She may, indeed, have been correct. However, on the basis of Dr. Gesell's data (which admittedly were limited), her hypothesis does not seem to hold.

Dr. Gesell's first publication on puberty praecox was a 28-page monograph on the subject titled "The Influence of Puberty Praecox upon Mental Growth," in 1926. Here for the first time he asked the question—does precocious sexual maturation have a demonstrable effect upon the course of mental growth? His conclusion based on two of his own cases was that:

> Though there may be an unusual increment in the sphere of social development, there is no corresponding increment in the sphere of general mental ability. Any changes concern personality as contrasted with intellectual factors.[24] (p. 536)

A second (1928) publication dealing with the same two cases reaches the same conclusion, and elaborates slightly:

> So far as we may generalize from two cases, we can conclude that precocious displacement of pubescence does not carry with it a coordinate deviation in the cycle of mental growth. Our study does not warrant the view which has been advanced that the whole period of growth may be regarded as a function of sexual development and differentiation. There is a high degree of specificity, even of independence, in the components of the growth complex. Pubescence plays its part, but not with unlimited autocracy.[25] (p. 408)

Much the same information is again presented in the *Journal of the American Medical Association* for the same year, and need not be repeated here.[26] The following year, 1939, in collaboration with three colleagues, Dr. Gesell reviews the literature on the subject and provides extremely detailed descriptions of the physical growth, menstrual history, and psychological development of the same girl featured in earlier papers. These authors conclude as earlier that:

> The stability of the mental development is interpreted as denoting a preferential immunity of the central nervous system to certain forms of endocrine imbalance. The developmental distortion of the precocious pubescence was most conspicuous in the skeletal system. Cranial development, however, followed an

average course. Growth is regulated by specific determiners. The evidence afforded by pubertas praecox indicates that there is no single pervasively controlled sex factor.[27] (p. 772)

Eleven pages on the subject in his 1939 book, *Biographies of Child Development*[28] do not add substantially to what has already been said. His final reference to the matter, and to this particular girl, appears 2 years later in 1941, in *Deveopmental Diagnosis*[29] and provides a succinct summary to this individual's life history.

> CASE 1 is an example of pubertas praecox, a remarkable endocrine disorder manifested in precocious development of sexual maturity. In over three-fourths of the reported cases menstruation began before the age of 5 years, as early as birth in 11 per cent of cases. In this instance, menstruation appeared at 3 years and 7 months. At that age the child's height was only slightly above the average for her age but she had the bodily conformation of an adult woman and all the secondary sex characters were well developed. She died at 18 years following removal of a cerebellar astrocytoma. This tumor probably was the etiological factor at the basis of the endocrine disturbance.
>
> Developmental measurements made at regular intervals between 5 and 18 years showed a striking approximation to an average course of mental growth. The emotional life and personality manifestations were in no way unusual. The stability of mental development in the face of the enormous dislocation in sexual development demonstrates the extraordinary immunity of the central nervous system to certain forms of endocrine imbalance.[29] (p. 163)

Clearly, a maximum of theorizing was developed in this instance largely from a single, even though unusual, case history. As to other special types of abnormal behavior, we find two titles having to do with hemihypertrophy. The first, already mentioned, is "Hemihypertrophy and Mental Defect," published in 1921,[16] describes in detail a single case of a mentally defective hemihypertrophied subject and also tabulates and summarizes the 40 cases recorded to that date. The second title, appearing in 1927, "Hemihypertrophy and Twinning: A Further Study of the Nature of Hemihypertrophy with Report of a New Case"[30] is self-explanatory.

Dr. Gesell's very special interest in both mongolianism and cretinism is expressed in the following three publications, all appearing in 1936: "Clinical Mongolism in Colored Races with Report of a Case of Negro Mongolism;"[31] "A Comparative Study of Six Infant Cretins under Treatment: Influence of Thyroid on Mental Growth;"[32] and "Effect of Thyroid Therapy on the Mental and Physical Growth of Cretinous Infants."[33]

The next year, 1937, saw publication of a series of articles on a subject which had become of increasing interest to Dr. Gesell—cerebral palsy. The following titles are pretty much self-explanatory: "Motor Disability and Mental Growth: The Psychological Effects of Cerebral Palsy;"[34] "Correlations of Behavior and Neuropathology in a Case of Cerebral Palsy from Birth Injury;"[35] and "A Behavior Study of Birth Injury: A Correlation of Psychological and Neuropathological Findings in a Case of Cerebral Palsy with Double Athetosis."[36] Dr. Gesell returns to this topic in three later papers: "Developmental Diagnosis and Guidance for the Palsied Child" in 1948;[37] "Cerebral Palsy Research and the Preschool Years" in 1949;[38] and "Foreword to Proceedings of the Annual Meeting of the American Academy for Cerebral Palsy" in 1954.[39]

In addition to these special papers, many of them research reports, Dr. Gesell continued his general interest in the diagnosis and management of retardation and other handicapping conditions throughout his professional life. In 1936 he contributed a chapter on "Developmental Diagnosis and Supervision" to *Brenneman's Practice of Pediatrics*.[40] In this chapter he addressed practicing pediatricians as to the methods of developmental assessment of behavior levels of infants and children, and gave special advice as to how adverse diagnoses should be given to parents.

Two major book publications written in collaboration with colleagues discuss deviations of development in two different ways. *Biographies of Child Development: The Mental Growth Careers of Eighty-four Infants and Children*[28] is a rather striking but little-known book. It demonstrates the consistency of behavior ratings of both normal and abnormal children as they are examined repeatedly over a period of years.

A second and widely used book, written in collaboration with Dr. Catherine Amatruda and first published in 1941, was titled *Developmental Diagnosis: A Manual of Clinical Methods and Applications Designed for the Use of Students and Practitioners of Medicine*.[29] This presents in great detail Gesell methods of developmental testing, behavior norms, and a full discussion of such abnormal conditions as mental subnormality, neuromotor dysfunction, minimal brain dysfunction, convulsive seizure disorders, autism, and infant psychosis.

This book has been repeatedly revised. The most recent revi-

sion was edited by two of Dr. Gesell's former students, Drs. Hilda
Knobloch and Benjamin Pasamanick.[41] An abbreviated version of
the book appeared in 1980 under the title *Manual of Developmental
Diagnosis* by Knobloch and others.[42]

One final book publication on the subject of handicap consisted
of an introduction to *Management of the Handicapped Child* by Michael
Smith, which appeared in 1957.[43]

With the exception of these several books, and of course incidental mention of the problems of defect and deviation which occurred in many of his writings, Dr. Gesell's contributions in this field
from 1939 on consisted primarily of a series of four articles, as
follows: "Early Diagnosis of Behavior Defect and Deviation" in
1939,[44] and "The Differential Diagnosis of Mental Deficiency in
Infancy" in 1943.[45] In 1947 a further article bore the same title,
with slightly different content.[46] Finally came "The Clinical Supervision of Child Development: Differential Diagnosis of Defect"[47] in
1957.

This last paper was apparently first presented as a lecture, since
the author speaks of "An audience of general practitioners and
pediatricians." As in earlier publications, he reviews the methods of
developmental diagnosis and then discusses such specific problems
as amentia, prematurity, pseudo-symptomatic retardation, sensory
defects, and cerebral palsy.

In summary, then, Dr. Gesell's main contributions to the field of
retardation and handicap in general may be said to fall into three
categories. In the early years, especially between 1913 and 1925, he
was concerned primarily with calling attention to these problems
and to encouraging schools and society in general to take responsibility for the education and vocational training of individuals with
less than normal endowment. He especially emphasized the importance of identifying and dealing with these problems in earliest
childhood.

Second, and this from the mid-1930s to the mid-1950s, he was
concerned not so much with retardation and abnormality in general
as with the special problems of mongolianism, cretinism, and, most
especially, cerebral palsy. His work here was less general than that
in the earlier part of the century, consisting primarily of research
reports. However, in the field of cerebral palsy he was also very
active publicly, serving, as earlier, on numerous committees and
commissions, and through his participation in numerous White
House Conferences, attemping to influence public policy.

A third main kind of contribution started early and lasted late —in fact, pervaded his entire professional life. Possibly his outstanding contribution of the many he made in his lifetime was the establishment of a series of clinical tests which outlined and evaluated the growing stages of infant and child behavior. These norms, first mentioned in the literature in 1923 but probably initiated around 1918, were throughout his life constantly being refined and improved. Their availability made it possible to identify retardation.

One of his most popular slogans was that "Development as well as disease lies in the province of clinical pediatrics." The basic message here was that pediatricians should be more skilled than many are in recognizing slowness of development at the earliest possible age, so that parents can be made aware of problems of development as soon as possible.

Though by the 1930s, if not sooner, Dr. Gesell's chief interest had shifted from the abnormal to the normal, his concern with deviation and defect continued through his lifetime, his final publication in this field appearing in 1957.[48]

DR. GESELL'S CONTRIBUTION TO
THE FIELD OF MENTAL HYGIENE

Dr. Gesell's contributions to the (then) new field of mental hygiene in the early decades of this century were substantial. However, in reviewing these contributions, we run into a problem in that in his writings Dr. Gesell used several different terms as he referred to the well-being of the child. "Mental hygiene" usually meant mental hygiene as we currently think of it. But "mental health," "child hygiene,"* "child welfare," and "child health" sometimes referred to the child's mental or emotional, sometimes to his physical well-being, and sometimes to both.

All of these terms were favorites of his and occurred frequently in his publications, often merely in the context that we must all do what we can to further the mental well-being of every child. We report here selectively on those references which seem to us substantive, and those that discuss mental health as separate from new physical health.

Mental health (or mental hygiene) was a major concern of Dr. Gesell's in the years between 1912 and 1930. His contributions to this cause went far beyond his published works. He served vigorously and tirelessly on numerous committees and commissions, among them:

* The term "child hygiene" will be discussed briefly in the following chapter.

Professor of Child Hygiene at Yale, 1915–1948.

Member Connecticut Commission of Child Welfare, 1911–1921.

Director Connecticut Society for Mental Hygiene, 1913. (Member of the Advisory Committee 1913–.)

Member of the Executive Committee and Vice President of the Connecticut Child Welfare Association, 1918–

Director of the National Committee for Mental Hygiene, 1922–1936.

Vice President of the Association International pour la Protection de l'Enfance, 1925–

Director American Child Health Association, 1925–1940. (Vice President, 1926–1928.)

Member White House Conference on Child Health and Protection, 1930.

Aside from casual mentions, 19 of Dr. Gesell's publications in the years from 1912 through 1930 dealt primarily with the topic of mental hygiene, though in the years between 1931 and 1943 there were only 7 such publications. In his books and papers after 1943 the term appeared infrequently, if at all.

Dr. Gesell made solid contributions to the general field of mental hygiene through his work in setting up special classes for "exceptional" children—both for defective children and for those with superior endowment. Most important of all, he provided norms by which psychologists, pediatricians, and others could evaluate the behavior of any child. He also, one assumes, supported the mental health of both parents and children by helping parents understand the stages through which each child develops.

His specific writings about mental hygiene as such tended to be somewhat philosophical and "talky" as the quotations in this chapter will show; but his actual contributions in the real world were extremely practical.

His very first mention of *child health* or *child hygiene* (in 1912) seems to refer primarily to physical health; but since he used various terms somewhat interchangeably, it will be included here. In his book, *The Normal Child and Primary Education*, he comments[1] (pp. 26, 27):

The new biological temper, which is the product of modern science, exalts hygiene and makes *health* the central solicitude in all the work of education.

Eleven years ago the school superintendents of America assembled in convention in Chicago discussed the problems then foremost in educational thought and action. Diligent search through the printed report of that meeting disclosed no single mention of child health, no word about school hygiene, no address devoted to the conservation or development of the physical vigor of youth.

The new biological temper in education is normalizing and training our humanitarism. . . . Historically, *Child Hygiene*, yesterday only a phrase, but already becoming a program for action, is a phase or an outgrowth of the scientific study of the child. In July 1909 there was held at Clark University a series of conferences which in the light of the history we have sketched from prescientific times to the present, takes on considerable interest. It was a general child welfare congress.[1] (p. 27)

The first full article to deal clearly with mental hygiene, child health or child hygiene, appeared in 1919 in the third volume of the new journal, *Mental Hygiene*. A few selected excerpts from this article will serve to suggest its content and mentions:

Mental power is one of our national resources. It is a rather intangible resource. . . . I do not wish to give the term mental hygiene too sweeping a connotation, and yet in its broadest and most positive aspect, this term stands for the protection of the mental health of individuals, and the constructive conservation of the native mental power of the nation.

The development of mental hygiene, both general and specific, in the public schools depends upon a consistent program of individual attention to individual children. This program must be more biological, more inquisitive and more solicitous than anything we have at present in our half-formed systems of school and child hygiene. . . . The only thorough-going remedy for this patchiness is a biographical interest in infants and children, which will regard the total and the continuing child and be primarily concerned in the healthy norms of his behavior. *This, and nothing less than this, spells mental hygiene.*

Such a biographical interest starts with the birth certificate and continues to the diploma. The mental hygiene of the child does not begin with his entrance upon school life; it goes back to the basic determiners, physical and mental, of the nursery years. . . .

We should build up a cumulative health and development record for each child, and into this record should be read not only pounds and inches but psychological observations and measurements which have a bearing on the mental hygiene of the child, his readiness for school life, and his major developmental needs when he enters school. . .

By way of conclusion, I will outline certain possibilities which seem to me workable, if we really believe that mental hygiene should be introduced into the public schools.

These possibilities include:

1. A hygienic supervision of the preschool period.
2. A psycho-physical entrance examination of every school beginner.
3. A reorganization of the kindergarten and first grade, which will place the first half year of school life under, systematic, purposeful observation.
4. The development of a new type of school nurse, who by supervision, corrective teaching, and home visitation, will further the concrete everyday tasks of mental hygiene.
5. The development of reconstruction schools, of *special classes* and vacation camps for certain groups of children who need specialized treatment.
6. A comprehensive system of mental conservation demands also that we discover and cultivate the superior intelligence which is at the basis of leadership and distinction in all the arts and sciences of life.
7. Finally we have the great mass of children who are not candidates for distinction, nor victims of mental defect or disorder. Their mental welfare will depend, as always, on the traditional influences of home and school. For them, education and mental hygiene are synonymous. That education is most hygienic which provokes and promotes their intelligence, and which disposes them to become good citizens.[2] (pp. 4–7)

A next mention of mental hygiene occurs in a 1921 report titled "Exceptional Children and Public School Policy, Including a Mental Survey of the New Haven Elementary Schools."[3] A part of this report was read at a symposium on mental hygiene and education at the annual meeting of the Massachusetts Society for Mental Hygiene in Boston on January 16, 1919. It reports the results of a survey of some 24,000 New Haven elementary school children. It was generally believed that this report had much to do with the development of a system of special classes in New Haven.

The next mention of hygiene, also appearing in 1921, is titled "The significance of the pre-school age for school hygiene." Here again, the "hygiene" being described appears to be rather a loose combination of physical hygiene and mental hygiene. Dr. Gesell notes that "The hygienic significance of the pre-school period may be interpreted from four points of view, the biological, the medical, the educational and the administrative"[4] (p. 25). These points need not be elaborated here as they pretty much speak for themselves.

In the following year, 1922, comes a rather substantive paper from which we will quote at some length, since it provides a good exposition of Dr. Gesell's thinking on the subject at this time:

> Now in addition to purely medical attention, all these children (the mentally deficient, children with special sensory or motor defects, and the mentally abnormal) need a special educational oversight and a supervision of their mental welfare. They are entitled to a kind of mental hygiene service. Precious time is lost, injustice is done, by idly waiting for the school years and the institutional years.
>
> What are some of the features of a mental hygiene service which are at least on the horizon? Periodic mental health examinations are a discernible possibility. The diagnostic and advisory functions of welfare and health centers should be gradually extended to include the hygiene of mental development. . . . We have undertaken a program of research at the Yale University Psycho-Clinic to determine the norms of mental or behavior development in children of pre-school age, with the hope of defining methods of clinical and social procedure in the field. . . .
>
> The new nursery schools in Boston and elsewhere will no doubt develop a very useful auxiliary service for the mental hygiene of pre-school children. Both nurseries and kindergartens have an important contribution to make. . . .
>
> It appears that a mental hygiene service for pre-school children can be realized if we extend and exploit the instruments which we have already at our disposal: (a) the consultation and health center to provide a more systematic supervision of mental development; (b) conferences for the guidance of parents; (c) public health nurses, psychiatric social workers, and pre-school visiting teachers to render more direct assistance in the home; (d) adaptations of nursery establishments, kindergartens, and special classes in behalf of the more exceptional, handicapped infants; (e) an active alignment of a reconstructed kindergarten with the public health and child welfare agencies

of the community; (f) an effective type of pre-parental education dealing with the mental hygiene of child care.

These possibilities are above the horizon. They will not all be realized tomorrow, but, perhaps, some day after tomorrow the agencies and movements mentioned may be coordinated to render a hygienic service—which will seek to conserve the mental health of the young child and which will increase his mental stamina.[5] (pp. 1030–1034)

The next mention of *hygiene* is found in Dr. Gesell's 1923 book, *The Preschool Child*, as he notes that:

> Psychology is the science of behavior. The future growth of preschool hygiene, both physical and mental, will see a more deliberate use of this great science to solve the behavior problems of child development and child care.[6] (p. 19)

Most discussion in this book has to do with services which could and should be offered to the handicapped, or in relation to the physical health of the child. However, on page 201 he speaks specifically about mental hygiene:

> The principles of mental hygiene are less nebulous and fugitive than is commonly supposed. It is not impossible to develop simple procedures in connection with health-center consultations, public-health nursing, and home visitation which will disclose many instances where the mental health is endangered or where the course of mental development is subnormal. The periodic health examination should, in time, broaden into developmental examinations. . . so that parents may, from the beginning, assist the child to achieve mental as well as physical health.[6] (p. 201)

In an important book entitled *The Normal Mind* by William H. Burnham, published in 1924 (possibly next only in importance to Clifford Beers's *The Mind That Found Itself*[8]), Dr. Burnham includes Dr. Arnold Gesell among the persons to whom he is indebted in the preparation of his book. He also comments, in discussing the D. Q. (or Developmental Quotient):

> This term is used to denote the relation between the chronological age of the individual and his general development, physical and mental. . . . Especially significant and valuable are

the investigations of the general development of young children now carried on at Yale under the direction of Gesell. The results already indicate that this is a specially significant relation both for hygiene and education and that it is possible to study this relationship and, in fact, apparently the best opportunity for studying this is presented in the early months of life.[7] (p. 252)

In this same year (1924), in a paper titled "The Nursery School Movement," Dr. Gesell has a good deal to say about the attention to mental hygiene principles that should be paid in both nursery school and kindergarten:

> Likewise the pre-school age falls within the scope of mental hygiene. We no longer think of mental hygiene as confining itself to adult abnormalities and juvenile defects and delinquencies. Mental hygiene in a preventive and regulative sense concerns itself with the whole developmental span. . . .
>
> Mental hygiene, like charity, begins at home. But it does not end there. Nursery school and kindergarten alike will have an increasing part to play in developing specific forms of mental hygiene services.* . . . During the past year we have been making a study of certain mental hygiene problems as they present themselves in children of kindergarten age. The teachers of 2,700 kindergarten children were asked to report all cases which they considered in any way exceptional from an educational point of view. . . . In addition, the clinic has recently made an intensive study of twenty-five children reported from two kindergartens. On the basis of evidence from all these sources it is certain that there is an appreciable minority of kindergarten children who, for reasons of mental hygiene, require special guidance provisions. . . .
>
> In an approximate way, it is safe to say, there are at least four children out of every hundred enrolled in kindergarten who constitute mental hygiene problems and who need special educational measures. It is highly desirable that a considerable amount of preventive and ameliorative work can be accomplished by beginning early and meeting the behavior problems, the mental hygiene problems, before the child reaches elementary school.
>
> We have given special consideration to these problems concerning the mental hygiene of the pre-school child because they

---

* It should be noted that in keeping with this point of view, Dr. Gesell named his own nursery school, begun in 1918, a "Guidance Nursery School."

represent a field of work on which nursery school and kindergarten can enter upon common terms.[9] (pp. 647–649)

In a radio talk given over Station KNX at the "Mother's Hour" on July 7, 1925, Dr. Gesell makes the following rather homey and perhaps slightly trite comments:

> The body of the growing child should be our first concern, but from the beginning—from the time of birth—we must remember the child's mind which is bound up in that body. Mind and body grow together, and from the very beginning of life we must protect the health of the child's mind.
> To study the mind of the infant, you must study his actions. These actions tell you what kind of nervous system he has., These actions show his capacity, his habits, his desires, his interests.
> We have taken hundreds of action photographs to show the normal characteristics of the young child at different ages. We have also taken a motion picture record to show the swiftness and richness of this early mental growth. The mind grows faster in infancy than it ever will again. That is the main reason why the child should acquire good habits from the very start.
> Begin early and nip bad habits in the bud. That is the way to give the child a healthy mind. The slogan, 'Get your child fit for school' is a good one. His mind, too, must be made fit in the pre-school years through healthy habits of everyday life.[10] (p. 19, 26)

In his historic book, *The Mental Growth of the Pre-School Child*, also a 1925 publication, Dr. Gesell has this to say on the subject of mental hygiene:

> Developmental diagnosis is essential to the mental hygiene of infancy.[11] (p. 8)
> Never again will the child's mind, his character, his spirit, advance so rapidly as in the formative pre-school period of growth. Never again will we have an equal chance to lay the foundations of mental health. From the standpoint of mental hygiene the pre-school period, therefore, appears to have no less significance than it has for physical vigor and survival.[11] (p. 11)
> Mental hygiene is chiefly concerned with the normality of personality trends and personality makeup. The key to the men-

tal hygiene of childhood lies in building up adequate self-reliance and independence. Even in infancy this principle must be regarded. Not only from the breast must the child be weaned.[11] (p. 227)

When development is made the key of child health supervision, our approach will be normative and regulative, just as it is in infant feeding, but on a wider scale which will include the mental as well as the physical aspects of growth. . . . Only in this way can mental health be brought within the scope of medical oversight. And there is a growing demand that mental hygiene be definitely incorporated into child-health procedures.

Can this be done with any success, or is mental hygiene too nebulous and fugitive to be made an objective? In last analysis, mental health even in young children proves to be a reflex or a compound of everyday habits of living. It is bound up primarily with wholesome habits of eating, sleeping, resting, elimination, exercise, and play. These habits are definitely within the province of medical control and advice. They are powerfully influenced by the family morale and by the attitudes of parents and brothers and sisters. But even these domestic factors can be reached by methods of parental guidance

When periodic health examinations broaden into developmental examinations, they will include a psychological inquiry into the health habits, the dispositions, capacities, and personality traits of the child, so that errors of development may be detected early and so that the parents may from the beginning assist the child to achieve mental as well as physical health.

A workable technique for administering this type of mental-hygiene service can undoubtedly be evolved.[11] (p. 435)

In the following year (1926) Dr. Gesell elaborated still further on one of his favorite topics, "The kindergarten as a mental hygiene agency":

The mental hygiene movement as we know it in this country began with a major interest in the conditions and care of the adult insane. But by a logic that has frequently expressed itself in the progress of public health, this interest has widened to embrace borderline and normal areas, and has deepened to reach juvenile and early developmental levels.

The mental hygiene movement was scarcely a decade old when it began to take an explicit interest in the mental welfare of children of pre-school age. This interest will undoubtedly become more systematic, and there will be an increasing utilization of community resources to further both the corrective and the preventive objectives of mental hygienists.

Of all these community resources, the American kindergarten is one of the most interesting, and potentially of great influence. . . . Also, the nursery school movement has had a stimulating effect upon the kindergarten situation. It has demonstrated the possibility of rendering concrete physical and mental-hygiene services to children of both kindergarten and pre-kindergarten age. It is awakening kindergarten leaders to the necessity of a change in outlook and procedure.[12] (p. 27)

The kindergarten is . . . in danger of crystallizing into just another schoolroom. . . . Instead of becoming fixed as a schoolroom, the kindergarten should evolve into an educational and mental-hygiene service instrument.[12] (p. 28)

There is a generous expectation that the child will outgrow his difficulties. From the standpoint of mental hygiene, however, these expectations are not always well founded. And it is precisely for reasons of mental hygiene that special guidance work for exceptional kindergarten children should be undertaken.[12] (p. 31)

The kindergarten has an opportunity and, still more, a responsibility in meeting the educational and hygienic needs of its exceptional children. . . . It holds a key position in the field of child hygiene. Revisions in technique and professional training will enable the kindergarten to prove its great importance as a public mental hygiene agency.[12] (p. 37)

A second 1926 paper may be a bit repetitive of what has been said before but nevertheless seems worth excerpting:

It happens that the mental hygiene movement, as we know it in the United States, traces very directly to the experiences of a Yale graduate who suffered from a mental illness soon after he left college. He wrote out of his experiences in a book entitled *The Mind That Found Itself* (8). In 1908, Clifford Beers, the author of this book, organized the Connecticut Society for Mental Hygiene, the first association of its kind which was ever formed in this field of public health.

The early use of the term "mental hygiene" was most fortunate. In the beginning, the major and almost exclusive emphasis was placed upon improving the care and treatment of the adult insane. But the impulse behind this movement was so deep and broad that an accumulative emphasis came to be placed upon the wider task of prevention. Crime, mental deficiency, juvenile delinquency were brought within the scope of the movement, and by gradual degrees there has grown up a conscious concern for the mental welfare not only of school children but of children of pre-school age.

If the conservation of mental health is a genuine watchword, it is necessary to recognize the developmental importance of infancy and early childhood. Since the growth of the mind has already begun at birth, it is necessary to safeguard mental growth from the very outset.[13] (p. 193)

Mental hygiene in a preventive and regulative sense concerns itself with the whole developmental span and does not underestimate the formative and the symptomatic significance of infant behavior.[13] (p. 194)

For several years we have been attempting at the Yale Psycho-Clinic to determine behavior norms of infancy, and to define diagnostic procedures which might enable us to make objective estimates of developmental status in early life.[13] (p. 195)

The behavior of the young child in the clinic, both the spontaneous and the elicited behavior, furnishes important evidence to those who are seriously interested in his mental well-being. In infancy behavior is a most sensitive and faithful index of developmental status. This gives us added assurance that procedures of developmental diagnosis will be found which will direct constructive, preventive mental hygiene measures on behalf of the pre-school child.[13] (p. 197)

One further 1926 reference to the topic of mental hygiene appeared under the title "Normal growth as a public health concept." Dr. Gesell comments that:

> This paper will deal chiefly with the feasibility and desirability of applying stardards of mental growth as an aid to promoting the mental health of normal children. Mental hygiene as a phase of public health remains a rather nebulous aspiration unless we can translate it into some of the same procedures and approaches which general health work for children now embodies.[14] (p. 394)

He then discusses, at some length, just what the concept of *growth* implies, and continues:

> The scientific attack on the problem of growth is of comparatively recent date. The countless studies now in progress will themselves grow in range and depth, and yield new insight into the factors which determine all growth.

One of the prevalent quasi-primitive notions holds that growth is predetermined, that it is so natural that it takes care of itself, and that there is little to be done about it. The too popular notion that the child will outgrow all his handicaps has a similar logic. Now the scientist would insist that growth is essentially lawful but also profoundly plastic. It is governed by certain limitations; but within those lawful limitations it is marvelously adaptive, and likewise lawfully responsive to both internal anad external conditions. If, in the laboratory, growth expresses this responsiveness at every turn, why can we not hope to bring the whole cycle of child growth gradually under greater control?[14] (p. 396)

A vast amount of research will be needed to give (our) norms precision. Meanwhile it is important to recognize that such psychological norms are attainable, and that standards of mental health are as legitimate and as feasible as standards of physical status.[14] (p. 397)

In a very brief paper published in 1929,* Dr. Gesell notes simply that:

There is a new and significant concern for the mental welfare of the young child. . . . The child has a mental hygiene as well as a physical hygiene. . . . To regard the mind as a natural and not a supernatural reality is the first step toward mental hygiene. Ample protection can come only through increased knowledge of the nature and laws of human growth. This knowledge is coming through modern science.[15] (p. 164)

In 1930 a short but quite substantive article titled "A Decade of Progress in the Mental Hygiene of the Preschool Child"[16] contrasts what is being done in the way of attention to mental hygiene of the young child in 1930 as compared with what was being done in 1920:

Immediately after the war, the hygiene of the preschool period was aptly characterized as a "no man's land" in the field of social endeavor. Lying outside of the ordinary limits of infant welfare work on the one hand and of public education on the other, the years from one to five were, in a sense, neglected. Even scientifically these years had received a secondary degree of attention. In the past decade, this situation has so profoundly changed that the preschool sector of activity has become an

* It appears to be in 1929 that Dr. Gesell dropped the hyphen from the word "pre-school" and from here on referred to "preschool."

'every man's land.' Psychologists, psychiatrists, kindergartners, primary school teachers, home economics and social workers, public health leaders, mothers' clubs, and mental hygiene organizations have found themselves side by side in the new interest in the preschool child. It is noteworthy, however, that nearly all these activities have been concentrated in the past ten years.[16] (p. 143)

In 1921, Congress passed the Federal Maternity and Infancy Law. The practical work under this law has inevitably widened to include incidental activities of a mental hygiene character.[16] (p. 144)

In 1930, Herbert Hoover called a White House Conference on Child Health and Protection to report on the present state of health and well-being of the children in the United States; on activities in the field of child hygiene; on possible steps to be taken in readjusting and supplementing community programs for child health and protection.[16] (p. 145)

Dr. Gesell then discusses progress that has been made in the nursery school movement, noting that a decade ago specific mental hygiene activities were largely limited to the adolescent and preadolescent age but now include the very young. He concludes this paper with his characteristic comments about the parent–child relationship:

The necessities of mental hygiene control of the parent-child relationship and of a development diagnosis of foster children prior to placement and adoption have put an added premium upon the downward extension of psycho-clinical methods. With the education of public opinion in the significance of behavior problems and in the importance of healthy mental growth, the preventive aspects of public health work and of private medical practice receive increasing attention. As a result, the general practitioner, the pediatrician, and the psychiatrist, both in the public clinic and in the consulting office, are concerning themselves more and more with psychological problems in young children and their parents.

The close of the nineteenth century witnessed the establishment of the principle of safeguarding the physical health of the newborn child. The twentieth century, and most notably the third decade of the twentieth century, is witnessing the extension of this principle toward a comprehensive developmental supervision concerned with mental as well as physical health.[16] (p. 147)

In an announcement of the First International Congress on Mental Health held at his clinic at Yale in 1930, Dr. Gesell listed "Current Studies of the Clinic." Among those that might be considered to deal with mental health were: Psychological Aspects of Child Guidance Problems; the Motor Difficulties of Left-Handed Children in Writing and Reading; Developmental Diagnosis of Dependent Infants; and Smiling and Laughing in Early Infancy.[17]

Also in 1930 Dr. Gesell discusses specifically "Mental Hygiene and the Public School System."[18] His position is expressed clearly in this paragraph:

> Mental hygiene as a medical and as an educational movement seeks to make a new approach upon the art of living. It seeks to increase mental health and mental efficiency by a better understanding and control of the laws of human behavior. The field is broad; but it is by no means as vague as the term suggests. It is full of practical possibilities, many of which can be adequately realized only through the public school. . . . We must use the public school for the preventive and constructive control of numerous forms of mental defect and handicap.[18] (p. 7)

He also notes that:

> There are one million young people walking the streets of the United States today who are necessarily doomed to spend some of their time before they die in institutions for mental disease. Such staggering figures suggest at least that the public agencies, including public schools, must with the aid of science evolve new measures for reducing the weight of the social burden represented by mental defect and disorder and delinquency.
>
> Special mental hygiene provisions (now in practice) are full of promise but they represent a mere beginning when the full needs of the population are considered. . . . Preventive mental hygiene must begin early to accomplish maximum results.[18] (p. 7)

Noting that the public school system must assume increasing responsibilities in the development of programs of child guidance and of mental health protection in the early years, Dr. Gesell outlines some of his own suggestions for what can be done in infancy, in the preschool period, in the kindergarten years, the elementary school years, in adolescence, and in the adult years. Since most of

these suggestions have been made in earlier publications, they will
not be elaborated on here.

A great deal that was said in this particular reference is repeated, and somewhat embellished, in Dr. Gesell's 1930 book, *The
Guidance of Mental Growth in Infant and Child*[19] and need not be
quoted here except to point out that in Dr. Gesell's opinion, not
remarkably, a strong basis for good mental health is found in the
parent-child relationship.

At this point we quote in full a rather unique letter which Dr.
Gesell wrote on February 17, 1933, extolling the work of the orig-
inator of the Mental Hygiene movement, Clifford Beers. The letter[20] speaks for itself:

YALE UNIVERSITY
School of Medicine
New Haven, Connecticut

*Office of the Director of the
Clinic of Child Development*

February 17, 1933

DEAR DR. WELCH:

It is a pleasure to salute the work of Clifford Beers on this
anniversary occasion. New Haven, of course, takes in him a local
pride which is accentuated by the worldwide recognition he has
received, and earned. Already he is something of a symbolic
legend, as well as an embodied dynamic force. As the world
know from reading his remarkable autobiography, much of his
fateful career was enacted here in New Haven, his native city.

I knew his father, a fine old gentleman, with a beard of
patriarchal length and whiteness, who lived and was active until
the age of ninety. He used to tell us about having ridden on the
first steam train from Schenectady to Troy in 1832, drawn by
the British engine, "John Bull," with her five-and-a-half inch
cylinders. How marvelously and prodigiously the machinery of
civilization has grown since those days! The conquest of environment goes on and we hear much about technology, and
economic engineering yet to come; but there is the disquieting
possibility that (even in a technocracy) man's control of the psychological factors of civilization may not keep pace with his
mechanical ingenuity.

Here, it seems to me, lies the present and the more remote
significance of Clifford Beers's work. The Mental Hygiene Movement, both in its scientific and its popular aspects, represents an
adjustment toward a more rational mastery of the psychological

energies of men. These energies, especially when socially conceived, call for new forms of "technology" which are becoming better defined through a mental hygiene approach.

On this occasion we should also recall the perceptiveness and courage of those, who, like yourself, came to such early support of a pioneering movement. It is extraordinary that this movement should have accumulated so much history and promise in so short a span of time.

Yours sincerely,
ARNOLD GESELL

In the following year, 1934, in a paper read a few months earlier before the annual meeting of the New York State Nurses' Organization in Rochester, New York, Dr. Gesell repeats some of his basic suggestions having to do with the promotion and safeguarding of mental health. As he has mentioned before:

> We need not think of mental welfare in mystical terms only—in the field of public health we must attempt to reckon with mental welfare with the same realism that we approach problems of rickets and diphtheria, knowing full well that nervously and mentally sick adults of today occupy as many hospital beds as do those who suffer from all other illnesses put together.[21] (p. 231)

He then makes his customary point that to make an approach to mental hygiene workable, we must have a working concept of the mind as substantial as our concept of the body. To do this we must understand and respect an understanding of the laws and stages of the growth of behavior which will be as clear and factual as our understanding of the physical body.

He concludes this paper with the comment that:

> In a sense the psychological hygiene of a large mass of our young children is at the same low level as their nutritional hygiene was in 1892 when Dr. Budin established in Paris the first infant welfare center.
>
> We can envisage a more or less complete system of mental hygiene protection which is already in the making and which includes these four distinguishable methods of approach: parental and preparental education, reconstruction of nursery and kindergarten, local clinics and guidance units, and periodic developmental supervision.[21] (p. 232)

From this time on (1940–1943), Dr. Gesell's papers or even comments upon the field of mental hygiene were few. His main contributions to this field, quite substantial in the early part of the century, had dwindled to a trickle. This was partly because the direction of the field had taken a psychoanalytic turn, partly because many or most of Dr. Gesell's suggestions in this area had already been implemented.

In 1940 there are two mentions of the topic. The first is a short article entitled, "The Day Nursery as a Mental Hygiene Agency."[22] Its point, which has been made before, is that:

> Mental hygiene is a term which is bandied about a good deal and frequently misused. But we can scarcely get along without it; because it sums up such an important concept. "Mental hygiene" looks upon the problems of child development and child behavior from the standpoint of health.
>
> Mental hygiene is a broad and elusive term; but it can be brought down to a workaday level whenever the nusery adopts an educational program deliberately directed toward improving the parent-child relationship of its clients. . . . The nursery becomes a mental hygiene agency if it conducts its work in a spirit of considerate understanding and focuses on the central objective of helping parents to interpret the child in terms of his growth characteristics.[22] (pp. 2, 3)

In his 1940 book, *The First Five Years of Life*, Dr. Gesell makes a brief comment on the subject of mental hygiene:

> A key to the mental hygiene of early childhood lies in building up adequate self-dependence. Even in infancy this principle of self-dependence must be respected. Not only from the breast must the child be weaned. By slow gradations he must develop fortitudes which lie at the basis of detachment. He cannot always play in his mother's lap, he must in time begin to play in his pen. He cannot always play in the same room with his mother; he must learn to play in an adjoining one, first for a few minutes, later for an hour at a time. If his mother must leave the house, he must be content to watch her through the window, even though it costs him a struggle. In time he must learn to go to bed alone, and later to school alone.
>
> These are elementary lessons in self-reliance, but the detachment must not be hurried, and all along the path of preschool development our demands should be tempered to meet the child's immaturity.[23] (p. 261)

In the following year, 1941, in *Developmental Diagnosis*, a textbook for use with students of medicine, Dr. Gesell makes the following brief commentary:

> For all infants and children preventive and curative medical services should be available. . . . These services, financed through private resources or public funds include:
> The supervision of health *and development* of infant and child at stated intervals throughout the period of growth
> Health instruction in schools and health education of parents in methods of conserving both physical and *mental health.*
> Effective nutritional services. Mental-health services when needed.
> The foregoing recommendations were adopted by the White House Conference on Children in a Democracy (1940). They were formulated by a medical committee which included national leaders in the fields of pediatrics, psychiatry, and public health. It is fair to say that these recommendations express the most modern trends in preventive medicine and child hygiene.
> We have italicized the two phrases, *and development, and mental health,* to emphasize the areas in which developmental diagnosis makes its chief contribution. Physical welfare, mental health, and development become indivisible concepts, and inseparable objectives. Optimal growth is the inclusive goal of child hygiene. This goal makes no artificial distinctions between mind and body; it recognizes the total economy of the child and places a premium upon a personalized, periodic type of developmental supervision.[24] (p. 323)

One further commentary, also in 1941, is titled "The Protection of Early Mental Growth: Some Social Implications in the Present Crisis." This article was first given as a talk at a meeting which addressed the question—"What can psychiatry contribute to alleviate national and international difficulties?" Dr. Gesell's solution, quite predictably, was that:

> An increasing volume of knowledge relating to the processes of growth awaits progessive application. When the insistence of military defense relaxes we may hope that the armamentarium of the life sciences which deal with the mechanisms and the measurement of human growth will be drawn upon to establish new safeguards and to surround the infant and child with optimal conditions of early development.[25] (p. 501)

One of Dr. Gesell's last and rather bland comments about mental hygiene appeared in his 1943 book, *Infant and Child in the Culture of Today*:

> It is too easy to forget that the infant has a psychology and that our methods of care affect his mental as well as physical welfare. The individualization of food-sleep-activity schedules is a basic approach to the mental hygiene of infancy.[26] (p. 56)

Later in the same book he makes a plea that not only the pediatrician but also the obstetrician assist the mother in furthering the mental hygiene of the growing child. And here he pushes the time when such efforts should be begun back before the time of birth to the period before birth:

> When does the baby's mental welfare begin? Before birth. And not, of course, because of the effect of maternal impressions upon the unborn child; but, rather because the mother, even during her pregnancy, is developing attitudes, expectancies, and decisions which will inevitably influence the course of the baby's mental growth, particularly in the four fundamental months which follow birth. It is well to make a good start.
>
> The mental hygiene of the child, therefore, begins with maternity hygiene, and for this reason the obstetrician has a more important role to play than he frequently suspects. Naturally his concern is focused upon the critical event of birth and the preservation of the mother's health in the face of this crisis. But granting this, the expectant mother still turns to him with many questions which have the potential importance for her own personal psychology and for the psychological welfare of the expected child. There are still other questions which she does not formulate at all, but which the obstetrician should formulate for her through his guidance.[26] (p. 80)

And now comes a 6-year gap. In a final article on the subject entitled "Pediatrics and Child Psychiatry," Dr. Gesell makes the point that:

> The problem of mental health conservation is a conjoint medical and social task so stupendous that it calls for an examination of the potential resources of clinical pediatrics. I shall limit this discussion chiefly to pediatrics as that sector of general medicine which is directly responsible for the protection of child development.[27] (p. 67)

Pertinent excerpts from this contribution follow:

Our present-day knowledge of the child's mind is comparable to a 15th-century map of the world—a mixture of truth and
error, with the heads of strange sea monsters ominously rising
out of the dark depths of uncharted seas. Vast areas remain to
be explored. . . . There are scattered islands of solid depend-
able fact, uncoordinated with unknown continents. Under the
mounting influence of biologic rationalism, however, the unfin-
ished map of the child's world is taking on more accuracy and
design.

A clinical science of child development is now actively in the
making. It will serve to coordinate knowledge and to put that
knowledge into usable form for the implementation of mental
hygiene. . . . Fortunately the very concept of development serves
to integrate and to simplify the multiplicity of data. This concept is monistic: it resolves the dualisms of organism and environment; of heredity and habit; of structure and function; of
mind and body. . . .

Should not the study of the normal infant be elevated to the
dignity of a clinical subject? This can be brought about through
a clinical science of child development incorporated into the
scheme of medical education. The fundamental preclinical
sciences are destined to bring forth new discoveries, which will
lead to great refinement in diagnostic technics. A developmental
pediatrics oriented to the supervision of normal growth will then
be in a position to utilize these discoveries and to implement
them for preventive and constructive mental hygiene.[27] (p. 671)

There are social and cultural reasons as well why pediatrics
may assume the role of leadership in mental health conservation. The pediatrician, in our American society, is most intimately identified with family life and as counselor he exercises
a profound influence upon the standards and practices of family
living. His influence will be far-reaching if he can function with
clinical authority in a purposeful form of developmental supervision which is concerned with the psychologic aspects of
health. . . .

So, in conclusion, we come back once more to the two alternatives which are open to clinical pediatrics. One road leads to
an emphasis on behavior disorders and psychotherapies; the
other road leads to a constructive concern for the normal and
wholesome potentialities of early human growth.

Pediatrics as a specialty of general medicine is concerned
with the promotion conjointly of mental and physical develop-

ment. Pediatrics cannot encourage the technical areas of child
psychiatry which are concerned with severe psychopathologies
and complex psychotherapies. It can encompass a preventive
and position type of mental hygiene through parent-child guidance and family counseling. . . . The principles and methods of
pediatric mental health conservation must be based upon a
clinical science of normal child development.[27] (p. 675)

After 1949 there were no further papers dealing with the topic
of mental hygiene, and the term was not indexed in any of Dr.
Gesell's subsequent books. His diminishing interest in the topic of
mental hygiene per se, at least as suggested by the decreasing number of mentions which we find in his writings after 1934, is in all
likelihood at least in part due to the fact that, as the years went by,
the entire field of mental hygiene (research, writings, clinical applications) took a marked turn, as we have noted, in the direction of
psychoanalysis and away from a philosophy and way of thinking
which was congenial to Dr. Gesell.

Thus his first substantial paper on the subject[2], as mentioned
above, appeared in 1918 in Volume Two of the journal *Mental Hygiene*, along with such other congenial papers as "Mental Hygiene
for Normal Children" by Dr. William H. Burnham[28] (p.19–22) and
"Supervision of the Feebleminded in the Community" by Jessie
Taft[29] (pp. 434–442). However, by 1954, this journal featured such
articles as "The Mental Health of the Educator" by Leo Berence,
which describes a situation in which groups of educators meet with a
group leader to discuss their "irrational emotional reactions, and the
unconscious motivations behind their behavior"[30] (p. 426). Quite
clearly the journal, the society, and the mental hygiene movement in
general were moving in a direction far from the area of Dr. Gesell's
personal or professional interests.

A further possible reason for the fact that Dr. Gesell, as the
years went by, wrote less and less about mental hygiene may have
been, as we have mentioned, that many of his own goals for the
field, as listed earlier in this chapter, had been at least to quite an
extent accomplished. Increased knowledge about the ways in which
child behavior developed (a body of knowledge to which his own
writings had contributed substantially) had made it possible for parents, teachers, child specialists, and pediatricians to deal with children in ways which presumably improve and preserve their mental
health.

The Gesell developmental norms were the first to define and measure the growing behavior of the individual child. Understanding of just where any given child is functioning presently contributes to his mental health because it helps those dealing with that child to know what to expect of him and thus to structure the environment in a way that will serve his best interests.

As Gesell and his colleagues wrote increasingly for parents, describing in detail what all kinds of behavior (eating, sleeping, toileting, socializing, learning) were like at different ages, it may be hoped that these writings improved the quality and effectiveness of parenting by familiarizing mothers and fathers with behavior to be expected at succeeding age levels. Today much of this information has become common knowledge. Even not too well-educated parents speak knowledgeably of the "Terrible Twos" or the "Wild Fours." At the time Dr. Gesell was writing, this kind of information was just beginning to be known even to the specialist.

Thus it is fair to say that Dr. Gesell through his research and writings contributed vastly to the general field of mental hygiene.

Chapter 4

CHILD HYGIENE AND
PHYSICAL HEALTH

CHILD HYGIENE

The topic of child hygiene should be included in this book because of the fact that it was a term sometimes used by Dr. Gesell. That this term was important to him is suggested by the fact that his title at Yale was Professor of Child Hygiene and Director of the Yale Clinic of Child Development. It seems quite possible that he chose this title himself.

Actually, over the years, the meaning of the term became somewhat ambiguous. On occasion it was used to mean the child's physical health. Probably more often it was used more or less synonymously with the term *mental health* or *mental hygiene,* or *child health.* Though it will not be necessary to report its every occurrence, we summarize here the major and more telling instances in which it was used.

The term first appeared in 1912 in the index of Dr. Gesell's early book, *The Normal Child and Primary Education.* The reference indexed suggests that:

> Some day, probably, laboratories of child study and educational hygiene will be regular features of every large public-school system in America. . . . The new biological temper, which

is the product of modern science, exalts hygiene and makes health the central solicitude in all the work of education.

Eleven years ago the school superintendents of America met in Chicago. Diligent search through the printed report of the meeting discloses no single mention of child health, no word about child hygiene, no address devoted to the conservation or development of the physical vigor of youth. At that time eight cities in America had systems of medical inspection in the public schools. Today the number of such systems is over four hundred. Historically *Child Hygiene*, yesterday only a phrase but already becoming a program for action, is a phase or an outgrowth of the scientific study of the child.[1] (pp. 26, 27)

Though Dr. Gesell's use of the term becomes rather ambiguous as the years go on, perhaps his clearest exposition of what he originally meant by it appears in 1913, in an article entitled "The Special Province of Child Hygiene in the Public Schools".[2] He appears to use the two concepts, mental health and physical health, together under the major heading *Child Hygiene*:

New occasions demand new phrases. Child Hygiene is a new and useful phrase which expresses the drifts of our best efforts and systematic intentions in the rearing of children. As a blanket term it covers all measures pertaining to the health of the child. . . . Child Hygiene. . . . will watch and register the careers of the individual school child. Here lies the deep and far-reaching distinction between Medical Inspection and the developmental supervision of Child Hygiene.[2] (p. 1)

Medical inspection follows up the defect; Child Hygiene follows up the child. . . . Hygiene is the art of maintaining health. The programming of Child Hygiene must be preventive in the most radical sense. . . . Child Hygiene requires psychological as well as medical insight and a personal interest in developing children.[2] (p. 2). . . . *The practical task of Child Hygiene will be to determine certain norms of development, both mental and physical.*[2] (pp. 2, 3). . . . *There is no need for the over-laboring of the distinction between Medical Inspection and Child Hygiene.*[2] (p. 6)

In short, Child Hygiene, as Dr. Gesell interpreted it, appeared to include the physical, psychological, and educational well-being, or health, of the child.

By 1919 there appears to be some distinction made between the term *child hygiene* and *mental hygiene*. In an article titled "Mental

Hygiene and the Public School,"[3] he describes the tasks of mental hygiene—a hygienic supervision of the preschool period, a psychophysical entrance examination of every school beginner, a reorganization of kindergarten and first grade, and the development of a new type of school nurse who will further the everyday tasks of mental hygiene[3] (pp. 8, 9). (All of this without mentioning the term *child hygiene*.)

In fact, from here on the concept of Mental Hygiene develops a life of its own and to quite an extent "child hygiene" seems to refer chiefly to physical health. Thus in the book *The Preschool Child*[4] most of the material indexed under "Child Hygiene" has to do with physical health, though it is noted[4] (p. 35) that "A division of child hygiene under the State Board of Health was established by law." However, the tasks and goals of an "organized bureau of child hygiene," as listed[4] (p. 181) have almost entirely to do with physical health including: regulation of obstetrical procedures, prenatal work, reduction of infant mortality, health supervision of preschoolers, school, medical inspection, and standards for child labor.

From this date (1923) through 1930, the phrase "child hygiene" is not indexed in any of Dr. Gesell's book publications, and does not appear in the titles of any of his articles. Thus in a 1930 article titled "A Decade of Progress in Mental Hygiene"[5] the term "child hygiene" is not mentioned.

By 1934 the matters of physical health and mental health seem separated, though conjoined, in Dr. Gesell's writings. In a short piece titled "The Mental Welfare of Normal Infants"[6] we find:

> Pediatrics, pediatric nursing and public health nursing will from sheer necessity have to take increasing cognizance of the mental, i.e. the psychological, factor of their common problems. . . . The problems of modern medicine cannot be solved through processes of professional subdivision. It therefore seems that pediatrics in one form or another is destined to take a controlling responsibility in the protection and supervision of the mental welfare of normal infants.[6] (p. 229)
>
> The close *relationship* between mental and physical welfare has been emphasized. Functional and psychological factors cannot be divorced from physical hygiene. . . . Favored sections of the community throughout the land are making increasing demands for the widening of this supervision of physical growth to include psychological development.[6] (pp. 230–232)

The same theme is repeated in 1941[7]:

> There is an unmistakable social trend toward enlarging the
> scope of health protection to include the mental as well as physi-
> cal welfare in all medical services for infant and young child.[7]
> (p. 501)

Clearly, nothing new is being said. And from now on we do not find the term "child hygiene" used conspicuously, if at all.

Though Dr. Gesell introduced the term "child hygiene" very early in his career—the first reference occurs in 1912—and though his official title at Yale was Professor of Child Hygiene, in actual practice this term was never used by him extensively. In most of his writings the terms he used were *mental health* or *mental hygiene* and/or *physical health*. He also referred to proper nutrition. Thus it seems fair to conclude that though the term *child hygiene* appears to have been a term which he favored, its use was infrequent and somewhat ambiguous—sometimes including both mental hygiene and physical health but more often referring to mental hygiene or mental health.

PHYSICAL HEALTH

It seems suitable, since Dr. Gesell was trained as a physician as well as a psychologist, and since for a substantial part of his professional life he was on the staff of the Yale University School of Medicine, that we should include here at least some comment on his contributions to the field of physical health. Interestingly enough, they were relatively few and in some instances did not go much beyond conventional comment. Though Dr. Gesell had vast respect for medicine, at no time did he or his staff undertake the practice of medicine.

On occasion, as outlined in the chapter *"Defect and Deviation,"* he did produce substantive papers, or chapters, on such physical ills as hemihypertrophy, pubertas praecox, mongolism and cretinism, cerebral palsy, and birth injury. However, such papers were the exception rather than the rule. For the most part his references to child health or child hygiene, as noted in the earlier part of this chapter, had more to do with mental health than physical health. Or, at most, he seemed to have combined the two concepts or to have discussed a combination of "health and educational needs."

That is, he extended his use of the term *child hygiene* to a feeling about the total welfare (mental as well as physical) of the whole child. Even as early as 1913 he emphasized the importance of understanding the *developmental needs* of the growing child:

> The school doctor of the future will not be an examining physician who comes and goes, but at least a semi-resident hygienist. We need biographical charts rather than consensus of defects.[2] (p. 2)

At this same time he gives a brief mention of the importance of dealing with special physical defects:

> The importance of the early discernment and the necessity for attention to all physical defects needs little argument. As for adenoids, the age of 5 or 6 is one of the most favorable for their removal. Hypermetropia, if neglected in the early years, is likely to bring on myopia; neglect of strabismus until the higher grades are reached usually means that an extremely serious defect and deformity is permanently established. Lateral curvature increases regularly through the grades from about 9 to 31 percent. This increase could undoubtedly be reduced if proper preventive measures were undertaken in the primary school.[2] (p. 5)

For the most part throughout his writing there is relatively little except routine and conventional comment about physical health. We have selected half a dozen or so typical quotations which contain conventional admonitions as to the importance of paying attention to matters of child health. Since they add relatively little to our knowledge or understanding of human health we shall keep them relatively brief.

In 1919, Dr. Gesell had this to say:

> Splendid accomplishments in our schools have been made through medical inspections and school nursing. . . . The child who matriculates in the first grade has been attending preparatory school for six years; the hygienic control of that period is both a logical and a practical necessity.
>
> The weighing and measuring campaign of the Children's Bureau was a definite step. We should make this campaign an established annual event. We should build up a cumulative health and development record for each child.[3] (p. 3)

In 1921 in a paper titled "The Significance of the Preschool Age for School Hygiene,"[8] he notes that:

> The medical significance of the pre-school age can scarcely be exaggerated. Certainly exaggeration is not needed. The problems of development and disease peculiar to this period are so numerous, that Pediatrics constitutes the broadest and in many respects the most important specialty in medicine. The curve of human mortality is of decisive import. Of all the deaths of the nation, over one-third occur below the age of six. Ten times as many deaths occur in the first half decade of life as in the full decade from five to fifteen years. . . . Medical science and public hygiene must continue to work on the assumption that it is in general a good thing to save the lives of babies. Consequently the infant mortality rate tends to vary inversely with the intelligence and prosperity of the community.
>
> Nowhere does the great object of medical science, namely life conservation, come more completely to realization than in the constructive work in behalf of infants and young children. . . .
>
> Many of the physical defects of school children originate in the pre-school period; even the quality of their permanent teeth is conditioned by pre-natal and pre-school factors; malnutrition, rickets, and diphtheria are or ought to be matters largely of pre-school control.[8] (pp. 25–30)

In his 1923 book, *The Preschool Child from the Standpoint of Public Hygiene and Education,* in a section titled "Psychology is the Science of Behavior," he notes specifically:

> The future growth of preschool hygiene, both physical and mental, will see a more deliberate use of this great science to solve the behavior problems of child development and child care.[4] (p. 19)

In 1923 a talk piece titled "The Kindergarten and Health" chiefly urges that the kindergarten teacher should make health development the supreme aim of her educational work.[9] (p. 5) Dr. Gesell recommends that this teacher "should come into working relations with all public and quasi-public agencies which are serving the physical and mental welfare of young children—with medical and dental clinics, with school physicians and nurses, health centers," etc. He suggests that kindergartens relate themselves to already established Infant Welfare Stations.[9] (p. 6)

In this same reference, in discussing "The Medical Importance of the Preschool Age," Dr. Gesell points out that:

> Most of the physical defects of the school age originate in the preschool period. . . . The preschool period, therefore, looms up as the field for basic prevention work. . . . And the kindergarten ought to become a supplementary, or integral, factor of the whole preschool system of child hygiene.[9] (p. 8)

He adds:

> Medical supervision of school children will always be indispensable, but the forces of preventive hygiene must be concentrated, shifted downward, and deliberately focused upon the pre-kindergarten and kindergarten child.[9] (p. 9)

In the same year, Dr. Gesell published one of his pieces which dealt most specifically with physical health, "The Preschool Child as a Health Problem".[10] His position in this short paper was that health work in the preschool years pays the highest dividend:

> The health significance of the preschool years can be quickly summed up. First of all, it is the period when death and disease pile up their biggest scores. . . . Even physical accidents, like being scalded, burned, injured, and run over by automobiles, bear with special weight on the preschool age. The susceptibility to infection is generally greater the younger the child. Over eighty percent of all cases of diphtheria and of all deaths from diphtheria occur before the age of five. Malnutrition, likewise, is more prevalent among preschool then among school children. Rickets, a disorder of nutrition, is almost as common as dental caries and is essentially a preschool disease.[10] (p. 1)

He continues with a paragraph on "Prevention of Malnutrition, Diphtheria and Rickets," which he labels as three of the most powerful foes of early childhood. He emphasizes that:

> Nutrition work as it is now recognized should not be limited to infant welfare stations and to public school classes. There should be a continuous sequence of supervision which will reduce malnutrition to a minimum by the time of school entrance. It is most probable that diphtheria, like smallpox, can be conquered by preventive practices.[10] (p. 2)

In the same year, in a short article in the *New York Times*, Dr. Gesell comments:

> *Medically* the preschool age is of critical significance because it outranks all other periods in mortality and morbidity. Most of the physical and development defects of school children originate or pre-exist in the preschool years. Practically every case of mental deficiency originates and is recognizable in the preschool period.
>
> Three fourths of all the deaf, a considerable proportion of all blind, one-third of all the crippled, and over three fourths of the speech defective come to their handicap in the preschool period. . . . Retardation, abnormal prematurity, normal precocity, superiority and normality all tend to reveal themselves well before the child cuts his sixth year molar.[11]

Dr. Gesell emphasizes the importance of periodic health examinations, that kindergartens and nursery schools are practical places for checking on health problems and that parents need guidance and direction helping to handle their children's health problems. And, as often, he stresses the importance of infant welfare or child consultation centers where doctors and nurses work with children and their parents. Thus one year later he notes:

> The fact that many children are started in school too soon and also that their health is not supervised grows out of the fact that we have been slow in appreciating the mental and developmental significance of the early years of childhood. We have intrusted these years too completely to the unaided home and to providence. . . . We must develop a consecutive kind of health service which starts at birth and will safeguard the child up to matriculation. Periodic health examinations throughout his preschool life, systematic parental guidance, preparental education and developmental child guidance will serve this end[12] (p. 6)

A pamphlet published in 1926 titled "The Baby in the House of Health"[13] "approved by" Dr. Gesell and a panel of other physicians gives routine information primarily on feeding the baby, but includes a short chapter on growth and training, sleep and play, health and comfort.

A book called, promisingly, *The Feeding Behavior of Infants*, by Gesell and Ilg, actually devotes itself primarily to mouth, tongue, and hand patterns of infant feeding. Nutrition is mentioned only peripherally. The authors do comment:

The chemistry of infant nutrition has made brilliant advances in recent years and the pediatric supervision of infant feeding contributes one of the most basic achievements of preventive medicine. But the *nutritional hygiene* of the infant has suffered from over-generalization. Physiology formulates the facts and principles which apply in general to the nutrition of all infants. Clinical pediatrics, however, must also give weight to those distinctive behavior traits and trends which express the individuality of the infant whether in sickness or health.[14] (p. 4)

They continue:

The protection of nutrition will still be the central objective (of periodic health exams) but the supervision of nutrition will be widened to embrace the total economy of the child. . . . The whole process of nutrition, indeed, is complicated by mental factors which arise out of the behavior equipment of the infant.[14] (p. 147)

A major emphasis of this book has to do with so-called "self-demand and self-regulation" schedules, whereby the child more or less makes his own schedule as opposed to a rigid every three or four-hour feeding schedule which had been traditional.

A major textbook authored by Dr. Gesell and Dr. Catherine Amatruda, *Developmental Diagnosis*[15], written as it was for medical students and practitioners, quite naturally does discuss at length various medical, as well as behavior, problems. Those covered include: amentia and retardation, endocrine disorders, convulsive disorders, cerebral injury, sensory handicaps, and prematurity. This coverage is too long and too detailed to be summarized here.

Physical health *is* mentioned in two of the three major books for parents published between 1943 and 1956, often referred to as "The Trilogy." In the first of these, *Infant and Child in the Culture of Today*,[16] neither the words "disease" or "health" appeared in the index. However in the second, *The Child from Five to Ten*,[17] he and his coauthors gave a short but thorough gradient on "Health and Somatic Complaints," reproduced here:

HEALTH AND SOMATIC COMPLAINTS

18 Months—Convulsions may accompany illnesses, especially those with high temperature.

21 Months—Elimination difficulties; frequency of both functions; diarrhea common.

2½ Years—Elimination difficulties. Long retention span; constipation more common in girls

Frequent colds with ear complications, especially in slow speech children.

Wants to be carried and treated like a baby (33 months).

3 Years—Expresses fatigue by saying, "I'm tired."

4 Years—May have one cold right after another, all winter

Stomach ache in social situations.

Need to urinate in difficult situations or at mealtimes.

May have "accidents" in emotional situations.

Knocks out front teeth if falls.

Breaks collar bone if falls (4½ years).

5 Years—Good, or even excellent health is characteristic.

Many have only one or two colds all winter.

Some increase in whooping cough, measles, chicken pox.

Occasional stomach aches or vomiting in relation to disliked foods, or just prior to elimination.

Constipation—girls.

5½ Years—Complains that feet "hurt."

Some have frequent colds.

Headaches or earaches beginning.

Stomach aches with some nausea and vomiting in connection with school.

Somatic symptoms may appear after a week or two of school.

Whooping cough, measles, chicken pox the most common communicable disease.

Hyper-sensitivity of face, head, neck region to washing, hair combing, etc.

Child may endure large pains yet fuss about a splinter or nose drops.

6 Years—More susceptible to disease and sicker with illness than earlier.

Frequent sore throats, colds, with complications (lung and ears); increase in allergies.

Chicken pox, measles, whooping cough. Diphtheria and scarlet fever; German measles and mumps.

Stomach aches and vomiting in connection with going to school.

Toilet "accidents" with over-excitement.

Breaks arm if falls.

Hyper-sensitivity of face, neck region if washed or touched. (Some become hysterical with laughter if tickled.)

Increased redness of genitals—girls.

7 Years—Fewer illnesses than at six, but colds of longer duration.

German measles and mumps frequent. Chicken pox and measles may occur.

Complaint of headache with fatigue or excitement; complaints of muscular pain.

Minor accidents to eyes, but fewer gross accidents; eye rubbing

Extreme fatigue.

8 Years—Improving health. Fewer illnesses and of shorter duration. Less absence from school because of illness.

Increase in allergies and otitis media.

Headaches, stomach aches and need to urinate in connection with disagreeable tasks.

Accidents frequent; from falls, drowning, and in relation to automobiles and bicycles.

Breaks leg if falls.

9 Years—Improving health and few illnesses, but marked individual differences.

Some have a prolonged illness or show marked fatigue.

Very few general somatic complaints, but innumerable minute ones related to the task at hand (eyes hurt when tested; hands hurt when gripping); often says "It makes me feel dizzy."[17] (pp. 268–270)

Because this information is also given, in more detail, in the chapters on the individual ages, it need not be included here for every age. An example from the chapter on five years of age will suffice to show the nature of the ground covered:

5 Years: On the whole 5-year-old's health is relatively good, with the exception of the communicable diseases which increase in number from the fourth year on. Whooping cough and chicken pox take the lead. Measles, once in the lead, is now better controlled. Some have a few colds during the winter months. Stomach-aches are fairly common and are related both to the intake of food and the need to have a bowel movement.[17] (p. 65)

A similar age gradient covering health factors at the various ages appears in the later book, *Youth: The Years from Ten to Sixteen*,[18] as follows (as in the just cited earlier book, the same kind of information is given in more detail in the chapters on the individual ages):

HEALTH

10 YEARS
Health is generally quite good; greatly improved in many who had poor health earlier. Many report that there was a very bad time around six years for trouble with ears, throat, contagious diseases.

Some stomach-aches and headaches, and a little hypochondria (all more common at nine years).

11 YEARS
The majority of Elevens themselves report *excellent* health, though parents of some say they take to their beds on fairly slight provocation.

Somewhat unstable body mechanisms in some: feel hot easily, develop headaches, vomit if have stomach-ache. Colds and infections may spread to involve other areas. Some contagious diseases.

12 YEARS
Parents often describe children's health as "unusual," "remarkable," "incredible." Many miss much less school than formerly.

However, there may be sudden, violent headaches or stomach-aches. Fatigue less frequent than at eleven, but may occur in more intense bouts. Sore throats and colds often develop at such times.

13 YEARS
Health, in general, continues to improve. "Didn't miss a day of school this year." Better able to carry on activity

when illness is only minor: "Doesn't give in to illness the
way he or she did."

Some difficulty with colds, fatigue.

Acne and allied complexion difficulties beginning in some.

14 YEARS

Health is excellent in most, "really wonderful," Occasional
use of health as an excuse: "I get sick every so often,
usually when I haven't done my schoolwork and don't
want to go to school." But this is less than earlier.

Major complaints are still colds and fatigue.

Complexion difficulties increase—pimples, pustules,
blackheads, blotches. A matter of real concern to some.

15 YEARS

Health is excellent in most. Some old complaints lessen;
many mention "no more hives," no asthma, etc.

Skin difficulties continue, and worsen in some, sometimes
requiring medical care.

16 YEARS

Health is excellent in most. Complexion starts to improve
in many, especially if aided by Sixteen's better ability to
control diet, and care for skin.[18] (pp. 290, 291)

This sampling shows that though Dr. Gesell certainly made
numerous references to the importance of physical health—his
substantive contributions were relatively few. Exceptions to this rule
are his papers on hemihypertrophy, puberty praecox, cretinism,
mongolism, cerebral palsy, and birth injury as reported in detail
in our chapter on "Defect and Deviation," and in his 1941 book,
Developmental Diagnosis[15] where he discusses endocrine disorders,
cerebral injury and special sensory handicaps. Clearly he was not
primarily concerned with physical health as such. Except for the
above, his most specific mentions of the subject appeared in two of
his latest books, *The Child from Five to Ten*[17] and *Youth: The Years from
Ten to Sixteen*.[18]

Many of the quotations given may sound rather obvious and
trite today. Now that so many of the things that Dr. Gesell spoke out
for and worked for are taken for granted in today's Society, it is easy
to underestimate his part in the campaign waged in the early part of
this century for more attention to both the physical and the mental
welfare of our children, especially of the very young.

Chapter 5

VISION

Dr. Gesell's major contribution to the field of vision, a book titled *Vision: Its Development in Infant and Child*[1] did not appear until 1949; but his earliest mention of visual behavior came more than a quarter of a century earlier, in 1912, in his book *The Normal Child and Primary Education.* Here he makes the following significant comment, one which in part his colleagues are still stressing in the late 1980s:

> *The eyes.* If the primary-school curriculum is very bookish and wordy, the visual mechanism comes in for a severe and unnatural strain, and the eye may not attain its full size and strength. "The eye was developed for general-purpose vision," says Dr. Terman, in an article on "Education against nature." "It is only in the last few centuries, since printing and literary instruction have become universal, that the eye has been generally robbed of its freedom—domesticated, so to speak—and harnessed into the wearying treadmill of the educational machine." The teacher must be on the lookout for both hereditary and acquired defects of vision, which are the result of these civilized conditions. If she were among primitive peoples, she would not have to be so alert.
>
> The chief varieties of eye defeat are *myopia* (near sight) and *hyperopia* (far sight), causing respectively a focusing of the image

65

behind and in front of the retina; *strabismus* (squint), due to a
deviation of the eyeballs; and *astigmatism*, due to imperfections
of the cornea, or lens, causing a blurred image.

The list of symptoms associated with eye troubles is rather
long, and includes inflammation, watering, congested lids,
crusts, twitching, dizziness, blinking, scowling, frequent headaches (especially in the frontal regions), lack of application,
cocking the head or holding a book close to the face, blurring
print and, according to Gould, many cases of lateral spinal
curvature.[2] (pp. 280, 281)

The following year, 1913, in a paper titled "The Special Province of Child Hygiene in the Primary School," Dr. Gesell notes:

> The importance of the early discernment and the necessity
> for attention to all physical defects needs little argument. . . .
> Hypermetropia, if neglected in the early years, is likely to bring
> on myopia; neglect of strabismus until the higher grades are
> reached usually means that an extremely severe defect and de-
> formity is permanently established.[3] (p. 5)

Dr. Gesell's later rather substantial interest in vision and in
blindness was further foreshadowed by very early comments on the
subject in 1921, 1922, and 1923.[4,5,6] In the first of these mentions[4]
he notes that the number of blind children in schools and classes in
this country in 1918 was 5,386. In some of these cases classes for the
blind were part of the public school system, with blind children
taught in the same classes with the sighted.

In the second of these brief mentions (5) he emphasizes that
though in over half the states general compulsory education laws
require that blind children be educated, most laws do not apply to
the preschool period. He emphasizes that "the preschool years are in
many respects the most important in the education of the blind
child"[5] (p. 233). He also emphasizes here that so far as possible we
should treat the blind child as if he were a seeing child.

In the third, a book publication, he again emphasizes his view
that "the education of the blind or partially sighted is a problem
which falls peculiarly within the scope of the public school"[6] (p. 90).
He then repeats much of what was said in his 1921 paper.

These early comments about vision were not immediately followed up. In the next decade we find no significant mention of eyes
or vision in Dr. Gesell's writings. Whenever normative behavior is

mentioned, it tends to include, but often only incidentally, some mention of a visual response. Thus in 1925, in a brief article titled "Monthly Increments of Development in Infancy"[7] (p. 208), he mentions in passing that "The four months' infant, for example, regards a cube on the table."

In that same year, 1925, in his first presentation of the Gesell norms[8] (p. 100) there are two visual items. At four months, eyes are expected to follow both a moving person and a moving plate. But vision is by no means featured in these 1925 norms.

In his first substantial revision of his norms, *Infant Behavior: Its Genesis and Growth*,[9] published 9 years later, in 1934, considerably more attention is paid to visual behavior. Though neither "vision" nor "eyes" is included in the index to this book, there are 18 indexed references to *regard*. These references for the most part do not go far beyond noting the age at which an infant may be expected to regard the various test objects.

The most elaborate discussion of the infant's visual response is found in information given about visual response to the one-inch cube[9] (pp.127–129), reproduced here:

Behavior Trends

Visual Regard. At 12 weeks less than one-quarter of the subjects fail to regard the single cube. At 16 weeks, *all* subjects regard the first cube. At 12 weeks, two-fifths of the infants show delay of regard; at 16, 20, and 24 weeks about one in four shows delay. Capacity for visual regard is present even at 8 weeks but to what degree we have not investigated. At 28 weeks and thereafter immediate and consistent regard for the first cube becomes almost universal. These statements sum up the general course of visual regard.

Some shifting of regard is observed in the first cube situation at all ages but is most marked at the highest and lowest age levels. Needless to say, the younger infant "shifts" his regard for other reasons than does the older. At 12 weeks eight out of ten, and at 16 weeks nine out of ten, infants shift regard from the cube to some competing focus like the tabletop, surroundings, own hand, or examiner. At these younger ages the shifts are twitch-like, and they go most frequently to the infant's own hand. At the advanced ages (52 and 56 weeks) these shifts are smoother and they appear more self-directed and less mechanical. They go preferentially to the examiner, and probably have a social as well as perceptual determination. But allowing for all of the deflections of visual regard at the extreme ages, there is a remarkable degree of sustained preoccupation for the first and the consecutive cubes. As early as 16 weeks the prevailing (that is, the preponderant) regard in two-thirds of the infants in the first cube situation is for cube itself.

At 12 weeks four infants out of five, and at 16 weeks five infants out of five, give regard to the cube. This means that at 12 weeks the infant is already beyond the nascent stage of cube perception. At 16 weeks the infant regards the cube more promptly and more frequently returns to the cube after eyes have wandered away. Momentary regard, however, is much more characteristic of both age levels than is prolonged regard.

At 12 and 16 weeks, the infant's own hand is the most powerful rival as the focus of regard. In one-fourth of the children at 12 weeks, and in one-half at 16 weeks, the regard shifts from the cube to the hand for several possible reasons: the hand has motion, is at a more favorable optical distance, is larger, or is more significantly related to the apperceptual organization then dominant. For that matter, hand inspection may have a relatively specific, innate basis, comparable to the hand-to-mouth impulse.

Hand inspection is a universal growth phenomenon among normal infants. It is not, however, to be interpreted as a fixed, hard and fast reflex. In its external form, this pattern of reaction changes obviously with age and with the expansion of associated patterns. The inner undiscernible aspects of the reaction also undergo change. Hand inspection fades out of the picture rapidly and has almost completely disappeared at 28 weeks. It becomes more snatchy as it becomes vestigial. At 20 weeks one infant in three, and at 24 weeks one infant in ten, may selectively regard his own hand (some time during the first cube situation); but if he does so to a conspicuous degree thereafter it is an atypical and sometimes an unfavorable developmental symptom. Exaggerated and intrusive sterotypy of hand inspection is often seen in mental deficiency.

Similarly a selective regard for the examiner's hand occurs in almost half the infants at 12 weeks but has almost entirely dropped out at 24 weeks. It is a more primitive focus of visual interest than the infant's own hand and possibly more important in the early stages. . . .

Consistent (sustained) regard for the first cube arrives slowly and does not become fully established until about 28 weeks. . . .

Because of its intimate dynamic and developmental association with the prehensory mechanism, the outward forms of regard show their most conspicuous changes from 12 to 24 weeks. It is significant that "active" regard, characterized by accompanying approach movements of arms and body, comes into sharp prominence at 20 weeks in three-fourths of the infants; whereas a prolonged "passive" regard is most characteristic of 16 weeks. Such a prolongation of ocular fixation suggests that for an object of this size the primary oculomotor system is at this period coming to a stage of relative perfection: and this is such a complex area of pattern differentiation that the most overt prehensory adjustments are for the time subordinated. The infant must grasp (apprehend) and hold the cube with his eyes before he does so with his hands. And apparently he gains as much satisfaction out of the ocular as out of the later manual performance. By the age of 24 weeks, passive regard is rarely seen, for he is already well on the path of prehension and manipulation.[9] (pp. 127–129)

This verbal description of what one may expect in the way of visual behavior is supplemented, for each of the test objects, with a table of expected behaviors.

Here[9] (p. 126) Dr. Gesell presents the percentage of infants at each age from 12 to 56 weeks who regard the test cubes when the first, second, and third cubes are presented.

Four years later (1938) a companion volume, *The Psychology of Early Growth*[10] presents much the same kind of information but in greater detail. Though neither "eyes" nor "vision" are indexed, we do find "Behavior, perceptual" and "regard." The information is presented in tabular forms as follows[10] (pp. 170, 171).

Table 5-1. Regard

				Critical age		
(a) FOCUS						
Supine						
Su 64	Stares vacantly	–	–	4:3	1*	0*
Su 66	Stares at window or wall	–	4*	6:3	2*	2
Su 65	Fixates definitely	–	1*	6:4	–	–
Su 69	Facial expression attentive	–	1	6:3	–	–
Social.						
so 2	Visually pursues moving person	–	1*	6:3	3*	–
Personal						
per 1	Regards hands	1*	1	12:3	4	–
Dangling ring						
RD 6	Disregards in midplane	–	–	4:3	2	2
RD 7	Regards in midplane	–	2*	6:3	3*	3

Table 5-1 (*continued*)

		Critical age				
RD 17	Follows past midplane	−	2*	6:3	3*	3
RD 20	Follows approximately 180°	2*	2*	12:3	3	−
Rattle						
Ra 13	Regards Examiner	−	2*	6:3	3*	4
Ra 12	Regards surroundings	3*	4	12:3	2	2
Ra 2	(If regards) regards only in line of vision or when shaken	3*	3	12:3	2	−
Ra 5	Regards in midplane (spontaneously or after shaken)	2*	2	12:3	4	−
Ra 8	Regards spontaneously in midplane	2	2	16:3	3	−
Ra 15	Regards rattle in hand	2	2	20:4	4	4
Cubes						
CCl 14	Regards Examiner's presenting hand	−	−	12:2	1	1
CCl 15	Regards hand	−	3	16:3	2	1
CCl 3	Regards cube	−	2	16:4	4	4
CCl 13	Regards predominantly	−	2	16:3	3	4
CM 12	Pursues visually to platform or floor	1	2	36:3	3	2
Pellet						
P 13	Regards Examiner	−	−	12:3	2	1
P 15	Regards table top	−	−	12:3	2	1
P 14	Regards Examiner's hand	−	4	16:3	2	2
P 16	Regards hand	−	2	16:3	1	1
P 1	Regards (s.m.p. or n.m.p.)	−	2	16:3	4	4
P 2	Regards with definite fixation	1	2	20:4	4	4
Pellet and bottle						
P-Bo 19	Attends to bottle only	−	3	36:3	2	2
P-Bo 21	Regards pellet after dropped from bottle	2	2	40:3	4	4
P-Bo 1	Regards pellet as dropped in bottle	2	2	40:4	4	4
P-Bo 3	Attends predominantly to bottle	4	3	44:3	1	1
P-Bo 2	Regards pellet in bottle	2	2	44:3	3	4
P-Bo 4	Attends predominantly to pellet	1	2	48:3	4	4
	(b) TYPE					
Stares						
Su 64	Stares vacantly	−	−	4:3	1*	0*
Su 66	Stares at window or wall	−	4*	6:3	2*	2
Ra 10	Regards starily	1*	2	12:3	1	1
Regards momentarily						
RD 3	Regards momentarily	3*	4*	8:3	2	2
Ra 9	Regards only momentarily	3*	3*	8:3	2	2
CCl 6	Regards momentarily	−	2	16:4	2	1
P 7	Regards momentarily	1	2	20:3	2	1
Regards prolongedly						
RD 4	Regards prolongedly	2*	2	12:3	4	2
Cp 5	Regards prolongedly	−	1	16:3	2	1
P 9	Regards prolongedly (increasing)	1	1	20:2	2	1
P 9	Regards prolongedly (decreasing)	1	2	24:2	1	1
Regards after delay						
RD 1	Regards after delay	3*	3	12:3	2	1
Ra 3	Regards after delay	2*	3	12:3	2	1
P 4	Regards after delay (increasing)	1	1	20:2	2	1
P 4	Regards after delay (decreasing)	1	2	24:2	1	1

Table 5-1 (*continued*)

		Critical age		

Regards recurrently					
Cp 3	Regards recurrently	− 2	16:3	2	1
CCl 7	Regards recurrently	− 2	16:3	2	2
P 8	Regards recurrently (increasing)	1 1	20:2	2	1
P 8	Regards recurrently (decreasing)	1 2	24:2	1	0
Regards intermittently					
CCl 8	Regards intermittently	1 1	20:2	1	0
Shifts regard to surroundings					
Rd 13	Shifts regard to surroundings	4* 3*	8:3	2	1
Shifts regard to Examiner					
RD 15	Shifts regard to Examiner (increasing)	− 2*	6:3	3*	3
RD 15	Shifts regard to Examiner (decreasing)	3* 3	12:3	2	2
CC 4	Shifts regard to Examiner	2 2	44:3	3	3
Cp-Sp5	Shifts regard to Examiner	1 2	56:3	−	−
Regards hand					
CCl 15	Regards hand	− −	12:3	3	2
P 16	Regards hand	− 2	16:3	1	1
Shifts regard to hands					
CC 5	Shifts regard to hand	− 2	16:3	2	1
	(c) EXTENT				
Su 65	Fixates definitely	− 1*	6:3	+	+
Rd 17	Follows past midplane	− 2*	6:3	3*	3
RD 7	Regards in midplane	− 2*	6:3	3*	3
so 2	Visually pursues moving person	− 1*	6:3	3*	+
Ra 5	Regards in midplane (spontaneously or after shaken)	2* 2	12:3	4	+
RD 20	Follows approximately 180°	2* 2	12:3	3	+
CCl 3	Regards cube	− 2	16:4	4	4
Ra 8	Regards spontaneously in midplane	2 2	16:3	4	4
RD 2	Regards immediately	2 2	16:3	4	4
CCl 13	Regards predominantly	− 2	16:3	3	4
P 1	Regards (s.m.p. or n.m.p.)	− 2	16:3	4	4
P 2	Regards with definite fixation	1 2	20:4	4	4
Ra 15	Regards rattle in hand	2 2	20:4	4	4
Sp 6	Regards consistently	1 1	24:4	4	4
B 8	Regards consistently	− 2	24:4	4	4
Cp 7	Regards consistently	1 2	24:3	4	4
CM 11	Shifts regard from cube to cube	1 2	24:3	4	4
RD 5	Regards consistently	1 2	24:3	4	+
Ra 11	Regards consistently	1 2	24:3	4	+

Two years earlier, in 1936, in collaboration with Dr. Eugene M. Blake, Dr. Gesell published a paper titled "Twinning and Ocular Pathology."[11] This paper reported in detail the case history of two otherwise relatively normal identical twin girls, twelve years of age, both with macular coloboma in both eyes. The paper discusses the probable cause of this deviation and concludes that, in all likelihood, the original single zygote or the constitutive factors in the twin embryos, which already held the hereditary determiners of all four eyes, *held also the specific factors* (or mutations) which delimited the development of the choroid.[11] (p. 1061)

The following year, 1937, an article presents the case of a boy who could not walk nor even creep and who because of his athetosis was in more or less constant motion. For all his handicaps, this boy seemed to have a more or less normal intellectual endowment. As Dr. Gesell says in summary:

> It may be argued that "the fullness of A.C.'s development depended upon the intactness of his auditory and particularly his visual functions. Visual experience was probably least affected by his brain injury. His eye grounds were normal and the early strabismus was self-corrected. He even attained the ability to make eye movements of a reading type. It is possible that the kinesthetic data furnished by his twelve oculo-motor muscles supplied the main scaffolding for his mental equipment.[12] (p. 531)

In a 1939 book titled *Biographies of Child Development*[13] Dr. Gesell mentions very briefly four children (including a pair of twins) who suffered from assorted "visual defects:" mystagmus, macular coloboma, and cataracts. He does not discuss the visual behavior of these children at any length.

There are brief mentions of vision in a 1940 book, *The First Five Years of Life*,[14] having to do with the earliest visual localization:

> *Reaching.* No one can say just how distances appear to the unsophisticated eye of the young infant. The indications are that his perception of depth is the result of the gradual integration of visual and proprioceptive cues, through the process of trial and error. Although information concerning the development of visual depth discrimination is scant, investigations on young children indicate an improvement with age. According to McGinnis,[15] visual localization is to some extent present at birth and improves rapidly during early infancy. Ocular pursuit in response to a moving light, objects, and persons is pretty well perfected at 6 weeks; whereas coordinate compensatory eye movements and fixational head movements undergo a somewhat slower development. True ocular fixation apparently does not function well until the third month. This is of particular

significance because it is at this time that directed arm movements in response to objects within the visual field are first observed.[14] (p. 76)

This book also includes brief comment as to the amount of difficulty a visually handicapped child tends to have in responding to
the Gesell Developmental Examination. The message here is that
though visual defect obviously interferes to some extent with a
child's response to (Gesell) developmental tests which require "real"
visual discrimination, children who are developmentally and intellectually normal have no major difficulty with the rest of the tests in
demonstrating their basic normality. But for the totally blind child,
that child's response to training gives more of an idea of his potential than does his response to the Gesell developmental examination.

In the following year, 1941, Dr. Gesell attacked the problems of
vision rather vigorously in his book, *Developmental Diagnosis.*[16] Aside
from incidental references to seeing, his major contributions here to
the field of vision come under the heading of normal visual behavior
to be expected at the early ages, and in a section titled "The Diagnosis and Early Management of Visual Defect" (which includes blindness).

Dr. Gesell notes that "In the early months, looking is half of
living"[16] (p. 253). He then describes, as in earlier publications, the
early development of visual behavior. He gives practical advice as to
the early diagnosis of various kinds of visual defect. Of the totally
blind child he advises:

> The blind baby needs extremely special care and yet the
> cardinal rule for parents should be *Treat the blind baby as if he
> were a seeing child.* . . . The important thing in the rearing of a
> blind child is the protection of his personality. He should not be
> made conscious of his handicap but rather of his obligation to
> take his place in the family circle.[16] (p. 258)

Dr. Gesell also discusses in this book the early diagnosis of visual
defect[16] (p. 257).

Next comes *Infant and Child in the Culture of Today,* a book written in collaboration with Ilg, Ames, and Learned. This book covers
the first 5 years of life and for every age level covered—4, 16, 28,
40, 52 weeks, 15 and 18 months, and 2, 2½, 3, 4, and 5 years—
there is a description of the visual behavior which can be expected.

The authors also devote two pages[17] (pp. 17–19) to eye behavior in general, in fetal life and in infancy.

It is here, to the best of our knowledge, that Dr. Gesell first makes his classic remark:

> *Vision is so fundamental in the growth of the mind that the baby takes hold of the physical world with his eyes long before he takes hold with his hands* [Italics ours].

In the two further books which completed his so-called Trilogy—*The Child from Five to Ten,*[18] and *Youth: The Years from Ten to Sixteen,*[19] the authors follow this same precedent of briefly describing normal visual behavior to be expected at each of the ages covered.

In 1945, in a picture-book story titled *How Baby Grows,*[20] Dr. Gesell devotes one page to a pictured summary of typical visual behavior in the first months of life. The brief accompanying text repeats the slogan, "Vision leads in the early growth of the mind. The baby uses his eyes before he uses his hands"[20] (p. 7).

In this same year, 1945, Dr. Gesell produced a more scholarly book titled *Embryology of Behavior.*[21] He describes visual behaviors that one may expect in the early stage fetal infant (28–32 weeks after conception)—"The eyes may be open or they may not"; in the mid-stage fetal infant (32–36 weeks postconception)—"Eyes move saccadically in brief after-pursuit"; and in the mature fetal infant (36–40 weeks). At this time:

> His ocular behavior at optimal moments suggests visual interest and even a seeking kind of inspection. He definitely follows the movement of a dangling ring through an arc of 45 degrees in the preferred sector of his visual field. He has a preferred sector because in the supine position he elects to lie with head averted to one side. At times, for brief moments, he immobilizes his eyes in pseudo-fixation, as though drinking in visual impressions, in a diffuse and passive manner. He tends to open his eyes wide when he hears the sound of a bell. He blinks to the flash of a strong light, but tolerates it far better than at an earlier age, and may even show mild interest in ocular pursuit.[21] (p. 127)

The text continues:

Transient strabismus is occasionally seen, but there is no well-defined ocular fixation. Under optimal conditions, the eyes follow a dangling ring through an arc of 45 degrees, and then stare in a shallow, vacant manner at a massive, strongly contrastive stimulus. It is difficult or impossible to elicit real regard for the examiner's face.[21] (pp. 139, 140)

Two years further along a special cinema study of the infant's visual response to his mirror image, developed in collaboration with Ames, was presented, in 1947, in two forms: a film[22] and an article published in the *Journal of Genetic Psychology*.[23] In both forms, visual behavior is featured strongly.

And now comes a somewhat surprising turn of events. In 1949, after Dr. Gesell's official retiring age from the University, at a time when many of his basic areas of contribution had rather wound themselves down, his interest in and his contribution to the field of vision increased. Three papers[24,25,26] and a major book[1] on the topic appeared in 1949. The book, *Vision*, provided even at this late date his major contribution in the field. These publications were followed in 1950 by a major film[27] and two more articles.[28,29] In 1952 came a further book[30] illustrating his film. A final brief article on vision appeared in 1953.[31]

The first of the 1949 articles[24] was an abstract of a paper delivered at the annual 1949 meeting of the National Academy of Sciences. It is a summary report and adds little new, as will be seen from the following quote, which gives this mention in full:

The Developmental Aspect of Child Vision:
Under a cooperative program of research over a period of 10 years, the Yale Clinic of Child Development has made periodic studies of the visual functions of normal infants and children of preschool and school age. These studies are concerned with the progressive organization of visual functions in their relationship to the action system of the growing child at a score of age levels. Five functional fields have been explored in a preliminary manner: 1) eye-hand coordination; 2) postural orientation; 3) fixation; 4) projection; 5) retinal reactions. The data were gathered by means of developmental examinations of behavior patterns; naturalistic observation of spontaneous and adaptive behavior at home, school, and guidance nursery; graded tests of visual skills; optometric tests; and examinations by streak retinoscope.

The retinoscopic findings in conjunction with other findings indicate that the visual mechanism is in a somewhat labile
condition, both dynamically and developmentally. Superim-
posed upon a basic delimiting refractive state there is a margin
of adaptability which is manifested in the brightness, the motion,
the direction, and the speed of the retinal reflex. Developmental
stages can be differentiated according to the child's visual manipulation of space.

The visual system and the unitary action system prove to be
intimately and reciprocally related. The child sees with his total
makeup. Acuity is only one aspect of the economy of vision.
From the standpoint of a developmental optics, visual functions
can be interpreted in terms of their dynamic relation to the
maturity and operations of the basic action system. This has
implications for visual hygiene. Eye care involves child care.[24]
(p. 342)

The second paper this same year, "The Developmental Aspect
of Child Vision" (apparently the same title), presents, in brief, information about the development of vision in infant and child, information to be found in more elaborate detail in Dr. Gesell's major
book *Vision: Its Development in Infant and Child*,[1] published also in
1949. In this paper, Dr. Gesell again emphasizes that:

The eyes take the lead in the conquest and manipulation of
space. The baby takes hold of the physical world ocularly long
before he grasps it visually.[25] (p. 311)

In addition to a clear summary of developmental stages which
occur in the child's visual functioning as he matures, Dr. Gesell gives
an important warning:

It should not be necessary to wait until belated adolescent
and adult years to determine the efficiency of visual functions.
With increased knowledge the developmental status of these
functions can be appraised and supervised throughout the period of infancy and childhood. In this sense the developmental
aspect of child vision has implications for preventive and super-
visory pediatrics.[25] (p. 313)

Dr. Gesell also briefly discusses here various kinds of visual
problems as strabismus, myopia, reduced acuity. He gives two special further warnings. First:

In considering the visual economy of a young child one does not think only in terms of refraction and fusion. One considers the over-all organization of his visual equipment, and asks whether he has the ability to meet the normal visual tasks demanded by the culture. A developmental approach to his problems puts us in a better position to give him the developmental support which will benefit him more than a full refractive correction would. Indeed, in some instances a full correction given too early and insisted upon too long may create a crutch which, in turn, becomes an impediment.[25] (p. 315)

Second, he warns of the danger offered when schools make excessive demands of the often immature visual ability of the school beginner.[25] (p. 316)

A third 1949 paper is titled "Development of Vision in Childhood."[26] This paper is brief (two pages) and adds little to what has been said before.

Dr. Gesell's major contribution in 1949, in fact the major contribution of his lifetime in the field of vision, is his book, *Vision: Its Development in Infant and Child.*[1] This volume clearly represents the culmination of all his earlier work on vision. Even in the late 1980s, 40 years after its publication, it is considered a classic in the field and is widely used by specialists in the area of vision.

Space prohibits a thorough review of this book, but the table of contents provides a good survey of what it has to say. In the introductory section, Dr. Gesell gives an overview which includes chapters on "The Eyes of Today and Tomorrow," "Orientation," "The Background and Scope of This Study," "The Evolution of the Human Action System," and "The Motor Basis of Vision."

Part One, titled "The Growing Action System," summarizes the development of visual behavior (most of which has been presented in earlier publications) from embryo and fetus through ten years of age. Part Two presents chapters on "The Visual Domain," "The Complex of Visual Functions," "The Young Eye in Action," "The Ontogenesis of Visual Behavior," and "Maldevelopment and Child Vision." Part Three is made up of chapters on "The Developmental Hygiene of Child Vision" and "The Conservation of Child Vision." The book is fully illustrated.

Anyone unfamiliar with Dr. Gesell's earlier publications in the field of vision will find here an excellent summary both of information about the way vision develops and of the Gesell approach to the field of vision. One specially valuable section presents in full detail the story of a totally blind child born with complete bilateral anophthalmia. That is, he had no eyes, and the optic nerve was lacking. This boy was followed by Dr. Gesell for the first four years of his life. In spite of his total blindness, most of his other behaviors developed in the same way and at the same rate as would those of a sighted child.

Dr. Gesell's conclusion about blindness, with special reference to this particular boy, is as follows:

> In the case history just outlined, we see, as though in a test-tube culture, the effects of uncomplicated blindness on the patterning of infant behavior. The developmental career of M.F. justifies the general conclusion that blindness in itself does not produce a serious degree of retardation. It profoundly alters the structure of the mental life, but not the integrity of a total growth complex. Despite congenital anophthalmia, the basic patterns of body posture, manipulation, locomotion, exploitation, language, and adaptive and personal-social behavior have taken progressive form, thus establishing conclusively the fundamental role of maturation in the mental growth of the blind infant.[1] (p. 273)

In the following year, 1950, came another substantial contribution—a 30-minute color sound film titled *The Embryology of Human Behavior*.[27] This film presents the beginning of human behavior both in fetal infant and in the first year of life. It features the development of the eyes in embryo and fetus, and the early development of visual behavior, especially in the first four months of life.

There was also in this same year a single paper called "Infant Vision"[28] written at the request of the *Scientific American*. This paper points out, rather amusingly, the ways in which human vision differs from that of a fish. It gives a comprehensive description of the evolution of vision over some millions of years, as well as the evolution of Dr. Gesell's own studies of the development of vision in infant and child. It is brief but comprehensive.

A single article on vision titled "Child Vision and Developmental Optics," again written on request, as part of a "jubilee" volume in honor of the French psychologist, Henri Pieron, appeared in 1951. It is a remarkably succinct summary of Dr. Gesell's earlier observations of visual behavior in fetus, infant, and preschooler.

Since the material is not particularly new, however, it need not be summarized here except to note Dr. Gesell's definition of Developmental Optics. This he defines, "in theory and in application" as being concerned with the ontogenesis and organization of visual functions in their dynamic relation to the total action system.[29] (p. 385)

In the following year, 1952, there was another single contribution on vision. Harper & Row published for Dr. Gesell a slim volume, *Infant Development*, based on his film, *The Embryology of Behavior*. Though supplied with adequate text, this is to a large extent a book of photographs based on the film. It describes, and illustrates, visual behavior as it develops in infant and young child. Here again, he repeats one of his favorite sayings:

> The infant takes hold of the world with his eyes long before he takes hold with his hands.[30] (p. 16)

A particularly pertinent chapter titled "Eyes, Hands, and Brain"[30] (pp. 49–56) gives one of Dr. Gesell's most succinct summaries of the physical and behavior development of the human eye during the prenatal period. This is followed by, again, an extremely succinct summary of the visual behavior of which the infant is capable in both the neonatal period and in the first year of life.

A final short paper on vision appeared in 1953, titled "Development of the Infant with Retrolental Fibroplastic Blindness." This is rather an anticlimax to his long list of major contributions to the field of vision, since it was an invited paper which discusses merely one single vision difficulty, as its title indicated—retrolental fiberplasia in infancy. Dr. Gesell notes that this disability is nearly always associated with prematurity. However, he assures his readers that "even a combination of extreme prematurity, blindness, and neonatal cyanosis does not necessarily produce serious retardation"[31] (p. 1). He then gives practical advice to the parents or caretakers of the young child suffering from this serious handicap.

Though for most of the topics discussed in this volume information is not given as to what took place after Dr. Gesell's retirement and death, in this instance the aftermath of his interest in vision seems worth recording. Shortly after the publication of his book on vision, the Gesell group left Yale University and colleagues founded the Gesell Insitute of Child Development in Dr. Gesell's honor. A major part of this new Institute was a Vision Department, headed by Dr. Richard J. Apell, still its director.

This department has continued to be active ever since that time. Its chief task is to examine children visually, to provide vision care and vision training, and to teach students the methods of developmental optometry which the Institute supports.

The most succinct description of the Gesell point of view with regard to vision, and of the way we would like to see it applied to children, is to be found in a chapter by Dr. John W. Streff, formerly of our staff, titled "What You Should Know About Your Child's Vision," from the book *Stop School Failure*, by Ames, Gillespie, and Streff[32] (pp. 89–119).

Chapter 6

KINDERGARTEN

Dr. Gesell very frequently mentioned the topic of kindergarten in his writings. It first appears in 1919, and last in 1946. His most frequent comments had to do with the kindergarten curriculum as contrasted with that of nursery school, or with the value of kindergarten in promoting related goals—such as the encouragement of the mental hygiene of the young child. Because many of these references are extremely casual and incidental, we have chosen to include in this chapter only twelve of his more pertinent mentions.

There appear to be two *major* themes in his comments about kindergarten. One is the somewhat obvious suggestion that kindergarten be considered as more or less a halfway station or link between nursery school and first grade. The other, more ambitious, and probably seldom realized, was that kindergarten be used as a mental hygiene center where careful evaluation could be made of the characteristics of young children, with the particular aim that such special qualities as superiority or handicap be recognized and dealt with.

This second theme appears in his first mention of kindergarten, published in 1919. He recommends:

A reorganization of the kindergarten and first grade, which will place the first half year of school life under systematic, purposeful observation. The teachers, program, schedule and equipment and administration of this induction period to be definitely adapted to such observation and to a system of record keeping and classification of pupils, which will determine their educational hygiene in the subsequent grades.[1] (p. 6)

A second mention in 1921 repeats this theme (and in fact some of the very words) but also introduces his persistent belief that the kindergarten program should not be too academic:

We should gradually reorganize the kindergarten and the primary school in such a way that the school beginner will be under systematic, purposeful observation. This means a gradual relaxation of our present zeal to teach him the three Rs, and the substitution of a much more wholesome solicitude, namely one to safeguard his health and to understand his psychology.[2] (p. 560)

His third discussion of kindergarten is by far the longest he gives, and is so general in nature that it is very difficult to summarize. He introduces the topic as follows:

The kindergarten. This was first introduced into the United States in 1855, and has had a notable development with us. It bears such important relations to the present problem of nursery education that this will be reserved for special treatment in the following chapter. Founded through the labor and vision of Friedrich Froebel, in the second and third decades of the nineteenth century, it has followed a rather independent course of growth, but has profoundly influenced other educational agencies and our relations to young children. Historically the kindergarten has accomplished much; it may have an equally important role in the future in solving the complicated problems of pre-school education and hygiene.[3] (p. 47)

There follows a 10-page chapter titled "The Kindergarten." Since this chapter is too long to reproduce, we present selections:

There is no agency concerned with the welfare of early childhood which, in America, holds more power for effective service than does the kindergarten. The kindergarten is strategically situated in our educational system. It is the very vestibule of our vast public school system. . . . Ever since its introduction into this country, the kindergarten has maintained itself as a kind of intermediate station between home and the nursery school.[3] (p. 57)

It remains to this day a silent, visible protest against the mechanistic tendencies and institutionalization of primary education. . . . It may again become the rallying ground for a forward movement in child hygiene, if it will assert in unmistakable terms the sacred right of young children to physical and mental health.[3] (p. 58)

There is need of more experimental work in kindergarten organization and administration. *School superintendents and boards of education in general have neglected this field.*[3] (p. 59)

The kindergarten is today distinguished by a kind of isolation which is becoming more and more unjustifiable. A gap separates it from the public school; a chasm separates it from the infant-welfare and public-health organization of the community. If it is to realize its destiny, it should become an organic part of a unified system of public health and education.[3] (p. 60)

Unfortunately, there has been a deplorable tendency to ignore the physical aspects of development, to disregard the symptoms of physical defeat and disease, and in actual practice to neglect even such fundamentals as sunshine, milk, free outdoor play and sleep.[3] (p. 61)

In principle the distinctions between nursery, nursery school, and kindergarten ought to disappear. The kindergarten must assimilate all that is best in nursery and nursery school and possibly even some of the actual functions of these two institutions.[3] (p. 62)

An effort could be made to conduct certain children's health centers in kindergartens or near kindergartens. Kindergartens could cooperate in developing methods for more parent-teaching in connection with the conferences. . . . The kindergarten might also become interested in developing an observation and information record of prospective kindergarten children while they are still in the infant-welfare period of development.[3] (p. 66)

A flexible type of kindergarten could readily assume certain nursery functions. . . . The principle of multiple use could be put into practice, also, by shortening and multiplying sessions and by having certain age groups or developmental groups report on alternate days.[3] (p. 67)

The following chapter in this same book, "School Readiness," presents the point of view discussed more fully in our chapter on School Readiness. Dr. Gesell's position, as outlined in that chapter, is

that readiness for first grade should and could be determined when
the child is still in kindergarten. Not only the child's developmental
status, but also his intellectual status and certain aspects of his personality or individuality and his general physical health could be
evaluated while he is still in kindergarten.[3] (pp. 68–77)

Dr. Gesell urges that:

> The organization of the primary department should be
> elastic enough *to permit full emphasis on the basic developmental needs
> of the child rather than on reading, spelling and arithmetic.*[3] (p. 70)

He recommends:

> . . . more deliberate and patient psychological observation of a
> non-technical type. . . observation of the child's behavior at play,
> games, handiwork, dancing, conversation.[3] (p. 177)

And he notes that:

> The social and constructive activities of the kindergarten
> give fine scope for this kind of observation. Through it we can
> discover the superior, the balanced, the inadequate, the unsta-
> ble, the speech defective, and all the exceptional children who
> need a specialized educational hygiene and a readjustment of
> procedure as to school entrance.[3] (p. 77)

He continues:

> Hygiene and education cannot do their best for the child
> unless his developmental history is known.[3] (p. 81)

And he recommends kindergarten as a place where emphasis
should be put on finding out more about each individual child. And,
importantly, he recommends that the primary school as well as kindergarten should:

> . . . modify its objectives, must relax its excessive emphasis on
> the so-called 'fundamental' (academic activities), and shift it to
> true fundamentals that is, to dealing with the whole child and
> not just his cognitive functions.[3] (p. 82)
>
> Individual differences in emotional and volitional traits are
> of more importance than those which are purely intellectual.[3]
> (p. 83)

Two statements still important to us in the 1980s, when length of kindergarten day as well as type of program are still highly controversial issues, are the following:

> Surely the primary teacher *ought not to attempt to teach the pupils to read and write before they have really learned to talk*, and kindergartens should make oral expression one of the chief objectives of their educational program.[3] (p. 125 [italics ours])

And,

> *It has not yet been demonstrated that it is educationally necessary or hygienic to send even first and second graders back to school in the afternoon.* Shorter and less frequent periods of institutional education may accomplish almost as much as longer and more frequent periods. (p. 206 [italics ours])

Finally, Dr. Gesell notes that at the time of his writing this particular book:

> The kindergarten is not a universal feature of American education. In some communities it has by tradition become an integral and cherished part of the public school system; in other communities it is altogether lacking. There are in round figures four million American children between the ages of four and six. About one in ten of these attends a kindergarten. California, New York, New Jersey, Michigan, and Connecticut enroll in their kindergartens a proportion of from 32 to 25 per cent of the children of kindergarten age. Arkansas, Tennessee, West Virginia, North Carolina, and North Dakota enroll from .19 to .53 per cent. Note the decimal point.[3] (p. 203)

A pamphlet titled "The Kindergarten and Health" by Dr. Gesell and Julia Wade Abbott[4] discusses primarily the role of the kindergarten in promoting mental and physical health and will be discussed elsewhere. A brief section on "Learning Through Doing" underlines Dr. Gesell's feeling that kindergarten teachers should not lay too much emphasis on academic learning but rather should make every reasonable effort to satisfy the child's curiosity and to help him to learn through play, through care of pets, through gardening, through dramatization, through "'conversation periods,' through stories and rhymes"[4] (pp. 24–29).

A 1924 article which deals primarily with the nursery school rather than kindergarten reminds us of the fact that all had not always been smooth sailing for kindergartens in this country. Gesell notes:

> If we have vague fears in regard to the nursery school movement, let us recall the kind of opposition which the kindergarten has had to meet. As late as 1900, a conservative formulated this protest: "The kindergarten encroaches, without justification or understanding, on these inalienable rights and duties (of the family), and thus injures the moral training of individual children, and also hinders the progressive moral development of parents.
>
> If we do not admit this as a sound criticism of the kindergarten, shall we count it as one against the nursery school?[5] (p. 650)

An article written in 1925, titled "The Downward Extension of the Kindergarten"[6] deals primarily with the importance of pushing preschool education down below kindergarten, and need not be reviewed here.

In 1926, a short piece entitled "The Kindergarten as a Mental Hygiene Agency"[7] appeared in the magazine *Mental Hygiene*. Its message, repeated in numerous other articles by Dr. Gesell, is that the kindergarten, if properly used, could be a tremendous mental hygiene resource in identifying and thus in trying to serve the needs of many different kinds of children ranging from the handicapped to the gifted. He urges[7] (p. 28) that it not be crystallized into just another schoolroom but should work with the home and community agencies to meet the "hygienic" as well as the educational needs of all children.

A second article in this same year[8] makes more or less the same suggestion, that the kindergarten, in addition to its usual functions, be used for the purpose of identifying and helping children with special needs.

The theme of the use of the kindergarten to promote mental hygiene needs—a concept quite clearly very dear to Dr. Gesell's heart—is repeated in 1930 in a brief article which concludes:

> The American kindergarten is in danger of crystallizing into just another schoolroom, when to meet the new demands it must develop a versatile, multiple technique which will bring it

into more effective contact with a wider range of childhood. Instead of becoming fixed as a schoolroom, the kindergarten may evolve into an educational service instrument, a kind of dispensary, that will be staffed to do a certain amount of routine but that will be organized and geared to render special educational guidance to parents and also to children of pre-kindergarten age.

The position of the kindergarten in the educational scheme is unique and strategic. The kindergarten is the recruiting station of the public school system. As such, there is every reason to hope that it will establish increasing contact with children of pre-kindergarten age and with their parents. By a judicious penetration into the region of the lower age levels, an articulation with infant welfare activities can be evolved.[9] (p. 8)

Lost from our files and unavailable at the Yale Library is an article with the promising title "The American Kindergarten," listed as having appeared in the *N.E.A. Journal* "after September 12, 1932."[10] This item was not included in the official Miles biography. Also, considering the title of the journal, and in view of what Dr. Gesell had been writing on the subject in the years just preceding, one may assume that it may well have continued with the theme of the kindergarten as a provider of mental hygiene service.

A final article titled "Looking Backward: To a Demonstration Kindergarten, 1876"[11] provides exactly what its title promises—a picture and description of a kindergarten class in 1876. It is a whimsical bit of history, but does not add to our knowledge of Dr. Gesell's feelings or ideas about the kindergarten as a part of our public or private school systems.

The topic of kindergarten is not mentioned again by Dr. Gesell in anything but the most casual fashion, not even in his book *Infant and Child in the Culture of Today,* until we come to a final rather brief mention in his 1946 publication, *The Child from Five to Ten.*[12]

Since this material gives a rather good summary of Dr. Gesell's view of what does, and presumably should, take place in kindergarten, we quote it at length:

> To the 5-year-old the kindergarten is a kind of extra-mural home. School does not yet mean the novel and exciting transition to a new world that it will a year later. Nor is the kindergarten truly a preparatory course for the first grade. Successful adaptation to the kindergarten does not always augur a compa-

rable adjustment to the first grade, but most children enjoy
kindergarten life. The child likes his teacher, obeys her as a matter of course, and quotes her as an authority. His relationship is
matter-of-fact and pleasant, and much less personal than it will
be later.

In the *language arts*, the 5-year-old is relatively facile and
well balanced. He not only likes to talk, he like to listen; and
loves to be read to time and time again. He also looks at books
alone and *may pretend to read*. He may recognize some of the
capital letters, pick out familiar words on a page or placard and
indulge in a little simple spelling. But he is probably more alert
with his ears than with his eyes.

He is beginning to use his hands languagewise, to delineate
figures and simple dramatic episodes, to trace, to paint at an
easel, to underline and to draw capital letters, and perhaps, to
print his own name.

In the *sciences*, he shows a dawning interest in meanings. He
has reached that stage of human culture when digits meant
digits; and so he counts the five digits on his hands. He may
count to ten; but his concepts are typically within the domain of
five. Finger counting should not be denied him now or later. It
is as natural as finger feeding once was.

His intellectual interests are varied rather than inquisitive
and critical. He does not distinguish readily between fantasy and
reality. He accepts "magic" as an explanation. He is fond of
stories in which animals act like human beings. Nevertheless as a
constant talker and listener he accumulates abundant simple
information in the areas of natural and social science.

His *personal-social participations* reflect the organization of
previous experience somewhat more than adventurous expansion into the unknown. He foregathers in fluid groups of two,
three, or four in his kindergarten play; he dramatizes familiar
events; he dresses up in adult clothes. He works creatively with
paint, clay and blocks, usually starting with a goal idea and
finishing with a recognizable product. Socially he shows an incli-
nation to establish friendships; and he can carry through on a
group project from one day to the next. He takes an interpersonal as well as personal pride in achievement; for he likes to
take home his kindergarten handiwork, and to keep the things
that he has made out of his own spontaneity in response to the
pressures of culture.[12] (p. 378)

In summary one may say that Dr, Gesell's chief emphasis with
regard to kindergarten seems to be that he saw it quite as much as a

mental hygiene center as a place for specific academic teaching and learning. He felt strongly that kindergarten was a place for children to go and enjoy themselves but also a place in which the adult world could become acquainted with the young child and could adapt to his or her individual needs and abilities.

As to controversial topics relating to kindergarten under discussion in the 1980s in schools throughout the country, he appears to be against both all-day kindergarten sessions and also against an overacademic curriculum.

Chapter 7

TWINS AND TWINNING

We find Dr. Gesell's first discussion of twinning in a paper on "Hemi-hypertrophy and Mental Defect"[1] published in 1921. Here he comments:

> It is natural that a discussion of the etiology of hemihypertrophy should finally bring us to problems of double physical personality and twins. Further researches into the biology of twinning may bring the remarkable phenomenon of unilateral hypertrophy more completely within our comprehension. By twinning we mean production of equivalent structures by division. . . . Hemihypertrophy is interpreted as a form of asymmetry due to a possible deviation in the normal process of twinning.[1] (pp. 13, 20)

A second major article[2] on hemihypertrophy appeared in 1927. In this article, "The medical literature on hemihypertrophy is reviewed and brought up to date. Thirteen cases are added to the original forty cases tabulated in 1921. And here hemihypertrophy is interpreted as a 'minimal form of twinning.' "

From here on the matter of hemihypertrophy is mentioned only incidentally, as in two single case histories included in *Biographies of Child Development*.[3] One of these subjects was followed from age 2 to 15; the other from 12 to 36 years. However, for this present review, the fact that twinning was first mentioned in a paper about hemi-hypertrophy may be considered largely incidental.

Dr. Gesell's first paper on twins as such, aside from the abnormality described above, was titled "Mental and physical correspondence in twins."[4] This appeared in 1922. Actually it was predated by a few months by the abstract of a paper given in December 1921 at the Thirtieth Annual Meeting of the American Psychological Association and published in the *Psychological Bulletin*[5] titled "Psychological Comparison of Superior Duplicate Twins." This paper described the forthcoming monograph.

This 1922 paper is primarily a historical review of the literature on twins and twinning. Dr. Gesell reports that:

> In 1918 the American Genetic Association announced its desire to communicate with twins living in our part of the world. Six hundred twins and parents of twins responded. The present writer (AG) in 1921 published a study of forty cases of hemi-hypertrophy and discussed this condition in relation to mental defect and twinning.[4] (p. 309)
>
> We report herewith a case which will serve as a basis for the consideration of the problem of resemblances in twins.[4] (p. 311)

He then discusses in detail the physical resemblances in a pair of highly superior twins and also the similarity of their responses to the usual psychological tests given at that time. These girls had been followed from infancy through eight years of age.

Here in 1922 he states, perhaps for the first time, the basis for his intense interest in twins:

> The problem of resemblance in twins is one of critical significance. *If we could solve it with any completeness even for one pair of duplicate twins, we should thereby gain much insight into more general problems of heredity, development and education.* Dr. Morton Prince has called double personality a veritable gold mine for the study of psychological phenomena.[4] (p. 331)

Dr. Gesell included this, his first paper on twins, with the following request:

> The reader of this article may be acquainted with an interesting pair of twins. The author will be grateful to receive any letters or photographs bearing on the problems of physical and

mental resemblances in twins. He is particularly interested in developmental correspondences observed in infancy and childhood. Address: Yale University, New Haven, Conn.

Two talk pieces, now unavailable, but presumably covering much the same ground[6,7] appeared in this same year. But it was not until 1929 that Dr. Gesell and his associate Helen Thompson published the first of two major monographs on the subject of twinning.[8,9] These and their sequel[10] plus two monographs by graduate students[11,12] constitute the body of Dr. Gesell's famous work on twins. This work quite obviously had its substantial impact on the literature more by its quality than its quantity.

This first Gesell and Thompson monograph, "Learning and Growth in Identical Infant Twins: An Experimantal Study by the Method of Co-twin Control"[9] is presented in two sections. The first and introductory section gives detailed evidence of the marked and striking similarity between these two identical twins, T (trained twin) and C (control twin). Not only were physical resemblances remarkable, but also weight curves (over a substantial period of time), dentition, and responses to Gesell Developmental Tests.

The main part of this monograph, however, is given over to an exposition of the so-called method of co-twin control (see Figure 7-1), and to examples of this method in action. The two developmental situations used for this demonstration were stair-climbing and cube behavior.

In brief, the purpose of this kind of experiment was to find out whether or not special training in any given kind of behavior, given when that behavior was about to emerge, actually resulted in improved or accelerated behavior for a trained twin over that exhibited, slightly later, by an untrained twin. In the stair-climbing experiment, for instance, the trained twin (T) was from 46 to 52 weeks given daily practice and encouragement in climbing stairs. The control twin (C) was kept in an environment which did not include stairs.

At 46 weeks neither had been able to climb even one stair. At 52 weeks, after 6 weeks of training, T could climb the stairs in 25 seconds. At this time, her training was discontinued and a week later, at 53 weeks, C's training began. Although hitherto untrained, and kept in an environment which did not include stairs, C, unassisted, climbed the steps seven times, a performance only approximated by T after 3 weeks of training and not surpassed until 5½ weeks of training. C's average time on this first day was 45 seconds.

More than this, both twins at 53 weeks climbed the stairs in the same manner, shifting from left hand and right knee forward to right hand and left knee forward halfway up the steps, though neither had seen the other perform.

To quote the authors:

> The climbing performance of twin C at 55 weeks was far superior to the climbing performance of Twin T at 52 weeks, even though Twin T had been trained 7 weeks earlier and 3 times as long.[9] (p. 116)

The same applied to the cube experiment. Twin T was trained daily in cube behavior from 46 to 52 weeks of age. At the close of this training period, when C was introduced to the cubes, her cube behavior patterns were highly similar to those of T. "It was impossible to demonstrate any significant influence of training upon the cube behavior patterns of Twin T."

The timing and precision of both stair-climbing and cube behavior were recorded explicitly by cinema, and cinemanalysis was used in analyzing and evaluating the results of these co-twin studies.

The main conclusions of the co-twin control experiments were that when an infant or child is just about ready to perform some new developmental task, rigorous training can sometimes cause that behavior to appear slightly sooner than it might have appeared without such training. However, if an identical twin, *untrained*, is presented with the same task at a later date, after a few weeks of growing, his performance at this later date will at that time equal that of the twin who was trained early.

This finding supports Dr. Gesell's basic belief that though one must always consider both nature and nurture in attempting to understand any child's behavior, environmental factors modulate and inflect but do not determine the progressions of development. Nature, at least in the case of co-twin control experiments, appears to transcend nurture in determining behavior.

Two monographs by graduate students, one by Strayer[11] and one by Hilgard,[12] apply the methods of co-twin control to language behavior and memory and motor performance. Their findings agreed with those of Gesell and Thompson—that early training has only modest and temporary effect in speeding up infant and child behavior.

The second major monograph on twinning[10] by Gesell and Thompson was written when the chief set of twins, T (trained) and

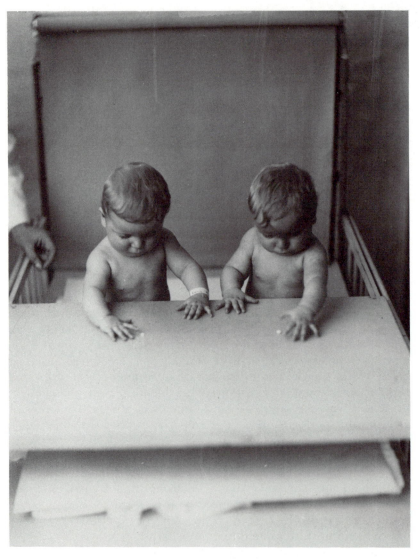

Figure 7-1.   Co-twin control.

C (control), were fourteen years of age. Its title, "Twins T and C from Infancy to Adolescence: A Biogenetic Study of Individual Differences by the Method of Co-twin Control", tells its story. After reviewing the many, often somewhat startling, similarities between the two girls, this monograph emphasizes chiefly the consistent personality differences between the two.

Thus when behavior was not identical, the twins differed virtually always in the same manner. Twin T was consistently right-handed; C mostly left. Twin T was quick, tense, direct, focused on a task, not particularly sociable. C was casual, relaxed, with roving attention and an extremely sociable manner, much more responsive to people than to things. As Dr. Gesell phrased it, "In posture, gait, and dancing, similar contrastive tendencies in angularity and curvedness display themselves." Even in drawing, T consistently drew straight lines; C, curved lines.

The impact of this second, major monograph on twins was not as great as that of the first. Perhaps the very wealth of detail obscured the basic and important message that even identical twins are individuals. At any rate, this monograph was quoted much less often in the literature than was its predecessor.

However, the original monograph, along with those by Hilgard and Strayer, did have a very strong influence in the field. This influence was bolstered by the fact that chapters by Dr. Gesell, and Drs. Gesell and Thompson, appeared in two influential compilations of studies on child behavior by leading specialists in the field.

The first, "Developmental Psychology of Twins",[13] appeared in Carl Murchison's *Handbook of Child Psychology* in 1931. This chapter, which came out very shortly after the first major monograph, includes such subtitles as "The Scientific Study of Twins," "The Diagnostic Classification of Twins," "The Pathology of the Twinning Process," "Physical Correspondence in Twin Development," "Behavior Correspondence in Twin Development," "Psychopathological Correspondence in Twin Careers": . . . *then*, as a grand finale, "Experimental Studies by the Method of Co-Twin Control and the Nature-Nurture Problem and Twins."

Murchison's *Handbook* was a classic, a standby in almost every college course taught in the field of child behavior, and thus gave great visibility to Dr. Gesell's early findings about twins.

A second *Handbook* chapter, "Learning and Maturation in Identical Infant Twins: An Experimental Analysis by the Method of Co-Twin Control" by Gesell and Thompson, appeared in Barker, Kounin, & Wright's *Child Behavior and Development* in 1943.[14] Both this volume and the Murchison *Handbook* were published in the days when there were just a handful of "leaders" in the field. And to some extent whether or not one was a leader was determined by inclusion in such compilations as these two.

In this particular chapter the authors point out that *they are concerned with twins as method rather than with twins as subject matter.* Since the material presented for the most part reviews earlier studies[9,11,12,] its contents need not be repeated here.

This relatively short list of Dr. Gesell's writings on twins and twinning may be completed by four further contributions. In 1941, Gesell and Ames edited two films—*Twins T and C: Similarities of Behavior*[15] and *Twins T and C: Differences in Behavior.*[16] In 1942, a piece titled "The Method of Co-Twin Control"[17] appeared in *Science, 94,* 446–448. Finally, in 1952, an article[18] which combined two of Dr. Gesell's favorite topics, "The Method of Co-Twin Control in Conjunction with the Method of Cinemanalysis", was published in *Acta Geneticae et Gemellogigiae,* 1952, *1,* 23–28. Since this was the last that he had to say on either subject, we shall quote briefly:

> Significantly enough, twins are not only a target of research, they constitute a tool of research for the exploration of problems which go well beyond immediate boundaries. I recall that in our early studies of twins we were chiefly fascinated by the correspondences, and the amazing identities of the pairs of twin children under observation. But in time we came to realize that the mechanisms which determined the almost uncanny identities were of greater scientific importance.
>
> This led us to devise the method of co-twin control for the objective study of biological and psychological factors in early human growth. . . . In identical infant twins, nature provides a stage for observing which can be confined to one twin. The co-twin can then be used as a baseline for comparison.
>
> *Cinemanalysis* is an objective research technique which capitalizes the almost magical time-space manipulability of flexible films to define the patterns of behavior in relation to spatial form and temporal sequences.
>
> The method of co-twin control and the method of cinemanalysis here briefly described can, of course, be used independently. But when the two methods are brought into conjunction, they reinforce each other and thereby sharpen our insight into the developmental mechanisms of the human action system.[18] (pp. 25–28)

Thus, in summary, it can be seen that Dr. Gesell's interest in twins and twinning followed a rather straightforward path. His initial interest in the subject had to do with such an abnormality of reproduction as hemihypertrophy, but very soon shifted to the more normal aspects of twinning.

His earliest publications combined a historical review of the subject with clear, objective evidence of the common-sense appreciation that identical twins tend to showing startling similarities not only in body but in behavior. He soon moved on to a concern with twins as a method rather than as a subject matter. Thus he pursued co-twin control studies in which he was able to compare the behavior of a twin who was trained in special activities with that of the untrained twin, demonstrating clearly the modest effectiveness of early and vigorous training. He then moved on in 1941, as his interest in individual differences increased, to a demonstration of the fact that even identical twins differ from each other in striking and consistent ways from infancy on.

Though the number of his studies in this field is not large, their effectiveness was tremendous. Hardly any review of Gesell's work omits reference to his co-twin control studies.His work on twins certainly helped substantially to strengthen his basic theoretical position which was that human behavior develops in a patterned, predictable way which can be influenced, but not substantially speeded up or altered, by environmental factors. It also substantiated his insistence that every human person is an individual, different in many ways from every other, even from his own identical twin.

Chapter 8

INFANTS ARE INDIVIDUALS

Many psychologists, unfamiliar with the detail of Dr. Gesell's writings, have complained that he does not "believe in" individual differences. Quite the contrary. A careful reading of his works makes very evident his respect for the fact that in his opinion "Infants are individuals," and that "Every child is different from every other— even his own identical twin."

The first of such statements appeared as early as 1922,[1] when he comments:

Individual differences among unrelated human beings are almost infinite in variety. We do not expect even two leaves from a forest to be alike, much less human beings.[1] (p. 331)

Two years later he states clearly:

Our normative and comparative studies have convinced us that there are irreducible individual differences in humanity which assert themselves even in infancy.[2] (p. 646)

In 1933 he goes rather beyond such statements, fleshing out his feelings about individual differences[3]:

The individual differences which manifest themselves among unselected, newborn infants, the individual differences

of prematurely born infants, the demonstration of sensory capacities and of postural reactions in the prenatal period, individual differences in the prenatal motility of twins, and many other
considerations suggest that the biological determinations of
individuality *trace back to the period of the fetus*.[3] (p. 68)

In 1938 he warns that:

> We tend to pay vastly too much attention to mere training
> and instruction. Our central task, particularly in the first five
> years of life, is to discover and respect individuality.[4] (p. 19)

The following year he states very clearly:

> The (observed) perpetuation of characteristicness is not
> incompatible with morphogenesis and maturing. It is, however,
> inconsistent with the idea that individual differences at birth are
> slight and increase with age. *Infants are individuals*. They differ
> as adults differ.[5] (p. 304)

Contradicting the opinion of John J. B. Watson,[6] Gesell warns
that:

> We must not jump to the conclusion that we can mould the
> child as though he were clay, for he is an individual with inborn
> propensities, with inherent characteristics.[7] (p. 198)

Later in the same year in his book, *The First Five Years of Life*,
he asks the important question, "How does individuality manifest
itself?" and answers as follows:

> Individuality manifests itself in the physical makeup of the
> child, in biochemical and physiological characteristics, and in
> patterns and dispositions of behavior, in distinctive methods of
> maturing and learning.[8] (p. 296)

Returning to his recurring theme of the individuality of infants
again in "Infant and Child," he repeats his basic notion that "Infants
are individuals. They are individuals from the moment of birth"[9]
(p. 39).

Referring specifically to the genetics basis of individual differences among children, in 1945 he writes:

> Many of the differences (among children) are attributable
> to ancestral genes. There are differences of body build, motor
> demeanor, temperament, aptitudes, and modes of mobilizing
> and of releasing energy which are based on hereditary or on
> constitutional determiners. Even one-egg twins may display
> consistent psychological differences from early infancy—differ-
> ences not traceable to social or educational factors.[10] (p. 196)

These typical examples, appearing over a period of a quarter of
a century, make quite evident Dr. Gesell's belief in, and concern
about, the importance of individual differences. It seems important
for students of his work to appreciate this concern in view of the
frequent criticism, made by superficial readers of his publications,
that Dr. Gesell thinks children are all alike and that they follow his
norms religiously. A careful reading of almost any of his works
makes very evident the superficiality of this criticism.

In fact, he states very specifically in 1939:

> Our data do not lend support to the concept of a relatively
> standard pattern of infancy. From the standpoint of embryol-
> ogy the infant is already far advanced in the cycle of life. *He is
> already stamped with individuality rather than a standard pattern.*[5]
> (p. 304)

In 1945 he repeats this warning:

> Every baby has his own way of growing up. No baby follows
> exactly an average time-table.[11] (p. 2)

Ways of Measuring Individuality

This review makes it clear that from his earliest days (as early as
1922), Dr. Gesell expressed full respect for individual differences.

The first published study which especially presented a method
for comparing children so far as individual differences (rather than
developmental differences) go appeared in 1937 under the title
"Early Evidences of Individuality in the Human Infant".[12]

This was a cinema study in which five infants who had been
studied intensively were arranged in rank order from 1 to 5 (best to
worst or most to least) on 15 behavior or personality characteristics,
as illustrated in Figure 8-1.

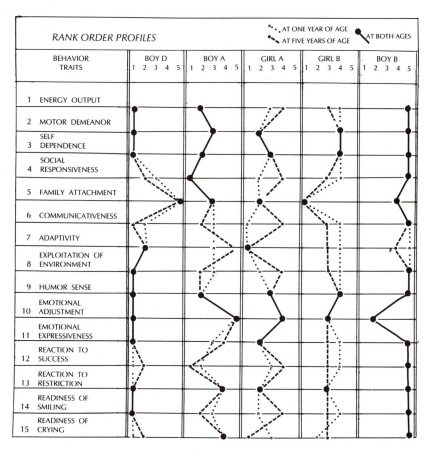

Figure 8-1. This graph pictures the predictiveness of individuality traits as appraised in infancy and at the age of five years. Fifteen behavior traits listed in the left column are rated for five children in the adjoining columns.

As this figure shows, there was marked consistency from trait to trait. As noted:

> Every infant seems to have what may be called a motor habitude or characteristicness which expresses itself in postural demeanor and modes of movement. This characteristicness is

difficult of description because it is the compound result of numerous factors, including skeletal form, disposition of musculature, speed, synergy, smoothness and precision of acts.[12] (p. 221)

Relative speediness was especially noteworthy in that the child who crept earliest crept fastest; the one who crept latest crept the most slowly.

Behavior ratings made during infancy were then compared with ratings on the same characteristics made when the same boys and girls were five years of age. As Figure 8-1 shows, there was outstanding consistency. For 48 of 75 evaluations, behavior was the *same* (first, last or at some specific point in between) both in infancy and at five years.

The conclusion was drawn that persisting traits of behavior individuality are observable in infancy and persist, very definitely, through at least the first five years of life. In fact this is so to such an extent that the child who had crept first, and fastest, at a five-year-old birthday party for the group of children was the first to reach out and take a cake from a plate of cakes in the center of the party table.

A second, more long-range approach to the precise study of individual differences was Dr. Gesell's use of the method of co-twin control, in which the behavior and personality of identical twins was compared over a period lasting from four weeks through fourteen years of age.[13]

This study, which is referred to elsewhere, in our review of Gesell's work with twins (Chapter 7), demonstrated that even in two identical twins, reared together from earliest infancy, no clear-cut and consistent differences were demonstrated. As Gesell concludes, these differences seemed to be the result of genetic rather than environmental factors:

In last analysis, the organism plays the primary role in determining environment. And the area of primary determination is equivalent to basic individuality. When human behavior is organized in a cultural milieu, there is almost an infinitude of available environments; the organism selects from this infinitude in much the same way that a living cell may or may not select potassium from a fluid medium. The structure of the organism, whether conceived in terms of biophysical waves or particles of stereo-chemistry, is attuned to what it selects and averse to what it rejects. For this reason it has proved difficult to find pure, thoroughgoing psycho-genic factors to explain the individual differences in the life careers of twins T and C.[13] (p. 119)

In spite of his strong and continued interest in individual differences, Dr. Gesell and his staff did not, during his years (1911–1950) at Yale University, develop any systematic method of evaluating individuality. However, they did make one stab at it in the book *Infant and Child in the Culture of Today* published in 1943:

> Temperament and growth are closely related phenomena. Each represents the characteristic manner in which an individual reacts to life situations. Growth type is particularly significant because it expresses the long-range individual way in which the organism handles the continuous task of achieving maturity. Some children, to use an antique word, are more "growthsome" than others. But they differ yet more profoundly in their styles of growth.
>
> These varied styles are manifested in emotional characteristics, in motor demeanors, in reactions to novelty, success and failure, in dependence upon environment and persons. Consider Children A, B and C as illustrations of three different modes of development and of self adjustment.
>
> *Child A* matures slowly: *Child B*, rapidly: *Child C*, irregularly.
>
> A approaches new situations cautiously and warily; B is incautious and cool: C is variably overcautious and undercautious.
>
> A is wise with respect to life situations: B is bright and clever; C is brilliant.
>
> A is equable: B is blithe: C is moody.
>
> A achieves orientation in total time and space; B is oriented to present time and immediate space: C is mixed and confused, while achieving orientation.
>
> A takes in the whole and works in from the periphery: B operates more in the immediate context: C takes in either too much or too little and holds on too long.
>
> A adjusts and shifts focus: B is in relatively continuous focus: C is well in focus or far out of focus.
>
> A can wait and bide his time: B is up and at it, does not need to wait: C does not know how to wait and is poor at timing.
>
> A assimilates gradually: B combines and adapts expeditiously; C overcombines and dissociates poorly.
>
> The foregoing traits are dynamic traits; therefore, they have wide and general applications. They come into expression

at all ages from infancy to adolescence and adulthood. They apply to all significant life situations, those of home as well as community—to the routines of feeding and everyday living in the nursery. They involve the vegetative as well as the sensori-motor and symbolic nervous systems. The traits, as listed, were not derived from an academic classification, but are based on observations of infants and young children in clinic and nursery school.

These A, B, C traits represent variations in the make-up of the "biological individual" but they also have significance for the "cultural individual." They determine to what extent the child is susceptible or immune to the stimulations of the cultural environment. By implication they even suggest adjustments which the culture must make in behalf of these individual differences in modes of growth and learning. The various traits overlap and do not fall into neat compartments. However, the A traits all tend to go together, and in the most typical cases are represented in one and the same individual. This is true of the B and the C traits also, so that we have, roughly speaking, three major *growth types*: A, B, C, and the solid, the facile, and the uneven. Which fact leads to a very interesting conclusion as to the responsibilities of the culture. It is clear that the C type will make the most demands, and require constant adjustments; the B type is less demanding. The A type asks little from the environment and depends on his own resources. The culture should be alert to offer him somewhat more than he asks for. The B type asks more from the environment; he knows what he wants and is so articulate that the culture does not need so much to foresee and plan. The C type is variably overdemanding and underdemanding. The culture must plan, foresee, direct, restrict, prod and channelize to bring about mutual accommodations between the individual and his environment.

Between these extremes lie the everyday problems of infant care and child guidance. The beginning of wisdom in the rearing of children is a realistic recognition of the growth factors which shape his conduct, and the acknowledgment that every child has a unique pattern of growth.[9] (pp. 43–46)

However, this effort at classification was not followed up, and was omitted entirely from the 1974 revision of *Infant and Child.*

Though Dr. Gesell thus did not develop in any depth his own system of classifying various personality or individuality types, in the late 1930s or very early in the 1940s he became interested in the methods of Constitutional Psychology proposed by Dr. William H.

Sheldon.[14] This interest was strong enough that he invited Dr. Sheldon to join his staff at Yale.

Dr. Sheldon did not accept this invitation, but in 1951 he helped to set up a somatotyping project at the Institute and later became a member of our Scientific Advisory Board.

Also, in three of his major book publications, Dr. Gesell made reference to Sheldon's systematic approach to individual differences. The first of these three references is given in the book *Infant and Child in the Culture of Today*[9] in 1943. It is short and to the point:

> Infants are individuals. They are individuals from the moment of birth. Indeed, many of their individual characteristics are laid down long before birth. In the shape of his physique the newborn infant already gives tokens of what he is to be. Physical measurements may show which of three body types he will most closely approximate as an adult: (1) round, soft body, short neck, small hands and feet; (2) square, firm body with rugged muscles; (3) spindly body, delicate in construction. Individual differences in physique are due to variations and mixtures of these bodily characteristics.
>
> There is a similar variety in temperaments, corresponding to differences in physique, and in biochemical and physiological peculiarities. Three traits or types of temperament have been distinguished. They combine in varying degrees in different individuals: viscerotonic, somatotonic, and cerebrotonic (Sheldon). The extreme viscerotonic has a good digestive tract. He is good-natured, relaxed, sociable, communicative. The pronounced somatotonic is active, energetic, assertive, noisy and aggressive. The fragile cerebrotonic is restrained, inhibited, tense; he may prefer solitude to noise and company. He is sensitive and likely to have allergies.[9] (pp. 39, 40)

In 1946, in the second major book on behavior characteristics of the various ages, *The Child from Five to Ten*, Dr. Gesell again makes glancing reference to Sheldon's work:

> There are enormous individual differences with respect to the strength of sexual characteristics among adults as well as children. Sheldon, for example, states that the viscerotonic temperament is "notably greedy for routine outward affect on from members of his family."[15] (p. 316)

As to posture:

Sheldon holds that postural preferences are unquestionably innate. He speaks in terms of three temperament types which are associated with three body types as follows: (1) viscerotonic: round, soft body, short neck, small hands and feet; (2) somatotonic: square, firm body, with rugged muscles; (3) cerebrotonic: spindly body, delicate in construction. The extreme viscerotonic has a good digestive tract. He is good natured, relaxed, sociable, communicative. The pronounced somatotonic is active, energetic, assertive, noisy and aggressive. The fragile cerebrotonic is restrained, inhibited, tense; he may prefer solitude to noise and company. . . . It is probably as natural and desirable for a cerebrotonic to sit round shouldered on the middle of his back as for a somatotonic to sit square shouldered on the end of his back.[15] (p. 230)

And, says Gesell:

Sheldon writes almost a paean describing the alimentation of the viscerotonic, who attends and exercises in order to eat. (While the cerebrotonic eats and exercises in order to attend; and the somatotonic eats and attends in order to exercise!) The viscerotonic has a love of food and a warm appreciation of the process of eating for its own sake, which is not to be confused with mere voracity of appetite. Digestion is excellent and is a primary pleasure.[15] (p. 242)

In 1956, in the third in his series of books about the various ages, *Youth: The Years from Ten to Sixteen*[16] Gesell again refers briefly to the Sheldon typology. Reflecting Sheldon's own shift in terminology, he now refers to endomorphy, mesomorphy, and ectomorphy, instead of, as earlier, viscerotonia, somatotonia, and cerebrotonia:

Physique and temperament. W. H. Sheldon approaches the problem of adult individual differences and deviations from the standpoint of variation of physique and temperament. There are three major body types: the roundish endomorph (soft body, short neck, small hands and feet); the squarish mesomorph (firm body with rugged muscles); the spindly ectomorph (slender and delicate in construction). Pure types are rare. Individual differences in physique are usually manifested in mixtures of the basic body types. Similarly there are three temperamental types. The temperamental traits combine in widely variegated degrees in different individuals. The extreme endomorph tends to have a good digestive tract. He is good-natured, relaxed, sociable, communicative. The pronounced mesomorph is active, energetic, assertive, noisy, and aggressive. The fragile ectomorph is restrained, inhibited, tense; he may prefer solitude to noise and company. He is sensitive and is likely to have allergies. Temperament denotes the distinctive mental character of a person.

Though all individuals present complex mixtures of components, the "typical" endomorph, mesomorph and ectomorph tend to express the ground plan of growth in characteristic ways which are now being investigated at childhood and youth levels. In the area of emotions, for example, the endomorph tends to show his feelings easily at any age; other people are too important for him to withdraw very far, even in the most withdrawing phases. The mesomorph, at any age generally described as less competitive, is non-competitive only in a comparative sense— that is compared *with himself* at other ages. The ectomorph is quicker to withdraw when troubled, takes pains to hide his feelings. He may show an alertness and fast reaction, but in many areas he tends to show immaturities. He seems to need more time to grow. *Our observations indicate that the gradients of growth take on added meaning when interpreted in the light of constitutional individuality.*[16] (pp. 28, 29)

In view of Dr. Gesell's consistent assertion that "Behavior is a function of structure," it is small wonder that Sheldon's system appealed to him. But it should be noted that Gesell, and presumably Sheldon as well, did not ignore the environment. In Gesell's philosophy, "environmental factors modulate and inflect but do not determine the progressions of development." Similarly, environmental factors do influence individuality; but it is the constitutional type or structure which determines the way in which and the extent to which they influence.

PERSONALITY VERSUS INDIVIDUALITY

It should be noted that Dr. Gesell was always firm with staff and students (and doubtless with himself as well) that a clear distinction be made between the terms *personality* and *individuality*.

Though he seldom used the term "personality," he appeared to be quite clear in his distinction between the two terms. He used "individuality" when he was referring primarily to innate constitutional characteristics; "personality" when he referred to the results of interaction between organism and environment.

The following references, over the years, set forth his definitions of the term *personality*. The first of these, in 1924,[2] was as follows:

> The traits and trends of the baby's personality are to a remarkable degree the product not of specific inheritance but of conditioning environment.
>
> The child's "personality makeup" so far as it is a describable subsisting reality, consists in the countless conditioned reflexes, associative memories, habits and attitudes which it acquires as a result of being reared by personal beings. If he were never touched by ministering hands, if he did not see and hear the evidences of humanity, if he could grow up in an absolutely asocial vacuum, it is difficult to believe that he would have any recognizable "personality makeup" at all. The balance, the topography, the well-being of personality depend to a remarkable degree upon the impress of other personalities. However, there can be no doubt that the first outlines and to a certain extent the very texture of a personality are laid down in infancy.

In the following year, he again[17] emphasizes the role which environmental factors play in structuring personality:

> The personality of the child grows like an organic structure which reflects in a marvelous manner the impress of the home and the social environment. Original nature, so-called, provides certain tendencies or materials, but the final patterns of *personality* are the result of education and experience.

In 1928[18] he gives the following rather poetic description:

> The image of the web of life is, in fact, applicable to the mechanics of personality formation. It is possible to think of each personal complex of mental growth as a brief compression of events staged in a little theater in which the individual achieves a unique but conditioned system of adaptations to the whole human family.

From this time on the term *personality* is seldom found in his writings, though in 1956 he comes back to it once again. At this time his distinction between "personality" and "individuality" is clear indeed.

In the foregoing discussion of *individuality* we have made meager use of the term *personality*. The two terms are not fully synonymous. Personality is the total psychic individual as manifested in action and attitude. It is the crowning product of the human growth process because it embodies all of the experience which the individual has assimilated—the remembered, the forgotten, the repressed. It represents a life history, an underlying, innate individuality which gives form and foundation to the developing personality and its life history.[16] (p. 32)

Chapter 9

GESELL DEVELOPMENTAL NORMS

The Gesell infant and preschool behavior norms, which substantiate Dr. Gesell's position that human behavior develops in a patterned, measurable way, are considered by many to have been his outstanding contribution. His effort to develop norms of child behavior was first mentioned in an article titled "A Clinical Preschool Psychology," published in the popular magazine *Mother and Child* in 1923. In this article Dr. Gesell reports that:

> The Yale Psycho-Clinic has undertaken a systematic program of research into the norms of development of children of pre-school age. With the aid of graduate students and with the cooperation of the Visiting Nurse Association and the pediatric department of the Yale Medical School we have at the present date succeeded in making individual psychological records of 300 children at the 6, 9, 12, 18, 24 and 36 months levels of development. Fifty children have been studied at each level, many of them retest cases. They were unselected "normal" subjects. The two- and three-year-old children were examined in their homes; the others were seen either at the clinic or at consultation centers.
>
> The purpose of the investigation is to secure data for defining more correctly and more accurately the behavior traits characteristic of the ascending age levels, in terms of motor development, intelligence, habit achievement and social reactions.

The method of psychological investigation which we have used with the babies is one of clinical observation rather than laboratory experimentation. The baby is seated in the mother's lap, before a small table. We present him with a series of simple objects and problem situations—an enamel cup, saucer and spoon to manipulate; a piece of paper to crumple, tear or fold; a small pellet to pick up; a cube concealed by a cup to uncover; a rod to put into a small hole; a dangling ring to pull down; a third cube to grasp when both hands are full, and so forth.

Simple as these materials and situations are they have been surprisingly effective in serving their psychological purpose. They have evoked behavior responses almost without fail and have revealed interesting developmental differences between adjacent levels and between individuals of the same age group.

To delineate these differences is the first task of mental measurement in this field. Although our investigation is preliminary in character we are confirmed in our belief that the phenomena of behavior occur according to laws, that individual differences assert themselves with prognostic import even in babyhood, and that a clinical type of psychology may hope to ascertain some of these differences and offer the findings as an aid in the timely control of human behavior[1]. (pp. 65, 66)

The second mention of norms also appeared in the popular press. In the *New York Times* for January 21, 1923, in a news release titled "Mental Development in Infancy: Its Measurement and Hygiene," Gesell had this to say:

Much of present child psychological literature consists of biographies or diaries of individual babies. . . . The procedure adopted in our own investigations has been designed to furnish a cross-section view of infants at the ages of 6, 9, 12, 18, 24, 30, etc. months [see Figure 9-1]. Fifty unselected "normal" infants have been studied at each age level, and we have strictly limited our cases to children who were precisely at these ages, or within 2 weeks thereof. It has been our purpose to secure data for defining more concretely and accurately the behavior ability characteristic of the ascending age levels, not only in terms of intelligence, but in terms of motor development habit achievement, social reactions and personality traits.

The method of investigation employed is one of clinical observation rather than laboratory experimentation. The baby is seated in the mother's lap before a small table. . . . We present him with a series of simple objects and problem situations. . . . Take for instance a child's reaction to a small red cube.

Figure 9-1.   Infant studies.

Babies are by no means all alike; but neither do they differ so radically that we are unable to delineate prevailing similarities for a given age level and typical distinctions between adjacent age levels. *The concrete formulation of these age characteristics provides us with norms or standards for defining individual and developmental differences.* Indeed how can we interpret or even describe the complex phenomena of behavior development without the orientation of orderly observation?[2]

A more specific dating of the beginning of this work is found in an article titled "The Nursery School Movement," published in *School and Society* in 1924. Here Gesell states:

During the past six years our psychological clinic at Yale has been making studies of norms of development in children from one to five years of age. Our subjects have been unselected infants who represent average conditions of life and training.

In all we have investigated some five hundred children (the number is growing) at ten different levels—the neonatal, four months, six, nine, twelve and eighteen months and two, three, four and five year levels.

Our normative data were secured through psycho-clinical examinations of each child, conference with the mother, and visitation of the home. These data relate to four major fields of development: (1) The child's motor development; (2) his language; (3) his adaptive behavior (intelligence); and (4) his personal-social behavior as indicated by his personal habits and general conduct.

These normative and comparative studies have convinced us that there are irreducible individual differences in humanity which assert themselves even in infancy. Such differences, however, apparently concern capacities and temperamental qualities more than they do the dynamic organization of the individual or his personality makeup.[3] (p. 646).

This report indicates an increase in the number of children studied, sets the date from the beginning of these investigations back to 1918, and for the first time lists the four fields of behavior studied as motor, language, adaptive and personal-social—a designation which has been continued up to the present day.

There are several mentions in 1925 of this pursuit of normative data. An article titled "The Early Diagnosis of Mental Deficiency"[4] notes that the Yale Psycho-Clinic is making a systematic investigation of the behavior of normal infants in order to determine norms of development *applicable to problems* of developmental diagnosis. (This may be the first use of this special term—*developmental diagnosis*—which later (1941) became the title of one of Dr. Gesell's most important book publications.)

Later in this same year, in an article titled "Developmental Diagnosis in Infancy," he elaborates on this concept of developmental diagnosis:

From the standpoint of developmental diagnosis we are primarily interested in all those forms of behavior, mediated by a nervous system, which are coherently related to the attained maturity of the nervous system. We may conceive such behavior

as being a functional index of developmental status. An infant is
as old as his behavior. *In this sense the mind becomes an observable
object within the scope of developmental diagnosis.*[5] (pp. 3, 4)

He then again describes, as earlier, the beginnings of his normative investigations, noting that his whole array of test items is over
150 in number.

In one further report in this same year,[6] Gesell mentions for
probably the first time his method of paired comparisons in which
he brought a pair of infants of adjacent ages into the laboratory for
simultaneous observation. This method was used from time to time
thereafter, and is elaborated in a 1926 publication[7] "A Comparative
Method for Demonstration of Normal Development in Infancy."

However, Gesell's outstanding 1925 publication was the book
"The Mental Growth of the Pre-School Child: A Psychological Outline of Normal Development from Birth to the Sixth Year Including
a System of Developmental Diagnosis."[8] This book presented for
the first time the Gesell developmental norms for the four fields of
behavior already referred to: motor, adaptive, language, and personal-social. Though these norms have continually been revised during the succeeding 50 years or so, they are present in their fundamental essence in this very first book publication.

Much work has been done on the developmental norms since
1925, and much has been published. However, in the more than 50
years since that time it has been chiefly a matter of sharpening and
polishing rather than of introducing new concepts. Each new book
shapes and refines the norms, but the basic test items and methods
remain very much the same.

Thus by 1934 the norms had come a long way, as will be seen in
"Infant Behavior: Its Genesis and Growth."[9] The number of test
items to be considered has more than quadrupled, and detailed
percentages are given to show the extent to which one may expect
success in any given behavior at any appropriate age.

A different method of presenting the infant norms is seen in
the ambitious *Atlas of Infant Behavior: Normative Series* by Dr. Gesell
and others, published in 1934 by the Yale University Press.[10] This
Atlas presents in pictorial form responses of children at every key
age in the first year of life to the customary test situations—prone,
supine, sitting, standing, cubes, pellet, bell, and all other situations
which make up the normative testing schedule in the first year of
life.

Much the same information as was given in *Infant Behavior* is repeated and elaborated in *The Psychology of Early Growth*[11] which to some extent may seem somewat superfluous in that it does not substantially further our understanding of the behavior tests or the norms. All three of these books, though extremely detailed, give norms only through 56 weeks of age.

The next publication which provides norms, and very nicely supplements books immediately preceding, appeared in 1940. *The First Five Years of Life: The Preschool Years*[12] gives verbal descriptions of behavior to be expected at key ages in the first year of life as well as at 18 months, 2, 3, 4, 5, and 6 years of age. Tabular norms and detailed information for giving and evaluating these tests are provided from 15 months through six years of age.

Dr. Gesell's final publication on the subject, and perhaps his favorite, appeared in the following year (1941). Written, as the title implies, primarily for pediatricians and medical students, *Developmental Diagnosis: A Manual of Clinical Methods and Application Designed for the Use of Students and Practitioners of Medicine*[13] provides detailed norms and specific instructions for giving the Gesell Behavior Tests at the key ages of 4, 16, 28, 40, 52 weeks, and at 18, 24, 36, 48, and 60 months.

Though this was the last of Dr. Gesell's books that dealt with the norms, colleagues and former students have continued to revise these norms. *Developmental Diagnosis* has been revised by Knobloch and Pasamanick.[14] Knobloch and others have also published a *Manual of Developmental Diagnosis*[15] which brings infant-through-three years of age norms up to 1980.

Three further books update and/or expand Dr. Gesell's normative contributions. *School Readiness* by Ilg and Ames[16] provides normative data and instructions for giving tests from 3 through 10 years of age. (This book was originally published in 1964 and revised in 1978.) *The Gesell Institute's Child from One to Six, Evaluating the Behavior of the Preschool Child* by Ames and others was published in 1979[17] and was dedicated "To the memory of our colleagues Doctors Arnold Gesell, Catherine S. Amatruda, and Helen Thompson." It updates norms from 2½ through 6 years of age. *The Gesell Preschool Test Manual* by Haines, Ames, and Gillespie,[18] published in 1980, covers much of the same material, but the format is strictly that of a test manual.

Thus one can say with certainty that the project of providing norms which will measure the developmental level of infant and

child, begun by Dr. Gesell in 1918, continues to be an ongoing and
ever-evolving project. Norms are now used by psychologists, pediatricians, educators, and others throughout the world in evaluating
the developmental status of young human beings.

Possibly the majority who use our tests actually use the official
Gesell battery. Others integrate some of our tests into their own bat-
teries. This is understandable, since though we can and do copyright our Incomplete Man form, one can scarcely copyright the
idea of copying geometric forms or of piling blocks. Probably the
most flagrant unacknowledged use of Gesell test items will be found
in the so-called Denver Developmental Test which, though it does
substitute raisins for pellets, was in its inception suspiciously identical with the Gesell Behavior Tests. We do consider that imitation is a
sincere form of flattery.

Though our norms are thus constantly being refined and improved, in essence they remain true to the original conception. As
Dr. Gesell expressed it, the mind has indeed shown itself to be an
observable object, within the scope of developmental diagnosis.

Chapter 10

ADOPTION

Both Parent and Child Must Be Protected

Dr. Gesell's position on adoption remained through the years clear-cut and consistent. It was that all adoptions should be carried out under the auspices of a responsible public agency. And that not only the child in question but the parents as well must be protected against ill-advised and hasty action.

In his first reference to the subject, in 1923, he mentions only one-half of this concern—the protection of the child:

> The benefits of adoption are great, acting mutually on parent and child. But the responsibilities are also great, and the child must be safeguarded against the effects of hasty, ill-advised legal action.[1] (p. 148)

He points out that the necessity for this is partly borne out by the fact that the Romans, "from whom our divorce laws descended" often had less than honorable motives for adoption.

In this very first reference to the subject of adoption, Dr. Gesell identifies the potential of 198 adoption candidates examined in or before 1923 by his assistant, Miss Margaret E. Cobb. According to her evaluation, only 2% of these children had "mentality that would qualify them for college training;" 7% might be expected to finish high school and 17% to do some high school work; 35% might benefit from vocational training; 25% might finish 5th or 6th grade; while 18% would not be suited for any level in the regular stream of education.

These findings may be compared with the findings of Ames as she examined 246 adoption candidates in the years 1941–1947. Of her subjects, nine, or 4% were "unclassified." Of the others, the median level of intelligence was "Low Average—i.e., 90–100"; the mean rating was 92. Five percent were classified as superior, 16% high average, 19% average, 26% low average, 28% dull normal, 2% borderline, and 3% were at the moron level.

In 1925, Dr. Gesell again emphasizes the importance and felicity of adoption: "Adoption at its best represents one of the finest human adventures in altruism." And at this early date he first emphasizes the importance of a careful, clinical evaluation of the quality of the child to be adopted.

> There are few situations which place upon us more exacting demands for prediction. The difficulties of prediction become greater the younger the child and the more definite the specifications of the adoptive parents. These difficulties cannot well be evaded nor should we seek to evade them.[2] (p. 424)
>
> The intelligent adoptive parent is entitled to at least reasonable assurance as to the *health* and *developmental potential* of the infant. An exhaustive medical examination, *including a thorough developmental diagnosis can be made in all cases of prospective adoption.* This initial thorough examination can be further safeguarded by successive follow-up examinations. If necessary the probationary period should be prolonged for this purpose.[2] (p. 425)

This suggestion is, of course, not unique with Dr. Gesell. As he notes:

> The improving standards of child placement work throughout the country are placing more and more demands upon psychological and developmental predictions. For example, the report on the mental examination of the child required by the Bureau of Child Welfare in Connecticut demands, in addition to ordinary data, a definite answer to the following questions involving not only immediate diagnosis but also prognosis:
> What is the child's intelligence? Superior? Normal? Dull normal? Inferior? Feeble-minded? (High grade? Middle grade? Low grade?) Imbecile Idiot?

Educational outlooks: Could child probably complete gram-
mar school? High school? College? Or should he have special
class work? Vocational training?[2] (pp. 426, 427)

In the first mention of the importance of a careful evaluation of
the potential of any adoption candidate, Dr. Gesell admits the possibility or even desirability of adoption even in cases where the prog-
nosis is not entirely favorable:

> We do not wish to suggest, in urging clinical safeguards,
> that child adoption should be made absolutely scientific and
> should lose altogether its fine element of faith and adventure
> and sacrifice. It is possible in certain instances that adoption of a
> mentally deficient child should be consented to.[2] (p. 427)

In the following year, 1926, in a pamphlet published by the
Children's Bureau of the U.S. Department of Labor, and titled
"Psychological Guidance in Child Adoption," Dr. Gesell again sets
forth, very clearly, his feeling that:

> In the interests of parents and child alike, purely impul-
> sive adoption should be discouraged and the whole procedure
> should be surrounded with clinical and supervisory safeguards.
> In all cases of adoption there should be an exhaustive inquiry
> into the health condition and developmental potentialities of the
> child. A thorough physical examination is essential, but no less
> desirable is a psychological estimate which will define in a gen-
> eral way capacity and developmental outlook. A probationary
> period of a full year, with follow-up examinations, may be uti-
> lized to correct this estimate, as well as to test the compatibility
> of the child and his foster parents.[3] (p. 1)

And he adds to the checks formerly deemed necessary, answers
to the questions: "Does the child show any evidence of epilepsy or is
there any history of convulsions?", and "Would the child be likely to
do well if placed in a family home?" "If so, would you recommend
an ordinary home or a superior home?"

Here he emphasizes what he calls the paradox that infancy is
the best time for adoption, but also the time when developmental
prediction is most difficult. However he believes that a probationary
period of at least a year, with a series of developmental examinations, can provide an adequate safeguard.

Here, as in future books and papers, he presents a series of case histories which illustrate both successful and unsuccessful instances of adoption, emphasizing especially the "cute" baby who is adopted without any psychological examination and who later turns out to be seriously defective.

He also gives warning but rather encouraging figures from two New York studies which followed up adopted children after adoption. In one such study only one out of nine children proved disappointing because of low intellectual level: in the second study, only one out of seven.

In 1927 came a short piece, significant primarily because it appeared in the *Bulletin of the Child Welfare League of America*, an organization which later, under the directorship of Joseph Reid, sneered publicly at the very notion of attempting to "match" adoption candidates to their prospective homes and parents.

The emphasis here was the same as in earlier publications. First, Dr. Gesell points out the necessity of protecting the child in question by ascertaining the sincerity and suitability of the would-be adopting parents. He then emphasizes the need of both careful diagnostic examinations and a protective probationary period:

> The greatest universal safeguard is a period of probation which will put the morale of the foster parents and the compatibility between parents and child to test. Legally and morally, in the interest of the child, no adoption should be consummated without an ample period of probation.
>
> When the period of probation is supplemented by careful clinical examinations, it is possible to determine in a precautionary way the normality of intelligence even in a young child or infant. Mental examinations are particularly necessary to forestall serious errors of selection in oversanguine foster parents who may have their hearts set on putting their child through high school or through college. It is a question whether any parent, adoptive or natural, should ever impose too specific a goal upon a growing child, and the adoption of an infant surely cannot be put on the same basis as vocational placement. However, it is desirable to learn everything we can about the constitution and capacities of the foster child.
>
> It is quite erroneous to suppose that excellent care and environmental advantages can in themselves determine the caliber of the child. Infants as well as adults differ in their native abilities, and only careful, consecutive examinations can deter-

mine the general developmental outlook of any child. Such examinations will confirm normality when it is obvious or taken for granted. They will also discover subnormality when it is altogether concealed in the general ambiguousness of infancy. They will sometimes reveal normal or even superior endowment when it is least suspected because of the poor repute of the child's origin.[4] (p. 2)

Thus by 1927, Dr. Gesell had already made the main points which he would continue to emphasize in his writings about adoption and in his clinical practice dealing with adoption over the next 20 years. These considerations include the necessity of protecting both parent and child. The child must be protected by determining the sincerity and suitability of the would-be parent. The parents would be protected by careful diagnostic examination of the child. A reasonably long probationary period will protect them both.

A 1928 mention of adoption emphasizes merely that though a certain amount of faith is needed in any case of adoption, it should not be blind faith and that:

... adoption cannot be kept under social control except through the careful exercise of prediction. Adoption cannot be entrusted altogether to good will or intuition, or to unaided common sense. The combined critical judgment of the social investigator, the court, the physician and the mental examiner should enter into the regulation of adoption.[5] (p. 385)

A somewhat long chapter in Dr. Gesell's 1930 book, *The Guidance of Mental Growth in Infant and Child*,[6] reviews at length points made earlier and concludes with a series of telling cases in which unsupervised adoption led to unhappy conclusions. Subheadings include: "An Attractive Infant but Subnormal," "Defective but Adopted," "Hasty Adoption and Antagonism Due to Mental Defect."

In 1939, in *Biographies of Child Development*, Dr. Gesell continues what many today might consider his overcautious theme:

Adoptions should, however, be protected and regulated. The first consideration should always be the child. That is why amateur placements by inexperienced persons are dangerous. ... To be a suitable candidate for adoption, a child should be physically and mentally normal; or to put it more realistically, he should have no *serious* physical or mental abnormalities (since) the ideally normal child is a fiction.[7] (p. 278)

He here again emphasizes the primary importance of a probationary period.

In *Developmental Diagnosis*,[8] a book written in 1941 for physicians and medical students, Dr. Gesell emphasizes the responsibility of the physician in cases of adoption. This individual must not allow himself to be drawn into "blind" and privately arranged adoptions, and should respect the fact that "a careful developmental diagnosis of status and outlook is an essential safeguard." In this book are listed numerous examples as well as case histories of unsatisfactory or tragic situations which have arisen from unsupervised adoptions.

Also in 1941, in an article in the *Journal of Pediatrics* we find the further comment:

> *Child Adoption.* The physician has certain professional responsibilities in protecting the standards and procedures of child adoption. Both for parents and for child, infancy is the most favorable time for adoption. But the hazards are great if the whole process of adoption is not safeguarded carefully at every step. Many infants offered for adoption are of inferior family stock, many have institutional backgrounds; their essential and innate normality definitely must be established before adoption can be recommended. There can be no guarantee that the good environment of an adoptive home will compensate for poor endowment.
>
> Careful developmental diagnosis and a probationary period of at least a year in the adoptive home prior to consummation of adoption are essential safeguards against unfortunate placements which can cause only unhappiness. The pediatrician is in an excellent position to reduce the risks of adoption. He should educate the parents to see the wisdom of dealing with responsible, accredited social agencies, of evaluating the family background of the child, of demanding an appraisal of the child's potentialities, and of considering all these factors in terms of the requirements and desires of the adoptive parents.[9] (p. 159)

In 1943, Dr. Gesell addressed a quarterly meeting of the Probate Judges of Connecticut on the subject of "Child Adoptions in Connecticut."[10] In this talk he reported on over 1500 dependent children examined at the Yale Clinic of Child Development prior to being placed in adoption, foster home care or an institution. He emphasized the "solemn responsibilities" of the court in child adoption; noted the various kinds of adoption—bootleg, commercial, blind, and safeguarded and court-controlled.

And he recommended a law which would safeguard all adoptions by demanding ample investigation of the home, a developmental evaluation of the child, and an adequate probationary period. According to Dr. Gesell, "Connecticut needs such a law."

In 1947, he wrote a letter to the Connecticut State Legislature[11] recommending that Senate Bill #117, which would eliminate compulsory investigation in cases of adoption, should *not* be passed. He stated specifically that in his opinion, investigation should be mandatory and not subject to the discretion of the Court of Probate:

> We can protect the adoptive child, the adopting parents and the State of Connecticut only by retaining a sensible, mandatory provision for prior investigation. It would be a step backward to make the provision permissive.[11] (p. 2)

He amplified this clear statement with examples of six cases in which disappointment, heartbreak, and tragedy resulted from unsupervised adoptions. Dr. Gesell's final statement on adoption, written in 1948, was brief and to the point:

> By methods of developmental diagnosis supplemented with clinical experience it is possible to diagnose in the first year of life nearly all cases of amentia, of cerebral injury and many sensory and motor defects and severe personality deviations. *One or two examinations in infancy* usually suffice to determine whether a child is suitable for adoption and whether the developmental outlook is favorable, highly favorable or unfavorable.[12] (p. 115)

Thus spoke Arnold Gesell on the subject of adoption. However, an interesting postscript by two of his former students, Knobloch and Pasamanick, in their revision of his major book, *Developmental Diagnosis*, throws certain light on, and to quite an extent explains, what some today might consider the rather rigorous standards which Gesell maintained in the 1920s, 1930s, and 1940s as to the suitability or nonsuitability of candidates for adoption. These authors note that:

> In modern times economic conditions and social attitudes have influenced profoundly the practices of adoption. Dur-

ing and immediately after the Depression, *there were many more infants available for adoption than there were families wishing to adopt.* Emphasis was on placement only of "perfect" infants who matched the adopting parents in ethnic and religious backgrounds, physical characteristics and purportedly in intellectual potential. After World War II, with improvement in economic conditions, the number of families wanting to adopt outstripped even the boom in births. Emphasis then shifted to restrictions on the type of people considered suitable adopting parents. Thus the "perfect" child required a "perfect" home.

But people continued to prefer to adopt infants—white, non-handicapped infants. By 1970 the greater percentage of children *not* adopted were non-white, over 6 years of age, mentally or physically handicapped or all three.[13] (p. 370)

Knobloch and Pasamanick feel, as do many today, that it is permissible to place a handicapped, or at least a "hard to place" child in adoption but they maintain, as did Gesell, that there is an increased risk of abnormality in illegitimate children, so that, before any adoption, a development assessment is essential so that before parents take on a child who is handicapped in any way this fact will be fully understood, as well as the nature and extent of the handicap. Physical handicaps are usually quite obvious, but intellectual, developmental, or personality handicaps are often revealed only after careful testing.

It may seem that Dr. Gesell's contribution to the field of adoption consisted pretty much of a single issue—that adoption candidates should be evaluated psychologically, developmentally, and intellectually before being given out in adoption. This was, indeed, his contribution, but it was a major one. Before he began his efforts, most adoption candidates were accepted or rejected on the basis of general appearance alone. To the uninitiated, many, especially infants, might give a surface impression of normality which obscured often quite serious defect.

In the earlier part of this century, as Knoblock and Pasamanick point out, there were plenty of adoption candidates available—and many people had not as yet come to the point of adopting handicapped children intentionally. So it made sense that adopting parents should have the protection of a behavior as well as a physical examination of the child they were adopting.

Gesell's efforts did for a while largely determine the policy of social agencies, certainly in Connecticut. His clinic alone examined hundreds of adoption candidates.

Then came a time when environmentalists claimed that it was the quality of the adoption home, not the genetic makeup of the adopted child, which determined how he turned out. Many social agencies adopted this notion and the concept of developmental examination was not only abandoned by many but even denigrated. Today, even though some couples actually choose to adopt a physically or mentally handicapped child, probably the majority of agencies do follow Dr. Gesell's directives, and at least make some sort of developmental evaluation, before placing a child in adoption, even though they may not be as concerned as he was in "matching" child and home.

Chapter 11

DR. GESELL OFFERS PARENT GUIDANCE

In the early years of Dr. Gesell's professional life, individuals who studied human behavior were extremely conservative about sharing their findings with the general public. He himself was by nature cautious about responding to requests that he should write for the popular press or even grant them interviews.

Nevertheless, and in spite of Dr. Gesell's strong feelings about "professional ethics," he was almost from the beginning of his career extremely concerned about parental and pre-parental education.

His contribution to this field was actually two-part. In the 1920s and 1930s he urged professionals to share their information with mothers and fathers to help them with the task of parenting. In later years he himself, with colleagues, wrote books and produced films whose purpose was to help parents be better informed about their boys and girls.

Thus as early as 1921 he commented that:

> The welfare of the pre-school child begins with his grand-mother and his parents. We need for these parents a new type of education, which will deal more directly and sincerely with the problems of infancy. . . . One of the major problems of the broader School Hygiene is the education of prospective parents in standards of child care. Such education will in a few years

fundamentally influence parents in the hygiene of the pre-school child.[1] (p. 30)

Two years later, in one of his first book publications, *The Pre-school Child from the Standpoint of Public Hygiene and Education*, he devotes an entire chapter to "Pre-Parental Education." His message here was that, important as the education and training of potential parents, boys as well as girls, for parenthood may be, very few schools and universities make any effort to provide such training. He comments specifically:

> If higher standards and improved methods of child care are so essential to the organization of an adequate program of pre-school hygiene, then must systematic parental and pre-parental education be made a major problem in civic administration.[2] (p. 211)

He also notes, in describing one of our early American nursery schools, the Ruggles Street Nursery School founded by Abigail A. Eliot:

> The school has two chief objectives. The first is to create the right environment for children of this age. The second is to demonstrate to the parents the value of right physical, mental and moral care for their children.[2] (p. 53)

The following year, 1924, he points out specifically:

> That health, mental and physical, has not been adequately supervised in preschoolers grows out of the fact that we have been slow in appreciating the medical and developmental significance of the years of childhood. We have intrusted these years too completely to the unaided home and to Providence. Since the World War, however, we have begun in earnest to bring preschool hygiene under judicious social control. . . . Periodic health examinations throught the preschool life, systematic parental guidance, preparental education and developmental child guidance will serve this end.[3] (p. 6)

In 1925, in discussing the importance of nursery schools, he nevertheless cautions:

> This does not mean that we must presently congregate all of our pre-school children into institutional nurseries. *The great*

problem is to assist the home and the parent, not to displace them. To make that home most effective in rearing the child for which it was really created is a durable social problem.[4] (p. 150)

In the same year, in an article about the nursery school movement, he notes that:

> The home needs more social recognition and support. Parents need more training and guidance in the socially significant problems of child care.[5] (p. 370)

The following year, in an article titled "The Pre-School Child and the Present-Day Parent," he comments:

> The re-discovery of the pre-school child has resulted in the discovery of his parents. . . . Although the development of the pre-school child must be brought more systematically under the control of society, that control should be achieved indirectly through his parents.[6] (p. 332)

In order to bring this about he recommends: courses in child development in high school and college; centers of parental training in connection with kindergartens and nursery schools; giving periodic developmental examinations from infancy to school entrance.

In the same year, in an article titled "Normal growth as a public health concept," he makes two significant comments about parenting:

> The welfare of the growing mind of the child hangs in no small measure upon the quality of the parent-child relation. It is possible to bring this factor gradually within the scope of infant welfare and child health center activities.[7] (p. 398)
>
> A calm, kind, consistent parent-child relation is the most important essential in improving the mental health of young children.[7] (p. 399)

In 1929 Dr. Gesell has this to say:

> In the age zone two to four, child guidance is parental guidance. The nursery school has been invented as a device for furnishing new educational opportunity to normal children and to their parents. . . . A guidance nursery functions like a dispensary unit, and focuses directly upon the guidance of the individual parent in relation to the individual child.[8] (p. 784)

Another brief comment, also in the year 1929, is found in an article titled "Child Mental Welfare Paramount":

> Growth is the key word in the psychology of child training.
> . . . Nature plays the primary role, but in the field of personality
> organization there is almost inexhaustible opportunity for the
> guidance of growth. . . . It is for this reason that preschool and
> parental education have so much importance for the stability
> and the happiness of the rising generation.[9] (p. 165)

In the following year, 1930, Dr. Gesell makes brief comment about the parent–child relationship in an article titled, "A decade of progress in the mental hygiene of the preschool child." He notes that though currently considerable progress has been made in interesting psychologists, psychiatrists, kindergarten and primary school teachers, social workers, mothers' clubs, and mental hygiene organizations in the preschool years, most of this interest has developed in the prior 10 years. He notes specifically that:

> The necessities of mental hygiene control of the parent-child relationship and of a developmental diagnosis of foster children prior to placement and adoption have put an added premium upon the downward extension of psycho-clinical methods. . . . As a result, the general practitioner, the pediatrist, and the psychiatrist. . . . are concerning themselves more and more with psychological problems in young children and their parents.[10] (pp. 143, 147)

A further 1930 publication, a book entitled *The Guidance of Mental Growth in Infant and Child,* abounds with references to the importance of the parent–child relationship. We include here just a few examples:

> From the standpoint of mental hygiene, the growth of the child's personality must be safeguarded not so much through sheer management of the child as through the preservation of a wholesome relationship between parent and child. . . . This association of parent and child is a kind of psycho-biological partnership. It is infinitely more complicated than a mere nutritional arrangement, but it obeys similar laws of nature.[11] (p. 158)
>
> Training in morale in the psychological sense must begin in infancy, because self-confidence is indispensable to mental health. Parent and child must continually share as partners, but

only in a manner which builds up mental fiber. The child must not only be weaned from the breast but must be gradually put on his own mental resources. He may not be altogether mature even as an adult if he does not achieve a full measure of independence from his mother.

From the standpoint of mental hygiene the family relations should be such that the child will not suffer either from undue dependence or conflict.[11] (p. 159)

To rear a child in the psychological sense is to regulate the parent-child relation in such a way that he has a maximum chance to grow up.[11] (p. 160)

The infant's well-being hangs not alone on vitamins and calories, but on his mode of living, on his habits, on the behavior of his parents. Accordingly, the administration of prenatal hygiene is bound to bring into its scope the psychology of the parent-child relationship.[11] (p. 257)

At this early age (the preschool years) child guidance is parent guidance.[11] (p. 258)

As the years go by, Dr. Gesell continues to hammer away as to the importance of parent education. Thus in 1934 he comments:

> There are endless opportunities for instruction and guidance of parents in the field of infant care and of child training. There is much to be learned in the practical art of child management. . . . Educational agencies can render most service by assisting parents to acquire a working philosophy of growth and learning, which will give perspective to the everyday problems of children.[12] (p. 499)

In 1935 he combined two of his favorite topics—parent education and use of the films—in an article titled "The Cinema as an Instrument for Parent Education." He pointed out that carefully edited motion pictures can not only instruct parents in the ways of growth and development and in methods of child care, but can also be used "to build up attitudes as well as knowledge"[13] (p. 9).

That Dr. Gesell sees the pediatrician as a key figure in providing help and advice, not only about illness but also about parenting, is evident whenever he discusses the role of the pediatrician. A typical statement in 1941 makes this quite clear. He comments:

> Since development is a continuing process, physician and parents must enter into a kind of partnership to keep pace with

behavior changes as they occur. Developmental guidance depends upon an intelligent interpretation of the behavior characteristics of infant and child in terms of growth, maturity, and social environment.[14] (p. 760)

Thus throughout the 1920s and the 1930s, in these and other writings, Dr. Gesell repeatedly and consistently advised that professionals dealing with young children must be concerned with both parental and pre-parental education. However, as early as 1934 and increasingly thereafter he made his own special contributions to this end.

For instance, in 1934 he published a series of five films for parents, accompanied by *A Handbook for the Yale Films of Child Development: Specially Released for Parent Education Leaders in Emergency Education Programs*. According to the text:

> The present series of the emergency program films is offered as a unit which may be used for adult groups. . . . These films are not intended to establish specific techniques of child care . . . or as absolute models for imitation. They stress individual differences as well as general growth trends.[15] (p. 3)

In 1940 came the first of five books written partially or primarily for a parent public. Actually, this 1940 book, *The First Five Years of Life*,[16] written like the others in collaboration with colleagues, was less directly addressed to parents than those which followed. It does give rather detailed descriptions of behavior to be expected at the various stages of infancy and throughout the first 5 years. But it is chiefly a presentation of norms of child behavior from eighteen months of age through five years, and thus was addressed primarily to specialists in the field of child behavior.

The first book written primarily for parents appeared in 1943. *Infant and Child in the Culture of Today*[17] attracted much popular acclaim and also considerable criticism from colleagues at the Yale School of Medicine who apparently felt it unprofessional for one of their staff to write, to parents, about eating, sleeping, and elimination.

This book, revised in 1974, which has been translated into many different languages and has sold very widely, spoke directly to the parent about the basic routines of everyday living, describing in detail behavior to be expected at various ages throughout the first five years of life, and discussing in detail both individual differences and nursery school behavior.

Next, in 1945, came a pictorial album of infant behavior titled *How a Baby Grows*.[18] This was followed in 1956 by the second volume of the so-called "Trilogy." *The Child From Five to Ten*[19] followed the pattern of *Infant and Child* in describing in detail, for parents and others, behavior to be expected at each of the yearly age levels for the period in question. The areas of behavior which it covers are: motor behavior, personal hygiene, emotional expression, fears and dreams, self and sex, interpersonal relations, play and pastimes, school life, ethical sense, and philosophical outlook.

The third book in this basic series for parents was titled *Youth: The Years from Ten to Sixteen*.[20] It appeared in 1956 and covered the same fields of behavior as did the immediately prior book. It was a significant popular success and was well accepted, so far as one knows, even by those professionals who had so harshly criticized *Infant and Child*.

Youth was the last of Dr. Gesell's own personal writing for the parent public, but in the years that followed, members of his staff, with his (possibly guarded) support, moved rather heavily into the parent and pre-parent guidance field through a syndicated daily column (at one time syndicated in as many as 65 of the major papers in this country), through several television series, and through a textbook addressed to high school boys and girls.[21] The column continues even to this date and the textbook has been "adopted" by numerous states.

This somewhat brief summary does not pretend to include every mention that Dr. Gesell ever made of the importance of parent guidance. Such incidental references as that "The home needs more social recognition and support. Parents need more training and guidance in the socially significant problems of child care"[22] (p. 370) abound in his writings and are not included in this chapter.

Chapter 12

DR. GESELL AND THE
NURSERY SCHOOL MOVEMENT

Dr. Gesell's interest in the nursery school movement in general, and in the nursery school in particular, was expressed early and strongly. Between 1923 and 1927 he published 13 articles on the subject. They both outlined the history of the nursery school movement and emphasized the great importance of paying attention to the preschool child and of recognizing the value of nursery schools.

In tracing their history,* Dr. Gesell points out that:

> The conception of a nursery school was anticipated four hundred years before Christ when Plato described a community nursery as a proper part of an ideal state. . . . Twenty-one centuries later an Englishman, Robert Owen, also drew a picture of the ideal state. More than that, he founded the very first nursery or infant school in England. This occurred in 1800 and in 1826 he founded a nursery school of over 100 children in New Harmony, Indiana.[1] (p. 644)

As Dr. Gesell emphasized:

* This summary is not intended as a complete history of the nursery school movement in the United States or elsewhere, but merely as a chronicle of Dr. Gesell's own recorded comments about or involvement with this movement.

>   In a sense the nursery school in America as well as in Eng-
> land is older than the kindergarten. Broadly interpreted, the
> infant school contained the germ of both these institutions as we
> know them today. . . .
>   In 1918 the Fisher Education Act conferred upon local au-
> thorities in England powers to supply nursery schools for chil-
> dren over two and under five years of age 'whose attendance at
> such a school is necessary or desirable for their healthy physical
> and mental development.'[1] (p. 645)

Bringing the story a little more up to date, in 1921[2] Dr. Gesell
notes that, "Legally the pre-school child has no status in this country.
The tacit assumption is that this is not an educational problem at
all"[2] (p. 27). In 1923[3,4] he comments that several experimental and
demonstration nursery schools have been established, although
unlike the situation in England, they are on a voluntary and pioneer
basis. One of the outstanding nursery schools was at that time established at the Merrill-Palmer School in Detroit which correlated its
work with a practical course in child care for college students.

    Other outstanding early schools include those founded by Har-
riet M. Johnson in New York and Abigail Eliot in Boston (The Ruggles Street Nursery School).

    As early as 1924, Gesell introduced his concept that a nursery
school should, among its other contributions, constitute a guidance
center for parents. Thus in 1924 he states specifically:

>   The durability of the nursery school will depend upon its
> capacity to develop vital relations with the home, the family, the
> family physician, the health center and the kindergarten. *Should
> the nursery school become a thinly disguised day nursery for the custody
> of children its future is doubtful. If, however, it becomes an educational
> adjunct to the home for the instruction and guidance of parents and
> ultimately for pre-parental training*, it will actually strengthen rather
> than weaken the modern day family.[1] (p. 651)

Also in 1924 he warns that:

>   The fact that too many children are started in school too
> soon and their health not supervised grows out of the fact that
> we have been slow in appreciating the medical and develop-
> mental significance of the early years of childhood. We have
> intrusted these years too completely to the unaided home and to
> Providence. . . . Since the World War, however, we have begun

in earnest to bring preschool hygiene under judicious social control.[5] (p. 6)

In 1925, Gesell mentions again the fact that:

The British Parliament has given legislative encouragement to the establishment of nursery schools for children from two to five years of age. A comparable nursery school movement has taken root in the United States, and it is certain that the whole pre-school period of childhood is gradually coming under some form of socialized educational control.[6] (p. 150)

Also in 1925 he warns that:

The nursery school as a nursery school is not a perfected entity which needs to be adopted as such. It is rendering a unique, invaluable demonstration of new types of educational service which must be inaugurated, but it is the service even more than the institutional organization which compels our attention. Moreover, the nursery school must be adapted to American conditions with due reference to established progressive kindergartens. At present there are two or three score enterprises called nursery schools now under way in this country.

Since the nursery school as at present constituted is not a finished device ready for universal, imitative adoption, it should be kept a formative, tentative tool. Our problem is not the multiplication of nursery schools as such; but the extension of nursery education and parental education. . . . The interest of leaders of home economics in the nursery school movement is a promising and a natural sign of the new preschool trend.[7] (p. 55)

Gesell's concern for what should be the shape and purpose of the nursery school is again expressed in another article, also written in 1925. He states:

In the present formative stage the nursery school raises a group of significant questions. Should the kindergartens begin to admit on a part-time arrangement children from two to five years of age? What should be the relation between infant welfare work, the health service of child health centers, community nurseries, clinics, kindergartens and prekindergartens? How can we relate homemaking education in all its forms to this vast field of pre-school education? How can we develop measures of parental guidance, which will safeguard the parent-child relation and increase the educational efficiency of the home?

These questions are so complicated and so vital that we should welcome rather than fear the nursery school in the present experimental form. For we may use this nursery school as an instrument to define our problems and to perfect our methods of approach. It would be unfortunate if at this early date the nursery school were accepted as a perfected device for uncritical imitation and duplication. Surely the nursery school should not grow into an altogether independent addition to our present social organization.[8] (p. 371)

In 1927, Gesell and Elizabeth Evans Lord conducted a research study in which they compared the behavior of nursery school children from homes of low and high economic status.[9] Not surprisingly they found that the children from homes of high economic status showed "a tendency toward superior mental equipment." It was not, clearly, a profound investigation.

In 1929[10] Dr. Gesell gives a detailed description of his own "Guidance Nursery of the Yale Psycho-Clinic," founded at 52 Hillhouse Avenue, New Haven, Connecticut in 1926. A direct quote from this report makes it very clear that parent guidance was at that time, as throughout the many years that this school—in slightly different forms and in different locations—continued, a major theme in Gesell's concept of the purpose of a nursery school.

The Guidance Nursery was established as an adjunct of the service divisions of the clinic. It is a device for the observation and guidance of young children and also for the guidance of parents who are perplexed with the behavior problems which their children present. The Guidance Nursery is designed to be an educational tool. It is operated like a service unit on an appointment basis. The procedure is constantly varied to meet the special needs of the individual child or parent. The guidance work is on a dispensatory basis.

The Guidance Nursery, therefore, has no fixed enrollment like the ordinary nursery school. Its activities and attendance vary from week to week and even from day to day. It is in charge of a guidance worker who has a background of experience with children of kindergarten and preschool age. Sometimes she works intensively with one child; more frequently she works with small groups of three, four, five and six children, usually from eighteen months to five years of age. The number of times which any given child comes to the nursery is indeterminate and depends upon the amount of adjustment or education which is needed.

Child guidance and parent guidance are carried on conjointly in natural relations with each other. One of the aims of The Guidance Nursery is to demonstrate methods of child care which can be carried out in an ordinary home and, to a large extent, in an ordinary schoolroom. These methods are simple in principle and require no special equipment.

There are plenty of opportunities for the child to "work" at problems requiring intelligence, motor coordination, conversation, and emotional control. With the oversight of the guidance worker he learns to make new adjustments. The worker does not "teach" the child in the ordinary sense but rather "guides" him. There are no set lessons but there are genuine life lessons in his new experience.

The mother may get a fresh and more detached point of view by observing his behavior through the segregative screen of the observation alcove. . . . The parents, like the children, are for the most part seen individually. The guidance takes the form of consultation and conference rather than formal group instruction.

The program of the nursery has been made flexible to permit a study of the normal aspects of social behavior, as well as of new methods of approach in child and parent guidance.[10] (pp. 105–106)

Also in 1929, supported by funds from the Laura Spelman Rockefeller Memorial, a committee was established for the preparation of a survey of the accomplishments and trends in the field of preschool and parental education. Dr. Gesell was a member of this committee, along with such other distinguished child specialists as Bird T. Baldwin, Lois Hayden Meeks, Douglas A. Thom, Helen Thompson Wooley, and others. Together they produced a volume of 875 pages dealing with the organization of preschool education, provisions for parental and pre-parental education, professional training of leaders, and child research and training methods.

In 1930 Gesell, backtracking a little, reviews the growth of the nursery school movement in America following the close of World War I. He tells us that according to a (then) recent report compiled by Mary Dabney Davis, a specialist in nursery-kindergarten-primary education, three schools were established in the period from 1914 to 1918; 16 were established in the next 5-year period; 108 in the period from 1924 to 1928. (This number includes the Guidance Nursery of the [then] Yale Psycho-Clinic.) Twenty-two more schools were established in 1929, making a total of 149 schools in all, reporting an enrollment of approximately 3000 children.

When the 139 schools were analyzed on the basis of their major functions, they were distributed as follows:

Class A. Schools organized to provide educational programs for young children (62)

Class B. Demonstration and training centers for students in teacher training schools and departments of education (42)

Class C. Laboratories for research in child development and parent education (9)

Class D. A combination of B and C (26).[11] (p. 146)

In 1943, in an article titled "The New Haven Child Care Center—an Account of its Origins and Organization," Gesell adds the following to a history of the nursery school movement in this country. He notes that in 1934 the first emergency nursery school was established under the Federal Emergency Relief Administration. The Yale Clinic of Child Development, the Yale Department of Education, and the Cannon Nursery School served as demonstration and advisory centers for the teachers who assumed supervision of these schools.

Three years later, in 1937, seven WPA nursery schools were in operation in seven public schools in New Haven. In 1942, the New Haven Child Care Center opened with a small group of children of working mothers. The hours were from 6:30 a.m. to 6:30 p.m.[12] (p. 368)

The next publication in which Gesell referred specifically to the nursery school as such was a major one, a book titled *Infant and Child in the Culture of Today: The Guidance of Development in Home and Nursery School*,[13] published in 1943.

For each of the age levels discussed—where it would be appropriate: two, two-and-a-half, three, and four—detailed information is provided as to what the nursery school day is like, techniques which a nursery school teacher may successfully use in working with children, and descriptions as to what one may expect of children of each of these ages in response to books, music, painting, finger-painting, clay, blocks, and their responses to their own possessions and to excursions which the teacher may arrange.

In the 1974 revision of this book, all material having to do with the nursery school, instead of being inserted into each age-appropriate chapter, is presented as a separate, nearly 100-page section of the book. Both editions constitute a fitting conclusion to Dr. Gesell's lifelong interest in and concern about the nursery school.

Before the 1974 revision of *Infant and Child* was published, two of Dr. Gesell's colleagues, Louise Bates Ames and Evelyn Goodenough Pitcher, published an entire book devoted to nursery school techniques and nursery school behavior: *The Guidance Nursery School: A Gesell Institute Book for Teachers and Parents*. This constituted a compilation of all that Dr. Gesell and his staff had to say on the entire subject. This book was prepared during Dr. Gesell's lifetime though it was not published till after his death.

SUMMARY

Dr. Gesell's contribution to the field of nursery school education might thus be considered to be fivefold.

To start with, he has given us a review of the history of the field, as it developed. Second, through his writing and speaking and work with various committees at local, state, and national levels, he encouraged the setting up of nursery schools in this country. Third, in 1926 he founded his own nursery school. Fourth, certainly as much as any other supporter of the movement he emphasized the guidance functions of the nursery school as opposed to its merely teaching or providing what in some amounted to simple day-care services. And, lastly, in his book *Infant and Child*, he has described in substantial detail the activity and levels of behavior which one may expect from the child attending nursery school.

His was a lifelong interest, personal as well as theoretical. There was nothing Dr. Gesell liked better than actually to visit in his own guidance nursery school. And his response to the children was personal and warm.

Chapter 13

FEEDING BEHAVIOR

Through the years, Dr. Gesell and colleagues wrote a considerable amount about feeding behavior. Most of these writings had to do with the actual mechanisms of eating, as in *Feeding Behavior of Infants*, by Gesell and Ilg, or with what foods children of different age levels preferred and what their appetites and table manners were like, as described in *Infant and Child, The Child from Five to Ten*, and *Youth: The Years from Ten to Sixteen*. Though nutrition, especially discussion of the value of breast feeding over bottle feeding, was frequently mentioned, Dr. Gesell for the most part wrote about feeding behavior rather in his role as a psychologist or child behavior specialist than as a pediatrician. Thus nutrition as such was not a main emphasis in his many writings about feeding behavior. And the term "child hygiene," used so often by Dr. Gesell, referred more frequently to mental health rather than to physical health.

However, though it was not a primary concern, as with respect to so many other aspects of child behavior, Dr. Gesell very early made an extremely pertinent comment about nutrition. In his early book, *The Preschool Child*, written in 1923, he notes:

> As Holt has said, "The younger the patient the worse the prognosis in all the diseases of childhood." Yet there is no more promising field in medicine, as this same authority has recognized, than the prevention of disease in this very period. First of

all, infections can in large measure be forestalled, delayed, or controlled. Secondly, the strength of the child to resist or to conquer disease can be safeguarded.

Successful reaction of his organism against infection depends primarily upon the nutrition of his protoplasm. Body maintenance, body growth, and immunization are all forms of metabolism, which are based on adequate food and proper feeding. *Nutrition is the key to prophylaxis and often to cure.* The role of nutrition in human welfare is always a great one; but it is of preponderant importance in the preschool period.[1] (p. 6)

In this same year (1923), in a pamphlet entitled "The Kindergarten and Health" Gesell and Abbott note that:

The child's growth has behind it the impulse of inheritance, but it will be achieved completely only if the proper conditions of health, diet, air, sunshine and play are forthcoming.[2] (p. 8)

In their immature but very real manner, even tiny children, for better or worse, are acquiring modes of wholesome or unwholesome activity, are assimilating healthy or unhealthy attitudes toward life; are forming habits of eating, reading, playing and social adjustment.[2] (p. 10)

So far as food goes, in this same booklet he makes the following very specific recommendations:

1. Eating three warm, wholesome meals regularly each day, with no candy or other sweets between meals. Sitting down to eat, chewing food thoroughly, eating slowly.

2. Every day eating some fruit and two or three vegetables including one green or leafy vegetable. At every meal eating some whole grain bread or cereals.

3. Drinking at least one pint of milk each day but no tea or coffee.

4. Drinking at least three and preferably four glasses of water every day.[2] (p. 15)

We find another brief comment in this same year to the effect that:

Malnutrition, diphtheria and rickets contribute three of the most powerful foes of early childhood. Nutrition work as it is now recognized should not be limited to infant welfare stations and to public school classes. There should be a continuous sequence of supervision which reduces malnutrition to a minimum by the time of school entrance. . . . (thus) rickets can doubtless be largely eradicated through fish oils and sunshine in any community which undertakes the task beginning with the baby's birth.[3] (p. 3)

In 1926, in a paper titled "Normal Growth as a Public Health Concept," Dr. Gesell included a list of characteristics of mental health—"wholesome habits of eating, sleeping, of relaxation and of elimination." He noted that:

> Even in the regulation of nutrition, the physician and the nurse must reckon in behavior terms with the parent-child relation. The supervision of nutrition can thus be broadened steadily to include certain psychological factors which affect mental health. . . . The nutritional supervision of infants did not begin with subtleties. The first step was to purify unclean milk and to cast out heavy solids like pickles and sausages.[4] (p. 398)

In his 1928 book *Infancy and Human Growth*, promisingly a chapter titled "Glandular and Nutritional Factors in Mental Growth" actually yields relatively little information about nutrition. Its main contribution has to do with rickets:

> Severe rickets, because of the disturbance in calcium metabolism and because of its recognized relation to tetany and childhood convulsions must inevitably have some effect upon the nervous system during the active stages of the disorder. . . . There are no conclusive data concerning the permanent effect of rickets upon mental development.[5] (p. 267)

This chapter concludes with the statement that:

> While some nutritional disorders undoubtedly disturb the course of development more than others, the nervous system apparently has considerable immunity against the adversities of faulty or impoverished nourishment. This is a factor of safety and fortunately protects the child from undue permanent handicap from the all too frequent disorders of early nutrition.[5] (p. 271)

The vital role of the doctor and nurse in supervising nutrition, and the close relationship between physical and mental welfare is emphasized in a paper read in 1933 before the annual meeting of the New York State Nurses' Organization:

> It is very significant that modern pediatrics is first of all concerned with the basic problem of nutrition both in the sick

and in the well child. . . . The close relation between mental and physical welfare has been emphasized by the recent Depression which is bearing with heavy weight upon the whole population including even infants and children of preschool age. Malnutrition and illnesses both among the young and the old have unquestionably increased. . . .

The point of view which needs to be stressed is that even the nutrition of the infant cannot be conceived narrowly in chemical or dietetic terms. It is surprising how rapidly and decisively the problems of nutrition become problems of psychology of the infant.[6] (p. 229)

A major photographic publication, *The Atlas of Infant Behavior*, Vol. II, by Gesell, Keliher, Ilg, and Carlson[7] illustrates with photographs taken from cinema the patterns of feeding behavior—bottle, breast, spoon and cup—from 16 to 80 weeks. But, like the feeding films produced in 1947, it describes the mechanisms of feeding rather than discussing nutrition as such.

In 1937 there were two major contributions to the subject of feeding and nutrition. In a short article published in France (and here in translation), Dr. Gesell discusses "The Psychological Factors in Infant Feeding." He notes that:

The regulation and supervision of infant feeding represents in many ways the most fundamental achievement of modern preventive medicine. Many nurses and physicians conceive this important work only in terms of bodily nutrition. But from a monistic medical standpoint, it is impossible to advance the hygiene of infant feeding purely on a physical basis. There are psychological factors. They are so ubiquitous that they demand attention.

The child's body consists of more than tangible tissue. It comprises those invisible chemical systems and patterned structures which are expressed in physiological processes and in behavior forms. By a thoroughgoing monistic concept "the mind," "the personality," "the reactions" of the infant are brought into complete identification with his nutrition and his feeding characteristics.[8] (p. 22)

In gathering data for the *Atlas of Infant Behavior*, the survey was planned to cover the main behavior aspects of the feeding situation, both in terms of the infant's abilities and of the mother-infant relationship, including breast and bottle, spoon and cup feeding. However, it was felt that a full perspective of the development of feeding behavior could be secured only by means of home visitations under medical supervision. Thus Dr. Gesell and Dr. Frances L. Ilg undertook the research which resulted in the book *Feeding Behavior of Infants.*[9]

It is difficult to summarize this fact-filled book. For the most part, it discusses the development of feeding behavior patterns, rather more than the actual nutritional aspects of feeding. However, in its introduction, Dr. Gesell makes clear his interest in the quality and nature of food consumed:

> *Chemistry is the domain of science which is most certain to make profound progress during the next century.* The exact nature of forth-coming forms of biochemistry cannot be predicted, but it is certain they will lead to marked advances in the control of early human growth. This control will be achieved through dietary means and through direct regulation of the growth process itself. The supervision of nutrition will have an augmented medical and social significance. It will become a more deliberate effort to bring to realization the hereditary potentialities of infancy.
>
> Altered methods of living and of thinking will create new cultural patterns and new social orientations for children and parents. But the infant will remain as he is now, a protoplasmic part of the evolutionary stream of life, subject to laws of growth. Surely biochemistry will envisage him in terms of human biology and will direct his development by more precise assays and alterations of his bodily composition.
>
> But biology has already demonstrated that bodily makeup is not a thing separate from the functioning of the organism. By a thoroughgoing monistic concept, "the mind," "the personality," "the reactions" of the infant are brought into complete identification with his nutrition and his feeding characteristics.
>
> His feeding behavior, broadly interpreted, becomes an indicator not only of his nutritional status in a narrow sense, but of himself. *In offering this volume, devoted to the behavior aspects of infant feeding, we do not wish to psychologize the problem nor to remove it in any sense from the domain of pediatrics or of clinical chemistry.* On the contrary, we should prefer to think that an objective study of the behavior symptomatology of the human infant will lead to a more discriminating appreciation of his "physical" health and his growth needs. He develops as a unit.[9] (p. 1)

Though the authors do state explicitly that "This volume is concerned not with nourishment but with feeding behavior"[9] (p. 3), they add:

The protection of nutrition will still be the central objective (of periodic health examinations) and the supervision of nutrition will be widened to embrace the total economy of the child.[9] (p. 148)

One of the most far-reaching and lastingly popular contributions of this book is its introduction of so-called "rooming-in" (the baby in the hospital remaining in the same room with his mother, rather than being relegated to the hospital nursery and brought to its mother only at regular intervals for feeding) and of the idea of self-demand feeding, that is, letting the child make his own schedule rather than forcing him to accept a 3-(or 4-)hour schedule, as was customary at that time, that is, 1937.

The actual origination of this dual idea (rooming in and self-demand) has never been definitely determined. Some attribute it to Dr. Edith Jackson of the staff of the Yale Medical School. Many, however, we among them, consider that the notion originated with Dr. Gesell and his associate, Dr. Frances L. Ilg.

The self-demand schedule is described in great detail in *The Feeding Behavior of Infants* (see Figure 13-1).[9] The basic principle of self-demand is that if the infant is allowed to feed when hungry instead of at definite pre-selected intervals which may or may not fit in with his own internal rhythms, he will quite soon settle himself into a reasonable pattern of feeding and sleeping, comfortable for both infant and parents. One of the most succinct descriptions of self-demand is given in a later book, *Infant and Child in the Culture of Today*[14] and is described below.

A section titled "Glandular and Nutritional Factors in Mental Growth" in *Biographies of Child Development*[10] by Gesell and others, consists of an update of material presented earlier in *Infancy and Human Growth*,[5] and need not be quoted again.

In *The First Five Years of Life*,[11] published in 1940, feeding behavior is discussed briefly under the headings self-feeding (cup), self-feeding (spoon) and "general response to meals." Similarly, in *Developmental Diagnosis*,[12] eating is described more from the point of view of the behavior itself rather than with respect to nutrition.

In 1941, writing specifically for pediatricians, Dr. Gesell makes the brief but pertinent comment:

The supervision of infant feeding is one of the major responsibilities of pediatrics. For the modern infant the whole

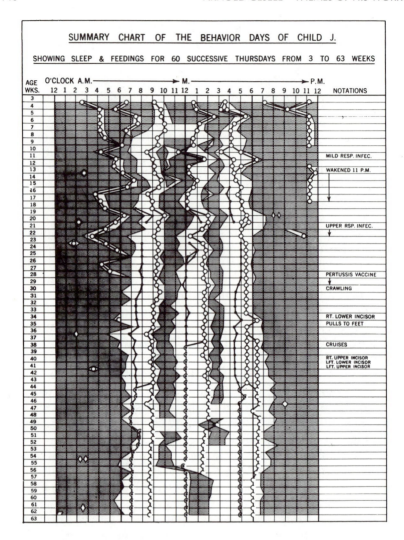

Figure 13-1.   Self-demand schedule.

problem of feeding has assumed new difficulties due to cultural reasons which are psychologic at bottom. The problem is not only dietary; it is also behavioral. Although the development of feeding abilities follows a general ontogenetic sequence, there are significant individual variations. Those which relate to the rhythms of appetite are particularly important because they are rooted in the emotional life—the strivings, satisfactions, and sense of security of the infant. When the rhythms are studied over a period of time, the infant on a self-demand schedule exhibits a capacity for self-regulation which casts doubts on the wisdom of imposed ironclad feeding schedules.[13] (p. 7)

Since perhaps the most succinct description of the self-demand schedule is given in a 1943 book, *Infant and Child in the Culture of Today,* even though it was introduced far earlier, this description is given here:

How does an infant register his self-demands? By his behavior. The well-being and the ill-being of his organism are summed up in his patterns of behavior and in the alternations of rest and activity which make up his behavior day. . . . The infant does not have words at his command, but he has two sets of signs and signals; the negative and the positive; those which express avoidance and rejection; and those which express seeking and acceptance. . . . By taking cognizance of these cues the culture (through the parents) can devise a flexible schedule of care adapted to the infant's needs as they arise. This would be a *self-demand schedule,* as distinguished from an imposed schedule. An inflexible schedule based on a more or less arbitrary norm would ignore the infant's signs and signals. It would insist on regularity of intervals despite the infant's irregular fluctuations. It would regularly insist on waking even when the infant insists on sleeping.

There are two kinds of time—organic time and clock time. The former is based on the wisdom of the body, the latter on astronomical science and cultural conventions. A self-demand schedule takes its departure from organic time. The infant is fed when he is hungry; he is allowed to sleep when he is sleepy; he is not roused to be fed; he is "changed" if he fusses on being wet; he is granted some social play when he craves it. He is not made to live by the clock on the wall, but rather by the internal clock of his fluctuating organic needs.

It is a relatively simple matter to initiate such a self-demand schedule, to keep it in operation, and to chart its course from day to day and week to week.[14] (p. 51)

It may be of interest to some readers to note that Dr. Benjamin Spock in 1945, two years after the publication of *Infant and Child,* and eight years after the publication of *Feeding Behavior,* had this to say about what he calls the "demand" schedule:

Some doctors and parents have been trying the experiment lately of going back to nature—never waking the baby, but feeding him whenever he seems hungry. . . . If more and more babies come to be fed this way, and it works well, it may possibly become, in the future, one of the "regular" ways to feed babies. Time will tell. If you are particularly interested, you can discuss with your doctor whether he thinks it is practical or advisable for your baby.[15] (p. 30)

However, in 1963, Spock warns that:

I had been very careful to give only *partial* approval to self-demand.[16] (p. 124)

Then, still later, in 1974, and again in *Red Book Magazine*, Spock states unequivocally:

I was one of the first pediatricians to *advocate* a reasonable respect for individual differences in babies' readiness to get to a four-hour feeding schedule." (That is, to advocate self-demand feeding).[17] (p. 29)

So much for self-demand. Dr. Gesell's book *Infant and Child in the Culture of Today*[14] was written in 1943 and was the first of his "popular" books of general advice written for parents. Its main emphasis, so far as feeding behavior is concerned, is on what feeding is like at each age in the first five years of life. It includes such subheadings as appetite, refusals and preferences, spoon-feeding, cup-drinking, self-help as well as, for the weeks of infancy, breast-feeding.

In the 1946 book, *The Child from Five to Ten*,[18] as in *Infant and Child*, feeding behavior is again very fully discussed under the topics of appetite, eating, preferences and refusals, self-help, and table manners.

Two films, edited in 1947, *Bottle and Cup Feeding*,[19] and *The Conquest of the Spoon*[20] have to do with age changes in bottle, cup, and spoon behavior, but do not include information about nutrition as such.

A specific mention of the importance of proper nutrition comes in 1948 in an article in the *Journal of Pediatrics*:

Shortly after the American Board of Pediatrics was established in 1935, a basic requirement in Growth and Development was set up for specialty certification. *When the medical history of the 20th century is written, we know this formal action will be regarded as a uniquely important event in the evolution of clinical medicine.*

The first five years are of supreme, overshadowing significance. It is in this area that society is demanding a concentration of medical and social safeguards.

Responsive to this deep-seated demand, the pediatrician and the general practitioner are becoming increasingly concerned with the pre-natal as well as the early postnatal period of development. The developmental welfare, the nutrition, and to some extent even the immunization control of the infant-to-be begins before birth. . . .

First and foremost, postnatal supervision will focus on nutrition and the biochemical status of the organism. But the regulation of nutrition, even at a physiologic level, inevitably leads to a diagnostic interest in the behavior characteristics of the infant —what he does, when he does it, and how he does it constitute a symptomatology. For the physician the behavior patterns of the infant are symptoms: to the parent they furnish clews and cues for intelligent child care.[21] (pp. 331, 332)

Breast-Feeding: The vital importance of breast-feeding, as opposed to bottle-feeding, in mid-century (1935 to 1970 or so), was by no means always emphasized by the medical profession. In many hospitals, in fact, mothers were actually discouraged from breast-feeding. And even well-known pediatrician Benjamin Spock in a *Red Book* column (date unavailable)[22] indicated that the method used in feeding infants did not really matter.

Dr. Gesell, however, in all of his writings about feeding in which the question of breast versus bottle feeding was discussed, consistently came down hard on the side of breast-feeding. His last and perhaps clearest statement on the subject appeared in 1974 in the revised edition of *Infant and Child in the Culture of Today*[23] (pp. 70, 71):

First and foremost comes the question of breast-feeding. Too often the decision on this crucial question is allowed to drift until a short time before the baby's birth. This dilatoriness has an adverse effect upon the mother's emotional orientation. It also tends to have an adverse effect upon her capacity for lactation. For one thing, the breast and nipples may require regular and systematic attention three months prior to birth, the anointing and massage of the nipples preventing the cracking that so often interferes with successful breast-feeding. This regular attention to the nipples also prepares the mother mentally for the duty of breast-feeding when the time arrives. Perhaps the word "duty" has been misplaced. Our culture in America in years not too long past showed a growing tendency to give the mother a choice between nursing and artificial feeding, and often weighted the choice in favor of the bottle.

However, within the last thirty years there has been an ever-increasing surge toward breast-feeding. Before that, mothers did not receive the supportive help they needed. Many had not fully realized the benefits of breast-feeding for both infant and mother. It is easier to make a choice when the mother realizes the advantages. Would any mother wish to deprive her infant of colostrum, the viscous substance that precedes the milk during the first two days after delivery, if she knew that this substance contains many protective antibodies? Early access to the breast, even in the delivery room, starts the process of interaccommodation between mother and child. We can destroy this by giving the infant fluid by bottle and separating him from his mother. The transitional milk can come in as early as twenty-four hours after delivery if the infant is allowed access to the breast when he cries.

The advantages to the child of a ready supply of nourishment from the mother, of a protein he can digest, of the close physical contact with the mother, of protection from illness (especially diarrhea) for the first six months before he has built up his own immunological protections, plus many other benefits, should alert mothers and physicians that breast-feeding may well constitute a fundamental requirement, not merely a method of choice. To be sure, the newborn can survive without breast-feeding, but only with certain very definite deprivations.

Fortunately the forces of influence are no longer restricted to those in authority—the obstetrician, the pediatrician. Grassroots forces have been organizing in favor of breast-feeding since 1956 in the mother-stimulated La Leche Leagues, including two in Canada, one in Africa and one in Mexico. The members give their personal service to those who have trouble continuing breast-feeding. There is a spirit in these organizations and a capacity to disseminate knowledge that defy all the forces which oppose breast-feeding.[23] (pp. 70, 71)

A final mention of feeding behavior, at somewhat older ages than had been heretofore discussed, is found in *Youth: The Years from Ten to Sixteen*,[24] by Dr. Gesell and his colleagues. Topics covered in detail, for every age during this time period, include appetite, preferences and refusals, snacks and sweets, table manners and, finally, interest in cooking.

Thus, in all, Dr. Gesell's writings on the subject of feeding behavior cover somewhat over a 30-year span and also cover many aspects of this basic behavior.

Chapter 14

DEVELOPMENTAL PEDIATRICS

"Development quite as much as disease falls within the science and the practice of medicine. To Developmental Pediatrics fall the manifold and interrelated problems of child development from the standpoint of medical diagnosis, prevention and control"[1] (p. 1058). This relatively simple statement by Dr. Gesell back in 1925 phrased his battle cry in a lifelong effort to persuade medical practitioners to become knowledgeable and effective in the development diagnosis of behavior.

His was at that time very definitely a voice crying in the wilderness. Many *psychologists* then did not even accept the idea that behavior develops in a patterned, more or less predictable manner. To suggest that *doctors*, who were actually *practicing medicine*, would do so was bold, and farsighted, indeed.

In 1929 Dr. Gesell elaborated on this basic theme:

> The supervision of nutrition in infancy is, and will doubtless remain, the central concern of pediatrics. . . . The protection of nutritional health of the child becomes the natural stage for a broader and equally continuous type of developmental supervision. . . . Although at first glance this seems like an expansive and abstract concept of the province of pediatrics, such an extension of scope is almost inevitable if pediatrics continues its

present position as a regional specialty converging the resources of general medicine and biology of infancy.[2] (p. 1071)

Looking well into the future, the scientific study of infant behavior from the standpoint of symptomatology becomes an important phase of preventive pediatrics. The methods of developmental pediatrics will naturally take shape slowly, but probably with the same steady and sound growth which has marked the advance of preventive pediatrics in the supervision of infant nutrition.[2] (p. 1073)

In 1932 he repeated this theme:

> Disease and development are related concepts. Pediatrics is compelled to reckon with both of them. . . . It is suggested that the periodic medical supervision of infant nutrition, which began meagerly only a generation ago, will continue to widen its' scope and embrace the total developmental well-being of infancy.[3] (p. 38)

> The protection and the promotion of optimum child development is a formula which expresses the more inclusive goal toward which pediatrics is tending. If this thesis is tenable it means that *mental growth* as well as physical growth will inevitably come within the range of pediatrics supervision.[3] (p. 41)

In 1936 he again stresses this concept:

> Since the physical and psychic aspects of development are so inextricably related, it is possible for the pediatrician to take cognizance of mental factors in all the supervisory phases of his work. . . . A view of the mind as a diagnosable entity puts us in a position to protect and to promote the mental growth of the infant.[4] (p. 32)

In 1940 he continued to voice his concern about the importance of development in the practice of pediatrics:

> Development, as well as disease, falls within the scope of clinical medicine. In recent years there has been an increasing tendency to look upon problems of health and disease from a developmental point of view. Development has ceased to be a vague abstraction, and is instead regarded as an organic process which yields to scientific analysis and to diagnostic appraisal.

The developmental diagnosis of infant behavior is certain to become a more routine feature of clinical care in office, dispensary and hospital. Timely application of norms of behavior makes possible the early detection and improved management of developmental defects and deviations. Almost all cases of mental deficiency can be diagnosed in the first year. Many cases, however, are never recognized because the physician relies on physical signs and stigmata alone.

Failure to use developmental norms results, for example, in serious errors in the diagnosis of cerebral palsy. Congenital and birth palsies often simulate feeblemindedness. . . . A careful examination of behavior symptoms may disclose considerable normality in the field of intelligence and of personality development. A complete survey of the neurologic status of an infant can scarcely be made without a developmental diagnosis of his total behavior equipment.[5] (p. 841)

Up until now one might say that Dr. Gesell has been firing only preliminary shots in his battle to persuade practicing pediatricians that, as he originally and repeatedly put it, "Development as well as disease lies in the province of clinical pediatrics." From 1940 he brought in his big guns.

He now began to stress the fact that if pediatricians are to be knowledgeable about child behavior, growth and development must be taught in medical schools.

From this time on he devoted a major part of his professional life to this cause. His friend and colleague, Professor Walter A. Miles, put it aptly when he noted that "Widening of the horizons for responsible departments of pediatrics may be considered the crown of Dr. Gesell's life work"[6] (p. 71)

The first step in this major effort was the publication of *Developmental Diagnosis: A Manual of Clinical Methods and Applications Designed for the Use of Students and Practitioners of Medicine*[7] co-authored by Dr. Catherine S. Amatruda. (This book was revised once by the original authors, and subsequently by his former students, Drs. Knobloch and Pasamanick. The latest of these revisions appeared in 1980.)

In 1941 Dr. Gesell published an article which deals specifically, as its title "Pediatrics and the Clinical Protection of Child Development" implies, with the importance for any pediatrician of a thorough awareness of problems of behavior development. He notes that:

Historically, pediatrics was at first concerned entirely with the symptoms of disease. But the very nature and needs of infancy necessitated a widening interest in physical growth and the origins of defects and deviations. . . . Also, we need simply to enumerate some of the conditions which first come under the eye of the pediatric physician to appreciate the enormous importance of mental factors. . . . The developmental consequences of defect, disease, injury and environmental handicap can be identified adequately only in terms of behavior. . . . The supervision and guidance of child development depend upon an orderly regard for the behavioral indices of maturity.[8] (pp. 755, 756)

It is clear that a clinical pediatrics which aims to protect the developmental welfare of infants and children must reckon with behavior patterns. Developmental diagnosis is primarily an appraisal of the functional maturity of the nervous system by the aid of behavior norms. Such an appraisal answers the fundamental questions upon which guidance and therapy are based. Is that child normal? How does he deviate from the normal? What is the cause of the deviation?[8] (p. 757)

He then goes on to discuss such aberrations as amentia. cerebral injury, sensory handicaps, environmental deviations. He concludes:

This brief survey of the practical applications of developmental diagnosis is sufficient to indicate the strategic position of pediatrics in the scheme of medicine. There is growing demand for a periodic type of developmental supervision which will require a more systematic diagnosis of behavior symptoms in the clinical protection of early child development.[8] (p. 761)

In 1942, in an article in the *Journal of Pediatrics*, Dr. Gesell emphasizes, as he will continue to do from then on, the importance of teaching growth and development to medical students:

Medical schools have not managed to give the integrated problems of child development adequate definition and interpretation. We do not need a new discipline in the medical curriculum, but we do need a reorientation of teaching which will bring the total embryology of the postnatal child into the focus of diagnosis and of understanding. The most fundamental function of an infant is development. We must get the medical student to think clinically in terms of development. We need to recruit more young men and women and train them for leadership in this field which has an inevitable future.[9] (p. 278)

This particular paper reports a panel discussion held in Boston, Massachusetts on October 11, 1941 at the Eleventh Annual Meeting of the American Academy of Pediatrics. Dr. Gesell was the chairman of a discussion group which included as speakers Drs. L. Emmett Holt, Jr., Winthrop M. Phelps, C. Anderson Aldrich, and Catherine S. Amatruda. In addition to chairing the meeting, Dr. Gesell (and his staff) also provided a booth in the Exhibit Hall of the Statler, which demonstrated some of his cinema techniques and cinema studies.

During the course of this meeting, and after the panel discussion, Dr. Gesell asked Dr. Catherine Amatruda, who was his chief assistant and a person in whose judgment he had great confidence, how she thought the panel went, and how many of the pediatricians were impressed with the idea that pediatricians should concern themselves with matters of development.

Her reply, direct as always, was that in her opinion possibly one third of the physicians present were impressed and interested, one third thought it a lot of nonsense, and one third really did not care one way or the other.

(Though he does not mention this in print until somewhat later, shortly after the American Board of Pediatrics was established in 1935, a basic requirement in *Growth and Development* was set up for specialty classification.) As Dr. Gesell commented in 1948,

> When the medical history of the 20th centery is written, we know this formal action will be regarded as a uniquely important event in the evolution of clinical medicine.[10] (p. 331)

In one further contribution in 1942, in a chapter of Brenneman's *Practice of Pediatrics* titled "Developmental Diagnosis and Supervision," Dr. Gesell defines Developmental Pediatrics as:

> A form of clinical supervision which is equally and coordinately concerned with problems of childhood disease and child development. The accurate diagnosis of growth needs is most fundamental.[11] (p. 28)

In 1947, in *Developmental Pediatrics*, he elaborates on this theme:

The concepts of development and disease cannot, of course, be divorced. In many diseases it is the developmental consequences which are of critical concern. The vast field of allergy and immunity involves developmental factors at every turn. . . . The practitioner never escapes problems of development, whether he is "merely" supervising the nutrition of a well baby or following the growth career of a chronically sick, handicapped or defective child.[12] (p. 188)

It is clear that a more fundamental training of physicians in the field of developmental diagnosis is indicated. This training should begin in the undergraduate years and may be carried through to a high level of postgraduate specialization. . . . A well-grounded pediatrician can be trained to expertness in one or two years of full-time participation in a diagnostic and advisory service which deals with a wide range of normal and ab-, normal developmental conditions. . . . For the vast work of preventive mental hygiene we must look to pediatric medicine.[12] (p. 191)

Also in 1947, in an article titled "Development Diagnosis of Infant and Child" he comments hopefully:

Developmental diagnosis is becoming a subspecialty in the domain of pediatrics. This is its logical orientation, since pediatrics is in itself a generalized form of medicine, which by tradition and necessity deals with the total child in his natural cultural setting.[13] (p. 35)

A final comment on this whole subject appeared in 1951 in *The Pediatrician and the Public*, where he notes that:

Like any other technique of clinical medicine, developmental diagnosis may be undertaken at various levels of skill and thoroughness. As a clinical specialty it demands at least a year of postgraduate preceptorship in training in addition to a basic internship in general pediatrics or neuropsychiatry. It is not assumed that the general pediatrician aspires to be in addition an expert clinical psychologist or an analytic psychiatrist. He can, however, acquire a working familarity with basic examination procedures, and a developmental insight into the symptoms of behavior deviations. He need not hesitate to make a few standardized behavior tests which may give evidence as to the maturity, and the organization of the underlying action system.

He cannot rely on incidental impressions and interviews alone, nor on intuitive speculation as to hidden psychological forces.[14] (p. 736)

In the final 10 years of his time at Yale, Dr. Gesell's attack on the problem of persuading medical schools to teach, and pediatricians to use, the methods of developmental diagnosis involved a three-part onslaught. In *Developmental Diagnosis* he had provided a basic text. In his more general writing he spread information as to the importance of developmental methods in the practice of pediatrics.

Of major practical importance was the fact that Drs. Gesell and Amatruda had set up a training situation at the Yale University School of Medicine whereby individuals who had already attained their M.D.'s could intern at the Yale Clinic of Child Development for periods of 1 or 2 years. Among outstanding pediatricians thus trained were Drs. Hilda Knobloch and Benjamin Pasamanick, Joseph Baldwin, and Arthur H. Parmalee of the United States, Dr. Cyril Koupernick of France, Dr. R. C. Illingworth of England and Dr. Alda Bencini of Italy, all of whom went on to carry out this kind of work.

Unfortunately, this training opportunity was cut short by the untimely death of Dr. Amatruda and by Dr. Gesell's retirement from the University. However, though by no means all medical students today receive a good grounding in growth and development, and by no means all pediatricians are interested in their patient's developmental status, many medical schools and practicing pediatricians are concerned with developmental diagnosis.

As to Dr. Gesell's own contribution, Professor Miles sums it up as follows:

> Dr. Gesell was a potent leader in making clear the important relationships that may exist between medicine and psychology, and he did much to establish the point of view that psychology is comparable to physiology as a fundamental partner of medical science. The developing human body is subject to profound laws of growth and an adequate clinical science must be founded upon good principles and methods of developmental diagnosis. . . .By the Gesell type of persistent study, research, and publication, the evolution of preventive medicine moves forward in its service to man.[6] (p. 71)

Chapter 15

DR. GESELL'S USE OF
FILMS AND PHOTOGRAPHY

USE OF CINEMA

The cinema cannot, of course, make the psychic essence of the mind visible on the screen. It serves, however, to sharpen our perception for the psychology of infancy and to confirm our faith in the dynamic importance of early growth and education.[1] (p. 150)

The cinema is in many ways an ideal instrument for the investigation of complex behavior forms because it captures the behavior in the outward totality. The films record and remember infallibly.[2] (p. 8)

When the history of current culture is written, it is certain that the historian will set down photography as one of the most pervasive and powerful instruments of modern civilization. In a shorthand way, one might even characterize the difference between primitive and technological culture as follows: the primitive culture lacks photography and other visual aids.[2] (p. 8)

Cinema analysis is an objective method of behavior research which was made possible only by the invention of the flexible film and other modern photographic techniques. Cinema analysis is a form of biopsy which requires no removal of body tissues from the living subject. Yet it is truly a study of the structuralization of the child's living being.[3] (p. 19)

159

The use of cinema was definitely one of Dr. Gesell's favorite methods of studying child behavior. He was certainly fascinated by, one might almost say enamored of, this medium. In the early years he made use of films as a means of recording behavior. But fairly soon, cinematography and cinemanalysis became for him a primary tool in his quest for an understanding of the ways in which behavior grows. His norms of infant and preschool behavior were based very largely on cinemanalysis. His photographic dome (see Figure 15-1) became almost a trademark and his photographic library was treasured by him as much as his book library.

In fact, the cinema was such a basic tool in much of his work from 1924 on that perhaps the majority of his scientific investigations were based on its use. A total history of his involvement with cinema would encompass nearly all of his major investigations. Only some of the high points in his use of this medium will be discussed here.

The first and perhaps most basic way in which the films were used was as a basis for the analysis which became the source for his norms of infant and child behavior.

A second product of cinemanalysis was the series of scientific articles he wrote with his colleagues, or which his students undertook under his supervision. In a 1933 publication titled "Infant Behavior Researches of the Yale Clinic of Child Development," he notes that "The methods of cinematography have been used in various genetic studies such as the following:

"The development of cube prehension,"

"An experimental study of learning and growth in identical infant twins,"

"The growth of adaptive behavior and insight in infants,"

"The growth of pellet prehension,"

"The development of eye movements in early infancy,"

"Clinical studies of the prematurely born infant,"

"Language and growth,"

"The relative efficacy of early and deferred vocabulary training, studied by the method of co-twin control."[4] (p. 542)

Though Dr. Gesell believed heart and soul in the method of cinemanalysis, he himself did not analyze his films. The seven main

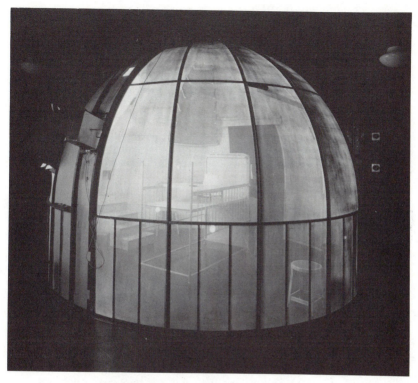

Figure 15-1.   Photographic dome.

studies which he published, in addition to his numerous twin studies with Helen Thompson, in which cinema was used as a tool, were in collaboration with colleagues. These were, first of all, in 1936 with Henry M. Halverson,[5] "The Development of Thumb Opposition in the Human Infant." This was followed in 1938, by "Early Evidences of Individuality in the Human Infant," with Ames.[6] Next, in 1940, came "Ontogenetic Organization of Prone Behavior in the Human Infant,"[7] also with Ames.

Then, in 1942, comes a major study, "The Daily Maturation of Infant Behavior: A Cinema Study of Posture, Movements, and Laterality," with Halverson.[8] This in turn was followed by three further studies with Ames: "Ontogenetic Correspondence in the Supine and Prone Postures of the Human Infant,"[9] in 1943, "The Development of Handedness"[10], and "The Infant's Reaction to His Mirror Image,"[11] both in 1947.

In 1943, in the Introduction to his *Atlas of Infant Behavior* Dr. Gesell reviews his use both of still photographs and cinema as follows:

> In connection with a psychological survey of the preschool period of childhood, in 1919, the writer used a Graflex camera, size 3½ by 4½ with rapid lens, to photograph infants in characteristic behavior situations. . . . In 1925 in the publication of our investigation we included some 200 action photographs as the first leaves of a clinical album which may be used for normative reference and comparative purposes. The album has expanded into the present Atlas.
>
> In 1924, with the cooperation of the Pathé Company, a cinema record was made, outlining "The Mental Growth of the Preschool Child." [This was mentioned first in the 1925 book by the same name.[12]] This venture confirmed our faith in the scientific potentialities of cinematography. Two years later, through the generosity of the Laura Spelman Rockefeller Memorial, a grant was made available for photographic research. This led to the installation of a photographic laboratory in the clinical quarters at 52 Hillhouse Avenue.
>
> In 1930, through a special grant from the Rockefeller Foundation, supplemented by a further grant from The General Education Board, it became possible to expand the photographic research to include the naturalistic aspects of the infant's behavior development. In this year the clinic was removed to the Yale School of Medicine at 14 Davenport Avenue and its old quarters were converted into a residential unit for a systematic cinema survey of the domestic life and social behavior of the infant. This survey was made by 35 mm. cameras and became the basis for the second, or naturalistic, volume of the Atlas.
>
> Both sets of records, the 16 mm. aggregating scores of thousands of feet of film footage, have been assembled, classified and indexed by library methods. Many of the records have been booked into edited reels. The present Atlas is in a sense a codification of selected materials from the Photographic Library of the Yale Clinic of Child Development.[3] (p. 13)

This entire Atlas project was a major undertaking. To bring it off, in addition to helping staff, Dr. Gesell engaged the services of two rather remarkable people. Dr. Alice V. Keliher, an educator, was in charge of assembling the subjects for each of the two Atlases. For the first, a group of presumably "normative" subjects came to the Clinic at monthly intervals and were photographed as they responded to the various test situations which make up the Gesell Developmental Examination. For the second, a group of "naturalistic" subjects came in, again at monthly intervals, and lived their entire day at the Clinic. They were photographed in various naturalistic situations such as being bathed, being fed, napping, and playing.

The films were taken and processed by Jules von de Bucher, reputedly the former official photographer for the Soviet Union.

The two Atlases themselves represent perhaps the pinnacle of Dr. Gesell's own use of photographs taken from motion picture films to present pictorially responses at various ages of infants to his test situations and in the normal activities of daily living.

Next, Dr. Gesell wrote five primary "talk pieces" about the use of cinema. The first of these, titled, "Photographic Studies in Child Development: A Clinical Study of Early Mental Growth,"[13] was written in 1927 and is no longer available. The second, appearing in 1935, was titled "Cinemanalysis: A Method of Behavior Study,"[14] a very thorough explanation of the Gesell use of cinema.

This was followed in the same year[2] by "Cinema as an Instrument for Parent Education." In 1946, at the request of the magazine *American Naturalist*, he published "Cinematography and the Study of Child Development."[15] And finally, in 1952, he combined two of his favorite topics in "The Method of Co-Twin Control In Conjunction with the Method of Cinemanalysis."[16] (Actually, nearly all of his famous co-twin control studies involved to some extent the use of films.)

These talk pieces were supplemented in 1947 by a pamphlet titled "The Story of Child Development in Motion Pictures: A Guide to the Yale Films of Child Development."[17] This pamphlet, co-authored by Ames, describes his Photographic Research Library as "Containing many miles of film depicting the behavior patterns which are typical of early human development," and also describes in detail 10 films edited at the Clinic and listed in the following section of this paper.

A final product of Dr. Gesell's use of cinema was the series of edited films themselves. A natural outgrowth of the vast amount of filming carried on at the Clinic, and of Dr. Gesell's extreme enthusiasm for this medium, was that he and his staff edited a substantial number of films. Some were used merely for teaching purposes. Others were edited in a more formal way—either for local showing or for widespread distribution to the public.

The first formally edited films were two 1,000 foot reels, both filmed and edited by *Pathé Review* in 1930. These films, made before Dr. Gesell had his own photographic facilities, were titled "The Study of Infant Behavior."

Next came 10 films, filmed and edited by Dr. Gesell and his staff in 1934, which were distributed by a commercial company called ERPI Classroom Films, of New York City. Each of these was 400 feet in length, on 16 mm. film (though some were reduced from original 35 mm. film). Each included a sound track by Dr. Gesell. Thus they were referred to as sound films, though they were not actually filmed in sound.

This series included the following titles:

The Growth of Infant Behavior; Early Stages

The Growth of Infant Behavior: Later Stages

Posture and Locomotion

From Creeping to Walking

A Baby's Day at 12 Weeks

A Thirty-Six Weeks Behavior Day

A Behavior Day at 48 Weeks

Behavior Patterns at One Year

Learning and Growth

Early Social Behavior

The presumably best of this footage was also made into a longer (1,000-foot) film, also distributed by ERPI and titled "Life Begins."

The next film was in some ways a more ambitious, though less scientific project, filmed and edited not by Dr. Gesell but by the *March of Time* of New York City. This 1,000-foot 16 mm. film, under the direction of Len Lye, was titled "Life with Baby." It was filmed at the Yale Clinic of Child Development in November/December, 1945, and first shown publicly on February 6, 1946. Thereafter it was shown in regular movie theaters throughout the world.

Next came a second series, edited in 1947 at Yale by Gesell and Ames. This series is described in the booklet "The Story of Child Development in Motion Pictures,"[17] already referred to. These films were distributed by Encylopaedia Britannica, along with the original series of ten ERPI films and the larger film, "Life Begins."

This 1947 series consisted of the following 400-foot 16 mm. silent films:

How Behavior Grows: The Patterning of Prone Progression

The Growth of Motor Behavior

The Growth of Adaptive Behavior

Infants Are Individuals

Twins Are Individuals

The Baby's Bath

Bottle and Cup Feeding

The Conquest of the Spoon

Self-Discovery in a Mirror

Early Play

Three further research films were edited, but not distributed publicly. These were two films on Laterality, made in 1946; and one on Reciprocal Interweaving in 1948, both in collaboration with Ames.

Then came what was in a way the crowning film of Dr. Gesell's career produced with his assistance, though not actually photographed by him. In 1949 the Medical Film Institute of America devised the notion of inviting outstanding individuals in various specialties. These films were to be distributed to medical schools throughout the country.

To Dr. Gesell's delight, his work was chosen as the first of these films. It was especially gratifying to him to have his work chosen as the basis for this series since one of his major campaigns had been to persuade pediatricians to be aware of the fact that, as he put it, development as well as disease lies within the province of clinical pediatrics.

This 28-minute color film, distributed by the Medical Film Institute, was titled "The Embryology of Behavior." It is still being distributed, though now by The International Film Bureau of Chicago, and is now available to the general professional public (educators and psychologists) and not merely to the medical profession.

The present location of Dr. Gesell's extensive Photographic Library should perhaps be mentioned at this point. When he and his staff were invited to leave the Unversity in 1948, there was some question as to the actual owership of the films. Yale felt that the films were theirs. The Gesell group felt that the films belonged to them. A compromise was reached. Yale, through Mark May, agreed that if the films could be left with them, L. B. Ames could be appointed Permanent Curator of the Yale Films of Child Development with a permanent Assistant Professorship. She in turn agreed to be responsible for the use of the films—that is, she would help students locate such films as might interest them and would refer them to related reading material.

At the end of a year, Yale decided they would keep the films but did not need a permanent Curator. Since proper humidification was not provided, some of the films deteriorated. However, about 1980 all films were transferred to the Child Development Film Archives at the University of Akron under the supervision of Dr. John A. Popplestone, where they now rest.

CINEMA—USE OF SPECIAL TERMS

Dr. Gesell's first reference to the word "cinema" appears in 1925 in his book *The Mental Growth of the Preschool Child*,[12] when he refers to the two reels of cinema film provided by the Pathé Review. These films were made at the Yale Clinic of Child Development. The phrase he uses here is *cinema film.*

He also speaks in this same book of a "Magster"—a device which enables the user to view stereoscopic stilled pictures of moving pictures. However, he notes that "lacking this luxury, we have assembled our action photographs as the first leaves of a clinical album." Thus the Pathé films were evidently not analyzed, at least not at this time.

Dr. Gesell did not refer to filming as *cinematography* until 1933, when in an article titled "Infant Behavior Research at the Yale Clinic of Child Development,"[4] in a section on "Systematic Cinematography" (p. 4, 5) he comments, "The clinic utilizes the cinema as a systematic instrument for research."

He notes, "Four feet of 16 mm. film embody 160 individual frames which depict 160 phases of behavior episode, 10 seconds in duration. *Cinematography* thus becomes a systematic tool for recording the phases of behavior pattern in their individual dynamic sequence. . . . The systematic cinema films of the Clinic of Child Development have been classified and catalogued by library methods, and are booked in 10-foot reels."

A full description and illustrations of his *photographic dome* (see Figure 15-1) with its two camera tracks permitting photography both forming the zenith and the horizon of the Dome, had appeared earlier—in 1928—in his book "Infancy and Human Growth."[18] It is clear that even by that date vigorous and systematic use of the motion picture camera was in full force.

However, the actual term *photographic library* did not come into his writing until 1934. In his book "Infant Behavior" he reports that "The films of the Yale Clinic of Child Development have been assembled into a *photographic research library.** The contents of the films have been catalogued by library methods and can be consulted by chapter and verse."[19] (p. 22)

Now for the important term, *cinemanalysis*. When did this first appear in Dr. Gesell's writings? He approaches it in 1934 in both *Infant Behavior*[19] and in his *Atlas of Infant Behavior*,[3] when he refers to *cinema analysis*. But the two words did not combine into *cinemanalysis* until a year later in 1935[14] in a comprehensive paper titled "Cinemanalysis: A Method of Behavior Study." Here, as earlier, in *Infant Behavior* he describes in detail the *analysis desk* invented by Professor Henry M. Halverson for use with 16 mm. film. He also describes the movieola with 35 mm. film, and explains the principles of what he called *cinemanalysis*.

A special use of film, popular with Dr. Gesell, was what he described as *coincident* (or *simultaneous) projection*. By this method a strip of film was split down the middle and two different original films—of a single infant at two different ages or of two different infants at the same age—were imprinted on it. He describes this method in a 1933 publication,[20] and probably earlier. This method was used more for demonstration and teaching than for analysis. Its forerunner, described as early as 1926[21] and used before cinema was available, was to seat two infants side by side in their mothers' laps and then to photograph them both at the same time. This was used especially in relation to the Gesell-Thompson studies of twins.

Use of Still Photography

When the history of current culture is written, it is certain that the historian will set down photography as one of the most

---

* It was somewhat later, in the mid-1940s, that L. B. Ames was appointed Curator of the Yale Films of Child Development.

pervasive and powerful instruments of modern civilization. In a shorthand way, one might even characterize the difference between primitive and technological culture as follows: the primitive culture lacks photography and other aids to vision.[2] (p. 8)

Though even his very first book publication, *The Normal Child and Primary Education*,[22] written with Mrs. Gesell in 1912, included a handful of illustrations, the first book which was (liberally) illustrated with photographs taken by Dr. Gesell or his staff was *Mental Growth of the Preschool Child*,[12] published in 1925.

Just earlier in that year he had noted that "In connection with our investigation numerous action photographs were taken of normal and of clinical subject. Specimens of these were shown by *stereopticon*"[23] (p. 1062). In *Mental Growth of the Preschool Child*[12] (p. 159) he explains that he uses the term "Action photographs because with few exceptions some form of action enters the picture." However, in spite of this terminology, the photos themselves did not move. He reports that in addition to these action photographs, "We have taken clippings from two reels of cinema film provided by the *Pathé Review*." Cinema was already in the picture.

Dr. Gesell's 1928 volume, *Infancy and Human Growth*[18] is also quite liberally illustrated with photographs from his own collection, as is *The Guidance of Mental Growth in Infant and Child*, published 2 years later. It is in this volume that for the first time he presents his famous "Montage"—a single infant shown first in supine and then in a tabletop situation in 14 photos at advancing ages from 1 week through 52 weeks.[24] (p. 87)

Through this period virtually all photographs used appear at least for the most part to have been taken with a still camera. But from here on, they were largely drawn from his films, as in *Infant Behavior*[19] and *The Atlas of Infant Behavior*,[3] both published in 1934.

Still photos made from the Naturalistic Atlas films were used for both the basic research underlying and the photos used to illustrate *Feeding Behavior of Infants*, written in 1937[25] with Dr. Frances L. Ilg. Both stills made from films and still photos taken specially for this particular book were used as illustrations for *The First Five Years of Life* in 1940.[26]

In the same year, 1940, Dr. Gesell's enthusiasm for photography spilled over into parent advice in an article titled "Plan Your Child's Picture," which appeared in *Popular Photography*.[27]

(Through all these years, but especially after 1940, photographs

—again both from cinema or taken as stills—were used as the basis for his formidable lantern slide collection. These slides illustrated nearly all of his basic scientific studies and he used them quite constantly both in public lecturing and in teaching.)

Though a less impressive publication than the Atlases, a book which made strong use of stills chosen from basic film records was published in 1945. *How a Baby Grows*,[28] a popular presentation for parents, covers such area as eating, sleeping, playing behavior, use of eyes and hands, and individuality of infants. This book consisted almost entirely of photos, with only very brief captions.

After this, only three of his book publications contained photographs. Also appearing in 1945, *Embryology of Behavior*[29] was generously illustrated with rather unusual photos both of fetal-infants and of neonates. As was customary, these photographs were from Dr. Gesell's own collection.

In 1949 he and colleagues published a volume titled *Vision: Its Development in Infant and Child*.[30] Like the majority of his publications, this book, too, was illustrated with photographs taken from his films.

And finally in 1952 came the book publication which accompanied the film "Embryology of Behavior". It was titled *Infant Development: The Embryology of Early Human Behavior*.[31] Photos here are taken from the 35 mm. film and, though not in color as in the film, are unusually beautiful. Like the film itself, illustrations in the book provide a rather elegant, certainly satisfactory conclusion to Dr. Gesell's quarter-century-long use of both photographs and films.

As an appendix to this summary, we present Dr. Gesell's own summary of his work with films, taken from the autobiography which he wrote in 1952.[32]

> I had come to the conclusion that cinematography should be used not only for purposes of documentation, but also as a research instrument for the analysis of the morphology of behavior patterns. Visible behavior is a form of motion, or, if you prefer, it is formed motion. Instantaneous photography freezes motion. Cinemanalysis is a method for systematic time-space study of frozen sections of motion, within a given episode, or in relation to a sector of the ontogenetic cycle.
>
> From a monistic standpoint, the primary problems of a developmental psychology are morphological. The fundamental scientific riddle is always one of pattern or form. The cinema helps us to capture this form and to define its lawfulness in

terms of (a) the behavior moment; (b) the behavior episode; and (c) a whole developmental epoch. Cinematography by itself bakes us no scientific bread, but as a tool for psychological research its potentialities are inexhaustible.

Our first contact with the cinema was in 1924 in our small laboratory at the Department of Education building at 28 Hillhouse Avenue. With the cooperation of *Pathé Review** we made the first photographic survey of the behavior development of the pre-school child, from early infancy to school entrance. The filming was done under the sputter of arc lights, and the infants made a surprisingly good adjustment to the novel situation. With the expansion of our research program, the clinic was moved in 1926 to the homelike environs of a spacious residence at 52 Hillhouse Avenue. Cinematography has an important place in this program. In collaboration with Professor Raymond Dodge, a member of the Institute of Psychology, and Professor Henry Halverson, Research Associate in Experimental Psychology on the clinic staff, we planned and installed a one-way vision observation dome for the systematic photographic recording of behavior at lunar month intervals. The sizzling arc lights were replaced with soft and cool Cooper-Hewitt illumination. The developmental examinations of infant behavior were made with careful regard for standard procedures by Helen Thompson, Ph.D., Research Associate in Biometry; by Catherine Strunk Amatruda, M.D., Research Pediatrician; and by myself. During this early period research and diagnostic examinations were also made by Elizabeth E. Lord, Ph.D., Ruth W. Washburn, Ph.D., and Marian Putnam, M.D., all of whom were especially interested in the clinical aspects of child development.

At first the cinema records were limited to the normative progressions of infant development, but from time to time instructive clinical deviations were similarly documented. In 1930 a supplementary Rockfeller grant made possible a parallel naturalistic survey supervised by Alice V. Keliher, Ph.D., which documented the infant's daily life under domestic conditions with the mother's immediate care. A homelike studio unit was constructed which permitted optimal 35 mm. cinema records of the baby's behavior day—his sleep, waking, feeding, play, bodily ac-

---

* In our later photographic program we made use of one of the original Pathé cameras which has been used in the historic filming of "The Birth of a Nation". Our film bore the title, "The Mental Growth of the PreSchool Child." The book bearing the same title was named after the film.

tivities and social behavior. The naturalistic survey was continued for two years in the Hillhouse unit. The two surveys, with
the accompanying stenographic and other protocols, supplied
the source data for *An Atlas of Infant Behavior* (1934). This work
in two volumes (Yale University Press) was illustrated with 3200
action photographs derived from the original films. The normative volume delineates typical trends from age to age. The naturalistic volume depicts individual differences.

Scientifically controlled cinematography fortunately is a
paradoxical form of embalming. It not only preserves the behavior in chemical balm, but it makes that behavior live in its original integrity. The cinema registers the behavior events in such
coherent, authentic and measurable detail that for purposes of
psychological study and clinical research the reaction pattern of
infant and child become almost as tangible as tissue.

Accordingly we have taken great pains to safeguard our
films with a view of giving them archive permanence and research accessibility. Each film was catalogued by library methods
and identified in specific footages and content. Over the years
we have assembled some 200,000 feet of 35 mm. film, and over
100,000 feet of 16 mm. film to constitute a Photographic Research Library. The photographic collection has recently been
taken over by the library of the Yale School of Medicine,[*]
where the Yale films of child development will be made available
for students and investigators.[32] (pp. 131–133)

---

* These films are now stored in the Child Development Film Archives at the
University of Akron, Akron, Ohio.

Chapter 16

FETAL BEHAVIOR

Dr. Gesell's interest in the behavior of the fetus began early in his career and lasted late. His first writing on the topic appeared in 1925 as a chapter in his book *The Mental Growth of the Preschool Child.* His last appeared in 1954. In 1945, he devoted an entire book titled *The Embryology of Behavior* to the subject. Throughout, his concern was for observation of as well as measurement and evaluation of fetal *behavior* rather than of the structure of the fetus as such.

His position was that behavior in the fetus, like that of the infant once born, develops in a patterned and highly predictable manner, influenced by but not primarily determined by its environment.

In his first discussion of the fetus, Chapter 13 entitled "The Foetus" in *The Mental Growth of the Preschool Child*[1] (p.187–195), Dr. Gesell asks the question, "Does the foetus belong to psychology?" and his answer is that it does. He points out that the first indications of the nervous system are found as early as the second week of prenatal development. He continues:

> Before the fifth month of the gestation period certain neurons, connected doubtless with the medulla, have established functional connections with cardiac muscles of the foetus and brought them under a rhythmic control which will not cease until death. The foetal heart sounds therefore indicate that an ap-

propriate group or network of neurones has in a sense matured. Such a group of coordinating neurones is called a "neurone pattern." *To the student of behavior the neurone pattern is as useful as the molecular theory was to the physician.* . . . The accurate observation and measurement of behavior of an infant (or foetus) will furnish an objective index of the maturity of the nervous system.[1] (pp. 192–193)

In 1928, in his book titled *Infancy and Human Growth* there is a short section on "The Behavior Growth of the Foetus." He notes that:

> Even the conceptual zero lies temporally very close to the earliest behavior observed in the human embryo. Pfluger saw activity of the embryonic human heart in the third week of gestation. Strassman observed slow movements of the arms and legs of a human embryo at the age of 7 weeks in a case of extrauterine pregnancy which came to his surgical attention. Minkowski, a Swiss neurologist, has made remarkable observations of early behavior in foetuses ranging from 2 to 5 months of age.[2] (p. 305)

He continues with a list of typical movements expected in the foetus at succeeding months during the fetal period, which in the interests of brevity need not be listed here. His general conclusion is that:

> Biologically considered the whole period of immaturity is a continuum. Postnatal infancy merges by backward reference into the stage of the foetus, which in turn derives from the embryo, which in its turn derives from the germ. The facts of human infancy cannot be grasped in true perspective unless the lineage of both body and behavior is traced back to the prenatal period. . . . So advanced are behavioral capacities that an infant may be born two or three months before the appointed time and still survive. The premature infant is a key to the understanding of the pre-natal portion of the developmental cycle.[2] (p. 10)

Further comment appears two years later, in 1930, in the book *Guidance of Mental Growth in Infant and Child*, when he points out that

> The lawfulness of psychological growth expresses itself in the tendency toward patterning which human behavior always displays. . . . Likewise with the foetus. Its behavior is in no sense

amorphous, but, as the studies of Minkowski have shown, manifests itself in fairly well-defined reflexes. . . . These patterns of behavior follow an orderly genetic sequence in their emergence.

The uterus is the normal environment of the foetus till the end of a gestation period of 40 weeks. But birth with survival may exceptionally occur as early as 24 weeks and as late as 48 weeks. . . . *Our normative studies of both premature and postmature infants have shown repeatedly that the growth course of behavior tends to be obedient to the regular underlying pattern of genetic sequence, irrespective of the irregularity of the birth event.*[3] (pp. 275, 276)

In 1933 he makes this significant statement:

Postnatal patterns of behavior may be envisaged in organic continuity with those which are laid down in the fetal period. Although birth brings numerous changes in the stimulus potentialities of the environment and introduces social factors, there is, biologically speaking, no fundamental, no unique change in the infant's method of growth. His developmental mechanics remains what it was *in utero.* Indeed the general physiology of his development is essentially comparable to the neuro-embryology of the amblystoma, which has been so significantly analyzed by the brilliant patience of Coghill.[4] (p. 68)

In 1938, in an article on the TNR (tonic-neck reflex) in the human infant, Gesell remarks that:

Torsion of the head to one side in a living fetus 20 weeks old arouses a movement of the arm on that side. This is a rudimentary T.N.R. which becomes better defined and elaborated in the latter half of the prenatal period.[5] (p. 460)

He continues:

Indeed, the T.N.R. is part of the ground plan of the organism, pervasively identified with its unitary, total action system. The T.N.R. accordingly has an ecology. More or less directly it subserves adaptations to the environment, prior to birth as well as later. The T.N.R. helps the fetus to accommodate in the conformation of the uterine cavity; and it may even facilitate the longitudinal presentation and orientation of the fetus at the entrance of the birth canal.[5] (p. 463)

In further comment about the TNR in a 1939 article, he notes again that Minkowski had observed in a 20-week-old fetus what may be considered a rudimentary TNR, and then continues:

> Davenport Hooker's cinema records show that the fetus with a developmental age of about 11.5 weeks, on unilateral stimulation of the lip will respond as follows: ". . . the head is rotated and slightly laterally flexed toward the contralateral side; the body is slightly laterally flexed to the contralateral side; both arms are slightly rotated outward, then sharply inward, so that the half flexed *forearms* are first *separated* then *approximated, as if to clap the hands*; the rump rotates slightly; both thighs extend and rotate slightly."
>
> The italics are ours, for we wish to call attention to the fact that the fetus is capable of a hand clapping reaction which is utterly foreign to the infant during most of the first year of life.[6] (p. 176)

(This mention of Davenport Hooker leads to a short parenthesis. During or around 1940, Professor Hooker lent Dr. Gesell an entire set of fetal films, showing the behavior of fetuses from somewhere around 28 weeks of age right up to 39 weeks. These films were analyzed in detail by a member of Dr. Gesell's staff [LBA]. This analysis revealed a great deal about the way in which fetal behavior developed. Obviously this development was cephalocaudad. But we also observed that ages when horizontal movements of the arms prevailed seemed to alternate with ages when these movements were predominantly vertical. Though some mention of Hooker's films was made in Dr. Gesell's later book, *Embryology of Behavior*, this specific analysis was never published or even mentioned in any detail.)

The theme remains the same, with respectful attention paid to the fetal period, in a chapter titled "The Nature of Mental Growth" in the 1940 book, *The First Five Years of Life*. Dr. Gesell notes that:

> The embryologist is particularly interested in the transformations of bodily structure; the genetic Psychologist, in transformations of behaviors. Both embryologist and psychologist investigate the shape of things to come and the shape of things becoming.

He adds that:

Even at the early age of 5 months the fetus has attained a high degree of behavior organization. It seems as if Nature hastens the growth of the organism as a safeguard against the contingency of premature birth.

He also suggests that:

It is permissible to speak of the *individuality* of the fetus for even newborn infants display significant individual differences.

And he concludes:

Even birth does not bring about a unique and abrupt transition, because *in utero* the fetus has already anticipated to a great degree the reactions of early neonatal life.[7] (pp. 10-12)

In a discussion of grasping, later in this same book, Dr. Gesell points out that:

Finger closure first appears at about 11 weeks in fetal life and is quite complete at 14 weeks. The gripping reflex appears during the 18th (prenatal) week and, according to Hooker, increases in strength up to 25th week. . . . The strength of the gripping reflex undoubtedly increases throughout the prenatal period.[7] (p. 80)

The next, and by far the most comprehensive, treatment of fetal life, is an entire book publication, *The Embryology of Behavior.*[8] In the interest of brevity we shall here merely indicate the main thrust of this volume. Dr. Gesell, in his own autobiography, describes his book this way:

In our publication entitled *The Embryology of Behavior,* the developmental approach was carried downward to the levels of fetal infancy and the neo-natal period. The neo-natal data were mainly based on a continuous study of a neonate who immediately after birth was transferred, with his mother, to the residence suite of the clinic. *Continuous observation and photographic documentation were maintained night and day over a period of two weeks* (by AG, CSA, and LBA).

A fetal-infant by definition is a viable infant, prematurely born and still living in the fetal period. Under very favorable hospital conditions we were able to make systematic observations of the behavior characteristics of a group of fetal infants ranging from twenty-eight to forty weeks in fetal age.

Many years ago Perez asked a blunt question: Does the fetus belong to psychology? The subtitle of the *Embryology* volume was intended to suggest an affirmed reply; it reads, "The beginnings of the human mind." Although this volume deals with the humbler spheres of behavior—with the developmental patterning of muscular tonicity, electro-tonic integration, respiration, sleep, body posture, ocular amd manual reactions—it is believed that these behavior phenomena have implications for a genetic psychology.[9] (p. 134)

According to Dr. Gesell, the purpose of the book *Embryology* is to describe the action system of the human individual in the making:

> . . . to indicate how an organic complexus of behavior is built up concomitantly with the bodily development of embryo, fetus and neonate.[8] (p. vii)

And he does so, in great detail, by picture and text. This book in its time may have represented the most complex description of fetal body and behavior to date.

In the following year, 1946, we find this brief comment:

> The action system of embryo, fetus, infant and child undergo pattern changes which are so sequential and orderly that we may be certain that the patterning process is governed by mechanisms of form regulation—the same mechanisms which are being established by the science of embryology. Experimental embryology is now one of the most active and flourishing of all the life sciences. It has undertaken the analysis of development, particularly as it affects the anatomy of the organism. *Investigators, however, are using functional and behavior criteria increasingly to define the somatic anatomy.*[10] (p. 337)

In a second paper on the tonic-neck reflex (TNR), published in 1950,[11] Dr. Gesell makes reference to fetal behavior. He points out that though in the very young fetus symmetrical postures prevail, in the early stage fetal infant (28–31 weeks), the mid-stage fetal infant (32–36 weeks), and the late-stage fetal infant, the TNR can be observed. (A fetal infant is a fetus born before its time and surviving. The age range of fetal infancy is from 28–40 weeks.)

During the years 1949–1952, Dr. Gesell and a staff member

(LBA) collaborated with the Medical Film Institute of America in the production of a film entitled *Embryology of Behavior*.[12] Unlike his book by the same name, this film does not deal primarily with fetal behavior. Though some of the film does portray the fetus, and there is some footage of a fetal infant, the films interprets the term "embryology" primarily as the roots or beginning of behavior and deals essentially with the period of infancy.

A final paper on fetal behavior, "Behavior Patterns of Fetal Infant and Child"[13] appeared in 1954, a few years after Dr. Gesell's departure from Yale.

A rather long quote from this paper will serve as a comprehensive summary of what he has to tell us about the development of fetal behavior, and it implications.

THE DEVELOPMENTAL STABILITY OF THE FETAL-INFANT

Manifest behavior begins with the fetal period and organizes with great rapidity. As an insurance factor against the contingency of premature birth, the capacity for breathing is laid down at about the fetal age of 28 weeks, which is 12 weeks prior to normal need. The *viable fetus becomes an infant* at birth. He is called a fetal-infant from the time of his premature birth to the fortieth postconception week

His precocious entrance into the world affords an opportunity to trace the course of behavior development which is usually concealed within the uterus. A total of 80 systematic observations supplemented by cinema were made on 22 subjects at post-conception ages of 28, 32, and 36 weeks. For convenience we regard these ages as marking the early stage, mid-stage, and late stage of fetal infancy. Our findings indicate that prematurity, uncomplicated by damage or disease, has no permanent dislocating effect upon the ontogenetic sequence of behavior development.

The early stage fetal-infant (post-conception age, 28 weeks), weighs about two pounds. The muscle tonus is minimal, flaccid, uneven, meandering. He neither truly sleeps nor wakes. His spontaneous activity occurs in brief ripples. His eyes are mostly closed; the eyeball moves conjointly; the lids flutter; the frontal brow, or only half of it, corrugates; the tongue protrudes; lips purse. Rarely he emits a faint bleat. Briefly, his face assumes a crying expression, a soundless cry. His postural activity is sporadic and meager. He lies with head turned to one side; he assumes quiescent and "floating" tonic-neck-reflex attitudes. Movements are poorly sustained. Torpor constantly supervenes.

At mid-stage, four weeks later, the fetal-infant is less fragile, more compact. His muscle tonus is less fluctuant and increases on manipulation. His head station is firmer and functionally more closely related to the trunk. He holds the tonic-neck-reflex attitude more tonically and at times windmills his extensor arm. On tactile cue he flexes on a rod with active grasp. His eyes open wider and more often. They do not fixate, but they respond saccadically in momentary pursuit of a moving object. Despite prevailing drowsiness, the mid-stage fetal-infant evidences a growing distinction between sleep and wakeness. There are brief periods of wakeful awareness and alertness.

During the late stage (from 36 to 40 weeks of post-conception age) the sleep-wakeness activity cycles become more clearly defined. Postural activity increases. Crying becomes more vigorous. The periods of visual and auditory awareness lengthen. The infant now falls off to sleep more decisively and clings to sleep more tenaciously. He wakes spontaneously (thanks to the primitive waking center of Kleitmann). He is physiologically more robust; his muscle tonus is now well consolidated. Having had some weeks in which to refine his adaptations to an extra-uterine environment, the late stage fetal-infant may function more smoothly than a full term new-born infant of comparable post-conception age. But this apparent advantage is transient and does not confer any permanent acceleration upon the precociously born fetal-infant. (pp. 115, 116)

This review of what Dr. Gesell had to say about fetal development is given at this length because his message seems important. His basic position was that behavior is a function of structure, and that structure develops according to a predictable and somewhat predestined pattern which does unfold, given even moderately favorable environmental factors, even in the period long before birth.

Chapter 17

RELATIONSHIP BETWEEN IQ AND DQ

Since the concept of the DQ (developmental quotient) played a major role in Dr. Gesell's normative work, and since the relationship of DQ and IQ (intelligence quotient) has not been fully understood by some workers in the field, perhaps the topic deserves special consideration.

That there is still some confusion in the minds of some is suggested by a 1985 quote from a book by Judith Rosenblith, who makes the following comment on the subject:

> The Gesell test can be used with separate evaluations for each of the four areas of performance, or those scores can be be combined into one and a developmental quotient (DQ) obtained. The latter was to provide an infant evaluation analogous to that of the IQ. Numerically it works like the IQ. The DQ, however, is psychologically quite different from the IQ. Many of the behaviors that go into the DQ score are decidedly nonintellectual. . . . The DQ and comparable scores on other infant tests are not, in fact, highly related to IQ scores. . . *Gesell's belief that the DQ and the IQ were highly related is one reason that psychologists have ignored his work in recent decades.*[1] (p. 324)

Rosenblith herself may indeed believe that Dr. Gesell believed that the two measures were highly related. However, Dr. Gesell's

180

own writings contradict her conclusion, as the following quotations make clear.

Admittedly, in his first book of norms,[2] he does not explain too clearly his concept of the relationship between the two measures. And three years later, in *Infancy and Human Growth*, he merely says:

> The term *adaptive behavior* approximates the term intelligence, but cannot be made strictly equivalent. Moreover, the data in the present chapter are not concerned with intelligence as such, but with developmental maturity levels. It is our general problem to inquire into the consistency of a series of maturity in relation to chronological age.[3] (p. 142)

In *Infant Behavior*,[4] published in 1934, the term *intelligence quotient* does not appear in the index, but in 1938, in *The Psychology of Early Growth*, Dr. Gesell notes:

> We have used the word intelligence sparingly, because its conventional connotation, transferred to the age period of infancy, might be misleading. There is no doubt that the genetic counterparts and precursors of "intelligence" manifest themselves in the functional fields of perceptual and adaptive behavior. But the intellectual abilities of the infant and preschool child are less individual, less specialized than at a later age. The young child functions more *as a whole*, and the evidences of his intellectual potentialities must be sought in the total tide and broad configurations of his behavior as well as in delimited problem-solving successes.[5] (p. 204)

The whole issue of the relationship of developmental quotient to intelligence quotient is made much clearer in 1941. In his publication *Developmental Diagnosis*, Gesell states specifically:

> A word is here in order concerning the ubiquitous and somewhat over-publicized I.Q. or Intelligence Quotient. Although the principle which underlies the D.Q. is similar to that of the I.Q., there are important differences in clinical application which should be pointed out.
>
> The I.Q. does not directly measure intelligence in any absolute way; it signifies rather the relative rate at which so-called intelligence is developing on the basis of a standardized psychometric scale which consists largely of verbal and problem solving tests. The tests are scored on an arbitrary basis of success and failure.

Developmental diagnosis does not attempt a direct measurement of intelligence as such, but should aim at clinical estimates of mentality based upon analysis of maturity status. We are interested in the biological equivalents of intelligence which we have called adaptive behavior; namely the capacity to use and to initiate experiences for present and for future adjustments. The infant, however, is so integrated and generalized that this adaptivity must always be considered in relation to the other aspects of behavior—motor, language, and personal-social. *Developmental diagnosis is consistently concerned with maturity status rather than with abilities as such.*

The D.Q., unlike the I.Q., is not limited to a single inclusive formula. A distinctive D.Q. can be derived for each of the four major fields of behavior; for specific functions like prehension, locomotion, manipulation, etc. This makes the D.Q. an adaptive device. The D.Q. registers change in the growing complex of behavior. Fluctuations in a general D.Q. or in specific D.Q.s denote intrinsic and extraneous factors which are subjected to interpretation.

The single formula concept of the I.Q. is inadmissible in the diagnosis of infant behavior. A single summative numerical value cannot do justice to the complexity and variability of infant development. *Any adaptation of our tests and methods which, for psychometric convenience would affix I.Q.s to infants is undesirable and is inadequate for the scientific study of growth processes.*

Errors of clinical application will be avoided if we remember that the D.Q. refers to the end products of development. It does not in itself take account of the etiologies of defects and deviations, the medical history of the child, environmental factors, personality liabilities and assets. The diagnostician therefore must weigh all these qualifying considerations and interpret the D.Q. accordingly. He must ultimately determine whether a given D.Q., general or specific, is really predictive or whether deflecting factors are present.

The Developmental Quotient has an additional merit. It reminds the examiner that, contrary to popular view, the younger the child, the more serious is the prognostic significance of every degree of true retardation. Two months is to 3 months as 2 years is to 3 years, and also as 6 years to 9 years—which in terms of D.Q. is another way of saying that 1 month of retardation in infancy may be the equivalent of a whole year or even of 3 years in later childhood.[6] (pp. 114–116)

These quotes would seem to make it quite evident that Dr. Gesell by no means, Judy Rosenblith to the contrary, believed that the

DQ and the IQ were highly related. However it is fair to admit that he did not perhaps, at all times, make the relationship entirely clear. Since in the minds of some there remains a certain ambiguity as to how these two measures relate to each other, it may be useful to explain our own (Gesell staff) interpretation of the relationship.

The Intelligence Quotient (IQ) is generally defined as a measure which presumably defines the relative brightness or intellectual possibilities of an individual more or less permanently. It tells us how bright the individual is compared to others of his own age. Some intelligence tests, as the Slosson[7] measure chiefly verbal ability. Others, as the better known WISC[8] include both a measure of verbal intelligence and a measure of performance ability as determined by pictorial arrangement, block design, object assembly and other tests.

The Developmental Quotient (DQ) on the other hand is intended to measure quite something else again. It is intended to measure the child's level of maturity or behavior age, that is the age at which he is behaving as a total organism.

As noted in our book *School Readiness*:

> It soon became evident that intelligence is only one part of the child's total endowment. A mere intelligence test does not and cannot attempt to measure a child's total level of maturity. Thus a child may be of clearly superior intelligence but may at the same time be behind others of his age in either physical or behavior maturity. This combination is so common that we have coined the term "superior immature" which indicates that a child is well above average in intelligence but below average in behavior maturity.[9] (p. 17)

The concept of using behavior age, developmental quotient, developmental level or level of maturity (the terms are used synonymously) instead of mere chronological age, or intelligence level, in determining school readiness was introduced by us in 1964.[9] Our position was that not all five-year-olds are behaving in a manner that is fully five, and thus may not be ready for the usual kindergarten curriculum which is based on the child's having reached a five-year-old level of maturity. We also hold that a high IQ alone, if it is not matched by a five-year-old level of maturity, does not guarantee success in kindergarten, since *much more than the child's sheer intelligence goes to school.*

We also hold that much school failure and many cases of sup-
posed "learning disability" are caused by sheer immaturity, by the
child's not being ready for the grade in which IQ or birthday age
may place him.

The practice of starting children in school based on behavior
age rather than chronological age or IQ is now being used in hundreds of schools in this country. Its success depends in part on making it very clear to parents that immaturity or a behavior age below
chronological age does not mean that the child in question has a low
intelligence. DQ and IQ are by no means the same thing, and immaturity should not be equated with "dumbness."

Whether one agrees with this basic principle or not, at older
ages—three or four years of age and following—the difference in
the meaning of intelligence quotient and developmental quotient
seems clear. And it seems quite understandable to most that IQ and
DQ may be equal or that either measure may be ahead of or behind
the other. It is at the earliest ages, especially during the first twelve
to eighteen months of life that some find the relationship between
these two measures a little confusing.

Since most intelligence tests rely very heavily on language alone,
rather than taking into consideration the four fields of behavior
used in determining the developmental quotient, many find it difficult to determine the IQ of children in the first two years of life.
Thus in evaluating the very young, many find the developmental
level not only easier to determine but also more objective and a
more reliable measure than the intellectual level.

However, even when only developmental or behavior tests are
used, there is often a temptation to try to hazard a guess as to the
child's intelligence. This is admittedly guesswork, but it goes as follows. Since language items are relatively sparse through the first fifteen months of age, we must rely chiefly for our estimate on motor,
adaptive and personal-social behaviors, motor and adaptive probably
giving us our best clues.

It seems fair to consider it likely that if the infant shows himself
to be behaving at age in all the ways we can easily measure that other
things being equal (favorable personality, good environment) he *may*
well be of at least normal intelligence.

If a 40-week-old baby can sit steadily for an indefinite period of
time, pull himself to standing, creep, match two cubes, poke at a pellet, and respond positively in others ways listed as characteristic of
40 weeks, it seems relatively safe to assume that he or she may be of

at least aveage intelligence. An infant whose maturity level is at or ahead of his or her chronological age seems to us to show good general promise. One whose maturity level is even a month or two behind his or her chronological age is considered to show less promise.

As the child grows older and language comes in more fully, and as adaptive behavior involves increasingly complex combinations of objects (as pencils and paper) some one area of behavior (especially language) often becomes increasingly likely to express itself as being out of line with the other kinds of behavior. That is, motor, adaptive, language and personal-social behaviors do not necessarily develop at the same rate. It is then that the possible divergence between developmental level and intellectual level grows potentially greater.

Though the IQ and DQ are and must be considered two quite separate measures, in the early months of life, due to the lack of an effective way of measuring infant intelligence and for lack of a better measure, we do tend to lean on behavior testing for clues.

This was particularly true in the 1940s when the Yale Clinic of Child Development did a great deal of examining of infants and young children who were being placed in adoption.

Infants who on developmental tests functioned at or near their age were considered to be developing normally and thus were considered to be good adoption risks. Those two months behind their chronological age were considered less suitable candidates for adoption.

It might be noted here that in our experience (though certainly not all investigators agree) developmental tests given in infancy and during the preschool years tend to be highly predictive of behavior in later years. Dr. Gesell's 1939 book, *Biographies of Child Development*, emphasizes:

> . . . the high degree of latent predictability in the early section of the life cycle. In this whole series of thirty developmental specimens (described in this book) there is no instance in which the course or trend of mental (developmental) growth has proved whimsical or erratic.[10] (p. 102)

In this book only developmental evaluations were considered at all ages. Throughout, Dr. Gesell was comparing a child's early Developmental Quotient with a later one. However, at the risk of complicating the entire issue, we report the results of a more recent (1967) study,[11] in which we again attempted to measure the predictive value of early behavior examinations.

Ideally of course early developmental examinations would have been compared with later developmental examinations on the same children, as Dr. Gesell was able to do it 1939. Since developmental data were not available on our own older subjects, what we did was to compare developmental quotients of infants and preschoolers for whom later (10-year-old) WISC scores were available. We quote from our findings:

> In spite of the fact that our infant and preschool tests aim to measure behavior level or developmental level rather than intelligence per se, there is a close, though by no means inevitable, correlation between the two kinds of behavior. Though it is possible for a child be both superior and yet immature for his age, for the most part infants who rate above average on infant behavior tests do turn out to be above average in intelligence in later years.
>
> Present subjects were 33 children examined in infancy on Gesell Infant Behavior Tests and 44 children examined in the preschool years on the Gesell Preschool Scale. . . . Twenty-one of the thirty-three infants, or 63.6% of all, had scores in infancy which fell within 10 points of the ten-year-old I.Q. score. Of these, sixteen (48.5%) fell within 5 points. The mean age for these first infant examinations was 33 weeks.
>
> In forty of forty-four preschoolers (91%), preschool and 10-year-scores fell within 10 points of each other. Twenty-one (or 48%) of these children had scores which fell within 5 points for the two examinations. The mean age of the first preschool examination for this group was 25.5 months.
>
> For all 76 children for whom preschool examinations were on record, 58 or 76% had scores within 10 points of the 10-year-old score.
>
> In very few instances did an infant examination overrate the child's later response. . . . Children are seldom worse in behavior than predicted by infant tests, and do often improve slightly. With present developmental tests, superiority cannot always be detected except in the so-called "quality" of behavior.
>
> Of the various parts of the early behavior examination, it is, as might be expected, the language items in the scale which correlate most closely with later I.Q. scores.
>
> Our conclusion is that if the complexity of what the infant or preschool developmental quotient (DQ) represents is kept in mind, if clinical judgments are taken into account, and if it is

remembered that the DQ and the IQ are different even though related measures, it can be shown that infant and preschool examinations are highly predictive of behavior which comes later.[11] (pp. 235–237)

In short, Dr. Gesell's position, and our own, has been throughout that IQ and DQ are by no means the same thing. IQ measures intelligence alone. DQ tells us the developmental level or developmental age of the total organism in action.

In the first year of life, since intelligence as such is hard to measure, we rely on the DQ to tell us whether a child is behaving in a manner appropriate for one of his chronological age, ahead of that level or behind it. Thus it seems permissible to hazard the guess that an infant who is behaving at age as a total person might indeed be of relatively normal intelligence.

However, the two measures are not identical, and as the child grows older in many instances they can be quite divergent. A child could be of superior intelligence as measured by sheer intelligence tests (IQ) and yet immature in total behavior (DQ). Or, of course, just the opposite.

Chapter 18

GESELL ON HEREDITY
AND ENVIRONMENT

One of the prevalent quasi-primitive notions holds that growth is predetermined, that it is so natural that it takes care of itself and that there is little to be done about it. . . . Now the scientist would insist that growth is essentially lawful but also profoundly plastic. It is governed by certain limitations; but within those lawful limitations it is marvellously adaptive, and • likewise lawfully responsive to both internal and external conditions.[1] (p. 395)

Though many critics through the years have attributed to Dr. Gesell this very notion that "growth is so natural that it takes care of itself and that there is little to be done about it," this statement of his made back in 1926 indicates that he is fully aware of the "plasticity" of growth. In fact from this date on, he phrases this hypothesized relationship in many publications and in various ways, but the message remains basically the same.

In 1928 he has this to say:

It is doubtful whether the basic temperamental qualities of infants can be *measurably* altered by environment influences.[2] (p. 372)

In 1929, however, he comments:

Environment may play a screening or selective role determining which of competing potencies are to be realized and
which suppressed, but the basic mechanism of realization is one
of maturation. . . . Much of the child's individuality is undoubtedly attained through the stresses of human relations, which
condition and habituate by the powerful influences of social
approval. But there is interdependence rather than conflict
between the extrinsic and intrinsic aspects of development.[3]
(p. 658)

Admittedly he does feel that maturation does play the dominant
role, but as further quotes will show, he definitely allows environment its place.
In 1933 he notes that:

I think the concept of maturation should not be used to set
environment and the intrinsic factors too much in contradistinc-
tion. There is alway a labile factor as well as a stabilizing one.
But it seems to me that the stabilizing one is intrinsic and depends upon what we would call for the present maturational
mechanisms.[4] (p. 77)

In 1934 Dr. Gesell comments more fully:

If we manage to envisage maturation as an active physiological process, we overcome the rather stilted antithesis of the nature versus nurture problem. . . . The heredity and environment
of an organism can be completely separated only in analytic
thinking, for in actual nature such separation would lead to in-
stant death of the organism, even though the philosopher making the analysis might himself survive.
There is a very reciprocal interrelationship between heredity and environment. The intimacy of this relationship may not,
however, prevent us from ascribing a priority and possibly even
some preponderance to hereditary factors in the patterning of
human behavior. Although it is a truism, it should be emphasized that no environment as such has the capacity of growth.
*Environmental factors support, inflect and modify, but do not gen-
erate the progressions of development.* Growth as an impulsion and
as a cycle of events is uniquely a character of the living organism and neither physical nor social environment contains any ar-
chitectonic arrangements even analogous to the mechanism of
growth.[5] (pp. 293–295)

He again expresses his feeling that one should not make too much of the distinction between the various forces that combine to make the individual what he or she is when in 1939 he comments further:

> Throughout life the manner in which the child profits by experience is influenced by inherent factors. It is impossible to resolve completely the antithesis of nature and nurture. It is artificial to press unduly a distinction between intrinsic and extrinsic factors, but it must be emphasized that environment as such cannot impart growth.[6] (p. 305)

In the following year, he again expresses his feeling that intrinsic factors are primary in determining behavior, but that too much of a distinction between outside and internal factors should not be made:

> In appraising growth characteristics, we must not ignore environmental influences. But these must always be considered in relation to primary, or constitutional factors, because the latter ultimately determine the degree, and even the mode, of the reaction to so-called "environment". The organism always participates in the creation of its environment and the growth characteristics of the child are really the end-product expressions of an *interaction* because intrinsic and extrinsic determiners. *Because the interaction is the crux, the distinction between these two sets of determiners should not be drawn too heavily.*[7] (p. 159)

Two years later, in 1942, he states very clearly his opinion of the relative contributions of genetic and environmental factors in determining individuality and behavior in infant and child:

> *Growth is a unifying concept which resolves the dualism of heredity and environment.* Environmental factors support, inflect and modify but they do not generate the progressions of development.[8] (p. 281)

(This early (1940–1942) emphasis on interactions is of interest in view of the fact that in the 1980s many students maintained that they "followed" Piaget instead of Gesell, because Piaget is interested in *interaction*, while Gesell ignores it.)

Three years later, in 1945, Gesell comments:

The child comes into his racial and familial inheritance through an innate process of growth which we call maturation. He comes into his social heritage of culture through a process of *acculturation*. The two processes interact and interfuse, but the process of maturation is the more fundamental in the production both of likenesses and differences among children.[9] (p. 196)

Also in 1945 he makes the very definite statement:

The baby is an individual from the moment of birth. He has inborn temperament and native constitution. They determine the way he will react to his environment.[10] (p. 2)

A few years later (1949) he reaffirms his position—that in trying to understand human behavior, one must respect both genetic and environmental forces, but that genetic factors play the predominant role in that they limit and prescribe what environment can accomplish:

No two infants were ever born alike. No two infants were ever reared alike. The individual differences which distinguish infants, therefore, have a double derivation—the genes of ancestral inheritance, and the endless variations in the personalities which constitute families, schools, and communities. However, no infant is so individual that he ceases to belong to his species and to racial stock. Although he is sensitive to cultural impress, he has a biological equipment which sets limits to that impress and which also determines the directions, the modalities, and the intensities with which he reacts to his personal environment.[11] (p. 548)

A final comment in 1956:

The organism comes by his individuality as he comes by his mind and body, namely, through the organizing process of growth. This insures him from becoming a mere creature of the culture into which he is born. In spite of all the cultural forces which make for standardization, the individual preserves a measure of the individuality with which he is endowed. This endowment comes chiefly through the genes.[12] (p. 26)

Dr. Gesell's basic position on the relative contributions of heredity and environment—that environmental forces modulate and inflect, but do not *determine* the progressions of development—has been clearly indicated in the above quotations. It is also implicit—if not elaborated—in a large proportion of his writings.

It is incorrect to believe, as some do, that he was not interested in or respectful of such contributions as the environment does make to the behavior of the individual. His position was merely that in order for the environment to act effectively, it must recognize and respect both the stage of development of any given child and also the personality or individuality of that child. His assumption was not (as some others hold) that the environment actually creates and determines individual behavior; but rather that *it can play its part effectively only when the primacy of individuality and growth factors are recognized.*

Dr. Gesell's assumption here is of course that those persons making up the environment of the child have a certain amount of control over this environment. On the other hand, strict environmentalists, and especially many anthropologists, appear to regard the environment as a dominant factor, which not only determines behavior, but is a force over which we have relatively little control.

One single book publication of Dr. Gesell's might be considered the epitome of his views on the priority of developmental forces, and the extent to which even environmental variations can be transcended by these forces. This publication was the book entitled *Wolf Child and Human Child: A Narrative Interpretation of the Life History of Kamala, the Wolf Girl.*[13]

This book tells the story of a girl named Kamala, who apparently in early infancy was carried off by a she-wolf to its lair. This child gradually acquired the ways of the wolf, which almost concealed her humanness, until 8 years later, when she was rescued from the wolf den and brought up by the Indian missionary, the Rev. J.A.L. Singh and his wife. According to the Rev. Singh's daily diary, which describes Kamala's development and behavior and her gradual return to human ways until the time of her death at the age of seventeen, she did acquire many of the characteristics and behaviors of a normal human child.

In fact, this is the main message of the book—that even when the behavior and personality of a human child has been grotesquely altered by environmental factors, once this child is returned to a presumably normal human environment, relatively normal human behavior does emerge. Not only does it emerge; it develops in more or less the usual patterned and predictable way even though at a reduced rate.

When Kamala was first allegedly rescued from the wolves, her behavior was in most ways more like that of an animal than of a human being. Since her mode of locomotion was creeping, her hands served as paws and she employed her mouth instead of her hands, as Dr. Gesell put it, "for prehensile purposes." She used her hands to pinion, her head to poke and pry. And when she was weaned to solids (she at first sucked from the udder of the mother wolf) she seized her food by mouth. What water she drank, she lapped, as a dog laps.

> She had developed not only a tolerance for raw meat, but a passion for it, and for carrion as well. The biochemistry of her retina was modified to increase vision in darkness and dim light. Her temperature controls became highly educated so that she was not unduly affected by heat or cold. She perspired scarcely at all; she tended to pant, and to extrude her tongue in the sun. . . . She growled and bared her teeth defensively when she was molested while eating. She took the offensive with the wolves when they chased the vultures from coveted carrion. She had no fear of the dark. . . . During the day she dozed and idled in the den.[13] (pp. 21–23)

Even after being rescued, three times in the dead of night, at 10:00 P.M., 1:00 A.M., and at 3:00 A.M. she would howl, as, presumably, her fellow wolves had done when she lived in the forest. Needless to say, she completely lacked human speech.

That all these changes not only in behavior but, to some extent, in her physical self were reversed and redirected toward customary human behavior once she came to live with human beings, speaks well both for the patient effort of the Singhs, but also for the force and strength of customary genetic factors.

As Dr, Gesell points out:

> In 1921 when first rescued, Kamala lived like an animal, in the dark. Except when she was passively receiving attention from Mrs. Singh, she either roamed around outdoors, in the night, or sat quietly in a dark corner, facing the wall. She shunned sunlight and human company. Her chief vocalizations were wolf howls. Though she preferred to remain in the dark she slept little, perhaps four hours out of the twenty-four, at noon and midnight. She spent no time in spontaneous social relations with people.[13] (p. 62)

By 1926, after 5 years in the Singhs' orphanage, her behavior day was comparable to that of other children in the orphanage:

> She now preferred daylight to darkness; human beings to animals. She slept through the night; not only did she not choose to roam around outside but was afraid if left alone outdoors.[13] (p. 62)

She walked like other children, preferred to wear clothes, and by the end of 1924 her vocabulary had increased "by leaps and bounds," and she even spoke in short sentences. She socialized with the older children and could be trusted to take care of the younger ones. She now actually seemed to fear the dark.

In view of these rather remarkable changes in Kamala's behavior, Dr. Gesell summarizes his, and Dr. Singh's, findings as follows:

> The career of Kamala teaches us that the relationships of heredity and culture are extremely interdependent. It is artificial to make a sharp and stilted antithesis of Nature versus Nurture. For we are not dealing with two sets of competing and incompatible forces, but with a physiological process which brings them into mutual interaction. We are dealing with the physiology of growth.
>
> The reciprocal relationship between heredity and environment should not, however, blind us to the priority of hereditary factors in the patterning of human behavior. It is the organism, and not the environment, which has the capacity of growth. Environmental factors support, inflect and modify, but they do not generate the progessions of development. They do not establish the primary potentialities of either physical or psychological growth. So inborn and ineradicable are these potentialities that even Kamala did not completely lose them.[13] (pp. 84, 85)

And in conclusion, Dr. Gesell notes, rather poetically:

> There is no insoluble paradox in the fact that Kamala both suffered and survived her fate. The seven years in the den took their toll. But when the life cycle of Kamala is contemplated in full perspective we must marvel at the insurance factors which protected her potentialities. We regain a tithe of further faith in Nature and by the same token in Man. He cannot transcend Nature; he cannot transcend heredity; *but by understanding Nature he can vastly improve his lot.* For in accordance with natural laws, human growth always seeks and finds an optimum.[13] (p. 98)

It is probably safe to say that no other publication of Dr. Gesell's attracted such stingingly negative reviews as did *Wolf Child*. Focusing directly, as it does, on the relative contributions of heredity and environment and on the question of the extent to which basic and innate growth factors can transcend even a striking, or even abnormally, adverse environment, it clearly aroused strong passions. Anthropologists were almost uniformly repelled by the book's message. Such humorists as Bergan Evans attacked it viciously, and in a personal communication to Dr. Gesell, Evans suggested that only advanced senility (Dr. Gesell was sixty-one at the time) could lead a reputable scientist to present the views espoused in this publication.

The basis of most of the contumely directed against the book was that Dr. Gesell had been taken in by a hoax, a hoax perpetrated by the Rev. J.S.L. Singh. In truth, Dr. Gesell had the courage to write his book only because he genuinely believed in the veracity of this same gentleman.

This belief was based on a number of factors. To begin with, Dr. Gesell was impressed by statements from the Right Reverend H. Pakenham-Walsh, Bishop, Christa Sishya Ashram, Tadagam, P.O. Coimbatore, India, to the effect that he was acquainted with the Rev. Singh and knew him as an honorable and reputable individual. Second, Dr. Gesell was highly impressed by what he described as the "internal veracity" of the diary which the Rev. Singh had kept of the behavior of Kamala from the time she was brought to the orphanage until the time of her death. Unless the clergyman was a total scamp and at the same time highly versed in the details of growing human behavior, he could not possibly have produced a diary so true to the ways in which young children develop.

In fact, of the diary, Dr. Gesell commented specifically, in an article written for *Harper's Magazine*:

> The diary strikes me as being a remarkable human document. In spite of omissions and a few inconsistencies, it bears internal evidence of sincerity and veracity. Its pages tell in unsophisticated detail what the Reverend Singh and Mrs. Singh did to reeducate the wolf-girl called Kamala. Her unique life history, as I reconstruct and construe it, gives ground for new faith in the stamina of human nature and the potentialities of human growth.[14] (p. 183)

Lastly, communications with the Rev. Singh through correspondence over a period of years gave the indisputable impression that one was dealing with a sincere and honest man. (After Dr. Gesell sent, as a gift to the Singhs, the fee he received for the *Harper's Magazine* article, they wrote to report that, since when the money arrived they were virtually out of food, the entire orphanage spent the day on its knees in prayer, in thanks for this timely gift.)

Admittedly, the value of the undertaking of writing the book *Wolf Child* does hang on the question—did things happen as the Singhs reported. Dr. Gesell believed that they did.

Chapter 19

PREMATURITY

A topic which ties in very closely with that of fetal behavior, and one which interested Dr. Gesell greatly, is prematurity. He first mentions it in 1928; last, in 1954. Though scattered comments occur throughout his writings, there appear to be 10 such references important enough to be included in this review.

The first allusion to prematurity appears in 1928 in Dr. Gesell's book *Infancy and Human Growth*, where he points out that:

> A considerable complement of behavior capacities has matured by the middle of the foetal period. So advanced are these capacities that an infant may be born two or three months before the appointed time and still survive. *The premature infant is a key to the understanding of the prenatal portion of the developmental cycle.*[1] (p. 10)

Two years later, in 1930, we find the following significant statements:

> The patterns of genetic sequence insure a basically similar growth career for full-term, pre-term and post-term infants. . . . Our normative studies of both premature and postmature infants have shown repeatedly that the growth course of behavior tends to be obedient to the regular underlying patterns of

genetic sequence, irrespective of the irregularity of the birth event.[2] (p. 276)

A premature postnatal and a protracted uterine environment might be considered as drastic deviations from normal environmental influence. *The relative immunity of the behavior patterns* from these environmental deviations again bespeaks the firmness of maturational factors.[2] (p. 289)

Two years later, in 1932, we find the title, "The influence of prematurity on mental growth." This, according to our card index, was published as a report of the *White House Conference, Part IV,* 1932.[3] The actual reference is missing from our files. Fortunately, however, the same information was given the following year in a paper entitled, "The Mental Growth of the Prematurely Born Infant," in *The Journal of Pediatrics.*"[4]* Here Dr. Gesell noted that:

Prematurity of birth constitutes an abnormal alteration of environment which might conceivably affect the developmental career of the infant.[4] (p. 676)

He then asks, and answers, the important question—"Does prematurity have any radical effect upon the character and the course of mental growth?" He carefully reviews the outstanding literature up to that date, quoting both investigators who feel that prematurity for the most part *does* have an adverse effect on subsequent development and those who find that it does not. He warns that:

The developmental fate of the prematurely born infant is *always an individual matter*, depending upon the severity of the complications produced by the prematurity and on his primary growth potentialities.[4] (p. 677)

His conclusion, both from his review of the literature and from his own clinical and research observations, may be summarized as follows:

Present data, though scanty and sometimes contradictory, indicate that *prematurity of birth in itself does not markedly distort, has-*

* A footnote to this article notes that "This paper in slightly moderated form was first reported in Part IV of the *White House Conference on Child Health and Protection,* 1932."

ten, or retard the course of mental development, when the age of the infant is reckoned from conception. Intrinsic organic factors of maturation, as opposed to environment, are so powerful and stabilizing that the infant tends to follow his inherent cycle of behavior development independent of the placement of birth. Deviations and defects of development occur when the conditions of the prematurity cause pathologic changes in organs or tissues. Deviations, such as imperfect postural and locomotor control, are not necessarily permanent; but frequently resolve in the first two years of life. . . .

Prematurity carries with it numerous hazards which may inflict temporary or permanent penalty; but fortunately the infant is also protected by the inherent factors of organic maturation, which make for a normal course of mental growth.[4] (p. 680)

The next substantive discussion of the topic of immaturity appeared in 1939, in Dr. Gesell's book *Biographies of Child Development.* Here he warns:

Too frequently prematurity is not recognized by physicians or nurses, and the child's welfare suffers in consequence. When more is known about the behavior characteristics of the premature, there will be greater accuracy in diagnosing both the presence and the degree of prematurity. Refinements in the hygiene of the premature infant will also come through a better understanding of his behavior limitations and requirements.[5] (p. 99)

In 1941 we find the following comment, which actually does not contribute substantially to the sum of our knowledge about prematurity:

A prematurely born infant is an anomalous, air-breathing fetus. Let us call him a *fetal-infant.* We have followed his development keenly because it reflects the behavior morphogenesis characteristic of gestation. We have made 80 behavior examinations of 37 fetal-infants with fetal or post-conception ages of from 28 to 40 weeks. . . . We have found that although the healthy fetal-infant makes a remarkably good adjustment to an abnormally untimely environment, the basic schedule of his behavior patterning is not upset. He remains faithful to his fetality.

In so doing he makes a fundamental contribution to the experimental morphology of behavior. Could any experiment more drastic be conceived to test the integrity of behavior form under the stress of a sudden, extreme and prolonged change of environment? If endowed with sufficient vitality the unblemished premature infant survives; but he gains no ontogenetic headstart. If he were born 8 weeks prematurely the general conformation of his behavior make-up at 28 weeks would be that of a normal 20-week-old infant. This indicates that the primary and predominant forces in the morphogenesis of early behavior are intrinsically determined.[6] (p. 472)

A further statement in 1941 from Dr. Gesell's book *Developmental Diagnosis* repeats succinctly his main thesis about prematurity:

Do the prematurely born infants who survive pay a developmental penalty for their survival? Uncomplicated prematurity exacts no penalty. Prematurity of birth, however, is often associated with malformations, asphyxia, birth trauma, intracranial hemorrhage. Such complications if not lethal may produce permanent defects and deviations. The developmental fate of the prematurely born infant is always an individual matter determined by the severity of the complications and by his primary growth potentialities.

Prematurity in itself displaces the time of birth, but it does not thereby dislocate the normal sequences of development when the sequences are reckoned from the fundamental base line of conception.[7] (p. 262)

Four years later, in 1945, in his substantial book *The Embryology of Behavior*, Dr. Gesell points out that by the time the premature infant has reached the post-conception age of 4 weeks, he will have been put in the world for several weeks, but this does not give him any developmental or behavior advantage. On the other hand, under favorable circumstances he should suffer no handicap from his premature birth. As he puts it:

Neither the full-term infant nor the premature, under normal conditions, has gained a striking advantage or suffered a permanent set-back because of the difference in the time of birth. By different but not dissimilar routes they both attain (eventually) the same level of maturity. The sequences of the growth cycle are not readily dislocated. The premature infant simply gives a slightly earlier prefigurement of what both infants will be when they reach the coequal age of 4 weeks.

Uncomplicated prematurity imposes no handicap on development. The majority of preterm infants are normally endowed and, given proper care early in life, their development is entirely normal. They cannot, as children and adults, be distinguished from individuals born after a full-term gestation. Their sensory equipment is intact, their motor development normal, and their intellectual achievements quite on a par with those of the general population.

Consider what might happen if prematurity of birth in itself (altogether apart from the attendant risks and complications) could dislocate and disarrange the normal progressions of development. Prematurity then would retard or blemish those progressions. Such consequences do *not* follow in the healthy premature.[8] (p. 142)

In short, the developmental status of the premature infant must always be appraised in terms of corrected age rather than his spurious chronological age. Born or unborn, the infant cleaves to the inherent sequences of behavior maturation. He remains faithful to his fetality even when birth has made him an infant. This is a striking example of a biological factor of safety.[8] (p. 143)

Dr. Gesell's next reference to prematurity, a paper titled "Behavior Aspects of the Premature Infant"[9] (pp. 210–212), appeared in the following year, 1946. Here he discusses viable fetal infants with post-conceptual ages of from 28 to 40 weeks, and discusses tonus at the varying ages, as well as such practical matters as clothing, cleaning, handling and bedding.

His conclusion to this paper repeats to some extent what he has said before:

The foregoing arrangements tend to personalize the care of the premature infant. Under the acculturating influence of one or two months of such care he may make consistent progress. In uncomplicated cases prematurity does not disturb the normal course of development. The healthy premature infant does not acquire any unnatural precocity from his head start; neither does he suffer any setback. This should be a great comfort to his anxious mother. She should be assured that the healthy premature infant follows the basic sequences of normal mental growth, making due allowance for his spurious age.

Fortunately, the maturational insurance factors are so

strongly entrenched that they protect the fetal infant to a great degree even from faulty methods of care. But if we are to bring his potentialities to the highest realization we must study more closely his total behavior economy by clinical methods of observation. His psychological needs are most clearly manifested in his basic muscle tonus and his patterns of tonal behavior.[9] (p. 212)

Final comment appears in 1954 in a paper titled, "Behavior Patterns of Fetal-infant and Child." Here Dr. Gesell describes in some detail the appearance and behavior of fetal-infants in the very early stage (post-conception age 28 weeks), mid-stage (32–36 weeks), and late stage (36–40 weeks.) His general comment here recaps what he has said earlier:

> The course of behavior ontogenesis is well ballasted by intrinsic maturational determiners, and it tends to run parallel to the equivalent developmental sequences of the full term infant. If, for example, the fetal-infant was born 8 weeks prematurely, we expect him to function at a 16 weeks maturity level when he reaches a chronological age of 24 weeks, his true age being reckoned as 24 minus 8 weeks. This expectation is confirmed by cinema and by our clinical studies of uncomplicated cases.
>
> The stability of early ontogeny has far-reaching implications for the problems of psychological inheritance and of psychic constitution. Maturation is the intrinsic stabilizing component of development which determines the basic patterns of species and individual traits. It represents the net sum of gene effects.[10] (p. 116)

Thus Dr. Gesell concludes as he began. From 1930 through 1954 the message remains virtually the same: Behavior develops in a highly patterned and predictable manner, even in the face of rather major environmental deviations and displacements. Accordingly, prematurity, if uncomplicated, does not distort, hasten, or retard the course of mental development, when the age of the infant is reckoned from conception. To predict what one may expect in the way of behavior and to obtain the child's "true" expected behavior age for any premature child as he or she develops, simply subtract the amount of the child's prematurity from his or her post-birthday age.

Most researchers today would probably still agree with this position. However, as the years go on, the vulnerability of the premature infant is increasingly being recognized, to an extent which was apparently not considered by Dr. Gesell. The consensus today appears to be that the fetus actually "needs" the full 40 weeks inside his or her mother's body for optimum development.

Chapter 20

INDIVIDUALITY OF THE AGES

A postscript to the notion that every *child* is an individual—a postscript which grew to be so substantial that it soon became a part of popular parlance—was the idea that every *age*, too, had its own individuality.

Dr. Gesell had in his early works written about the patterned changes which occurred from age to age as the child developed in terms of what the child could do at each age, rather than in terms of what his personality was like.

Gradually, however, his summaries of behavior to be expected at the various age levels began to include personality or individuality characteristics of these ages. The first strong indication of this appeared in 1940 in *The First Five Years of Life* by Gesell and others.[1] Though the important half ages—two-and-a-half and three-and-a-half—had not yet been recognized, nor had such important characterizations as "out of bounds" for *Four* come in, qualitative descriptions of the various ages were creeping in.

Thus in "First Five Years" we find such descriptions as the following:

Eighteen Months: Eighteen is rather resistant to changes in routine and to all sudden transitions. He is a nonconformist, egocentric, negative.

Two Years: Two can stick to confining tasks somewhat longer than Eighteen months. He shows finer discernments, is conscious of the family group.

Three Years: Three is a delightful age. You can bargain with him. Three is cooperative.

Four Years: The four-year-old is highly imaginative. He likes to ask questions. He may talk to attract attention. He is at times assertive, bossy, and silly. He may tell lies.

Five Years: The child of this age, on the other hand, is self-dependent, serious, reliable, and obedient.

Such descriptions constitute a small start, but a significant one. Age pictures given are made up of behaviors or behavior characteristics found at any given age, and to some extent imply the kind of personality or individuality to be expected. However, it was not until 1943, 3 years later, that his and his colleagues' summaries of behavior characteristic of the advancing ages took on the form of personality portraits.

In 1943, in collaboration with Drs. Ilg, Ames, and Learned, he published *Infant and Child in the Culture of Today*,[2] the first of a trilogy. In this book, for the first time, Gesell and colleagues gave strong emphasis to the quality of behavior at each of the succeeding ages. (It should be noted that there is no question as to the major contribution made to the characterization of the various ages by Dr. Frances L. Ilg. Her ideas about the qualities of the succeeding ages were fitted neatly into the framework of the Gesell/Ames notion of reciprocal interweaving.)[3,4]

According to this principle, as any behavior develops it appears to do so through a system of paired opposites—flexion and extension, symmetry and asymmetry, equilibrium and disequilibrium, for example. Thus as the ages of childhood appear in succession, the organism goes through alternating stages of equilibrium and disequilibrium, outwardized and inwardized stages of behavior.

Applying this idea to the early ages of childhood,* 18 months was found to be an age of disequilibrium, 2 years an age of equilibrium, 2½ of disequilibrium, 3 of equilibrium, 3½ of disequilibrium, 4 an age of expansion, 4½ a transition age, and 5 an age of inwardized equilibrium.

From 1939 on, Gesell and colleagues had expressed these

---

* Infants, too, go through alternating stages of equilibrium and disequilibrium, but the changes occur more rapidly and individual differences in timing are greater.

changes as an upward-going spiral, and referred to the entire process of development as "a progressive spiral kind of reincorporation
of sequential forms of behavior."[3] However, in his 1939 publication,
Dr. Gesell was referring to physical postures only, and not to the
entire quality of behavior at any single age. In the 1940s this concept
of the spiralling of development, or reciprocal neuromotor interweaving, as Dr. Gesell called it, applied to general behavior or personality characteristics of the ages as well.[4]

In 1943, in *Infant and Child*, the first publication which applies
this concept to the ages as a whole, only the levels of 18 months, 2
years, 2½ years, 3 years, 4 years, and 5 years were described. It was
not till 1949 that Ilg, Ames, and others introduced the idea of 3½ as
a special, separate age of disequilibrium.[5]

Dr. Gesell wrote further, and substantially, about the individuality of the ages. In 1946 he published *The Child from Five to Ten*,[6]
coauthored by Ilg and Ames. In 1949, in an article titled "Human
Infancy and the Ontogenesis of Behavior,"[7] in a section called "The
Interpersonal Self," he clearly describes the personality characteristics of every age from 2½ through 10, with strong emphasis on such
qualities as the following: the interest in opposite extremes of the
2½-year-old, the instability and tentativeness of 3½, the out-of-
boundness of 4, the self-containedness of 5, the overdemanding and
explosive qualities of 6, quietness of 7, expansiveness of 8, self-
consciousness of 9, self-possession of 10.

Possibly the most succinct description of salient characteristics of
ages 18 months to six years appeared somewhat later, in 1964, 7
years after Dr. Gesell's death, in a paper titled "The Developmental
Point of View with Special Reference to the Principle of Reciprocal
Neuromotor Interweaving," by Ames and Ilg.[8] Though Dr. Gesell
himself was, obviously, not an author of this paper, he had been
influential in determining these characteristics. To make this chapter complete we include this description at this point. (Figure 20-1
shows graphically the alternation between periods of disequilibrium
and equilibrium as the child matures in the age period from 18
months to 10 years of age.)

18 Months

The 18-month-old child walks a one-way street, and this
street more often than not leads in a direction exactly opposite
to that which the adult has in mind. It is difficult for the child to
mind when spoken to, to respond to commands, to keep within

Disequilibrium   Equilibrium

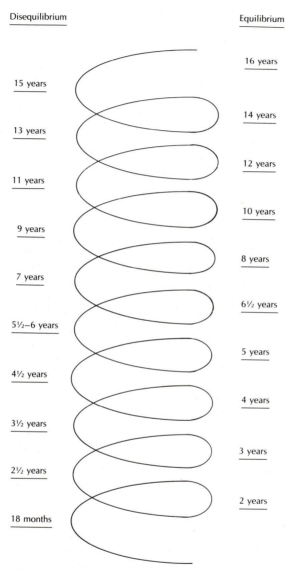

Figure 20-1.   Equilibrium versus disequilibrium.

reasonable bounds. And he is extremely strong-willed. His immaturities in motor, adaptive, language, and emotional fields may lead to tantrums. This is a marked stage of disequilibrium in many children.

2 Years

Things are much smoother in nearly every field of behavior. Added maturity and a calm willingness to do what he can do and to not try too hard to do things he cannot manage result in rather good equilibrium. The child is now surer of himself both motorwise and languagewise. Emotionally, too, he finds life easier (as his demands are not so strong as earlier), and he has developed an ability to wait and to suffer slight or temporary frustration if need be.

2½ Years

This is an age of marked disequilibrium. The child of this age tends to be rigid and inflexible—he wants exactly what he wants when he wants it. Everything has to be in what he considers its proper place, everything done exactly so. He sets up rigid routines which he expects everyone to follow. Furthermore, he is domineering and demanding. *He* must make the decisions. His emotions are violent. And, most of all, this is an age of opposite extremes. The child has no ability to choose between alternatives, so he shuttles back and forth endlessly between any two extremes: "I want—I don't want," "I will—I won't."

3 Years

Things quiet down briefly at 3 for most children. Whereas the 2½-year-old loved to resist, Three loves to conform. The child now likes to give as well as take. He likes to cooperate. He wants to please. He seems to be in good equilibrium not only with those about him but within himself. People are important to him and he likes to make friends. His increased language ability allows him to enjoy language and to respond well to language cues.

3½ Years

In many, there is even more marked disequilibrium than at two-and-a-half. The child at this age exhibits an extremely strong will, and any sort of compliance is hard to obtain. He may resist any and every routine. He insists on having his own way and seems to resist for the sheer pleasure of resisting. Though quite unwilling to please, he is emotionally very vulnerable and is quick to question: "Do you love me?" He cannot stand to be ignored; but too much attention, also, disquiets him: "Don't laugh! Don't look at me," he commands.

4 Years

This is an expansive, out-of-bounds age. Motorwise the child may hit, kick, throw stones, break things, run away. Emotionally he exhibits loud silly laughter or fits of rage. Verbally he is extremely out-of-bounds; he lies, swears, boasts, resists. He loves to defy parental commands and seems to thrive on punishment. A terrible toughness comes over many: they swagger, swear, boast, defy. And yet within himself the child of this age does not seem to be in any great trouble, and he can be quite delightful and enjoyable in spite of his out-of-bounds qualities.

4½ Years

Halfway between Out-of-Bounds Four and Calm Five, the child of this age often doesn't seem to know where he *is* functioning, and, as a result, his behavior can be extremely variable and unpredictable. It is this extreme variability and unpredictability that makes life difficult for the child himself and for those around him.

5 Years

A period of extreme and delightful equilibrium. The child of this age tends to be calm, stable, reliable, well adjusted. He is friendly and undemanding with others. He loves to please. His mother seems to be the center of his world and he likes to be with her, to do what she asks, to please her. "Today I'm going to do all the good things and none of the bad things," a five-year-old will say. Five likes to be instructed and to get permission and then to obey. He likes to help. Briefly he is a delightful social being.

5½ to 6 Years

Equable Five is followed by Tumultuous Six, the breakup starting around 5½. Behavior resembles that seen at 2½ in that the child is violently emotional and tends to function at opposite extremes: "I love—I hate." He himself is now the center of his own world and he wants to be loved most, to be first, to have everything.

When anything is wrong he blames his mother and takes things out on her. He cannot stand to lose, to wait his turn, to share. He has to be right, needs to win, demands praise. If things go well he is warm, enthusiastic, eager, ready for anything. If they go badly, he resorts to tears and tantrums.

This same kind of description of the ages, easy years following difficult ones, ages of equilibrium alternating with ages of disequilibrium and inwardized ages alternating with outwardized ages continues in two other publications—"The Child from Five to Ten"[6] and *Youth: The Years from Ten to Sixteen.*[9] We present here brief descriptions of behavior characteristic of the ages after five and up through sixteen, adapted from these two books.

6½ Years

The often difficult and contrary 5½–6-year-old emerges, somewhere around 6½ and, on his way to Seven, and often appears as a truly delightful creature indeed. Expansive, exuberant, friendly, cheerful, he proves to be a rewarding companion to adult and child alike. Temporarily secure in himself, he projects real friendliness to others. He is positive as well as friendly. He is giving. He enjoys other people and attracts positive attention to himself. He has quieted down considerably from the bumptuous exuberance of 5½ to 6, but has not as yet pulled in with the minor withdrawal so characteristic of Seven. This period may be fleeting but while it lasts it is truly delightful.

7 Years

There is a quieting down at seven. The 7-year-old goes into lengthening periods of calmness and self-absorption, during which he works his impressions over and over, oblivious to the other world. It is an assimilative age, a time for salting down accumulated experience and for relating new experiences to the old.

Seven is a pleasant age if one respects the feelings of the child. However, these feelings are all too often on the minor side. SEVENs quite characteristically feel that people don't like them, are mean to them, are picking on them. Children of this age like to spend much time by themselves.

8 Years

We think of the typical 8-year-old as expansive, speedy, and evaluative. He covers much ground, tries many new things. He covers the new ground speedily. But with his increasing ability to evaluate, he tends to feel that he has not done well. Though much less minor than at seven, he is apt to burst into tears if he is disappointed or feels that he has disappointed others. However, on the whole this is rather a positive age. Eight-year-olds will tackle anything in their own enthusiastic way. Relationships with others are now extremely important, close and intimate, especially the relationship with Mother.

9 Years

Nine may be thought of as an inbetween age—in between the exuberant expansiveness of Eight, and the calm, smooth composure of Ten. It resembles in some ways the unpredictability of Four-and-a-half. The child is by no means in the best of equilibrium, varying markedly from one day to the next. Nine has been described as an "embroidery" age, the child going on and on with whatever he may have started. And since it is a time of unpredictability, often neither adult nor child can be certain what may happen next.

Some child behavior clinics report that they see more 9-year-old child patients than those of any other age. This may be partly due to some inner disequilibrium on the part of the child. It may come partly because at this age many are making a real thrust to be free from adult supervision. But a child of this age may seem extremely self-sufficient at one minute, quite dependent at the next.

10 Years

Ten has been described by Dr. Gesell as a golden age, an age of unusual equilibrium, when the child appears to be friendly, confiding, comfortable and highly accepting of parents and others. "My Father is the most wonderful man in the world" Ten will tell you. Or, with enthusiasm, "Every Sunday our whole family goes for a ride." TEN is accepting of adult direction. If "Mommy says" something, that is the way it should be.

There are bursts of happiness and bursts of demonstrative affection. Earlier fears and worries lessen. This is indeed a sunny age, a time when such adjectives as nice, happy, casual, unselfconscious, straightforward, sincere, relaxed, comfortable, self-possessed, poised, frank, and open, are all applied.

11 Years

The sharp shift from equilibrium to disequilibrium is seldom seen more clearly than when the "good" little 10-year-old turns eleven. At Ten, as earlier at Five, the child's parents represented the center of the world for him. At Eleven, as at Six, the child himself holds that position. He wants everything for himself, wants to be best and first, wants everything to go his way.

Instead of going with the flow the child of this age seems to work *against* what is expected of him especially what his mother expects. TEN admired his mother vastly. ELEVEN criticizes and works against her, is often extremely rude and resistant. He is more adept at challenge than at acquiescence. However, away from home many ELEVENS are said to be "wonderful"—active, outgoing, enthusiastic, friendly, happy.

12 Years

At Twelve we find that many boys and girls emerge from the tangles and resistances of Eleven onto an entirely new plane of friendliness, confidence, and equilibrium. No longer resistant to Mother, the child may merely shrug off what he considers to be her faults: "Oh, you know you when you have a headache, Mommy."

TWELVES have themselves much better in hand than they did a year earlier, tending to be friendly, expansive, enthusiastic, outgoing, energetic, understanding, able to show considerable emotional empathy with other people. Most are good with their family but starting to move away: "I like to spend some time with my family but some time with my friends."

Though on an even keel emotionally, TWELVE tends to go to emotional extremes at times. He LOVES some things and HATES others; may find life WONDERFUL or TERRIBLE. Girl or boy tends to express a comfortable sense of self.

13 Years

Compared to his friendly, sociable, outgoing 12-year-old self, THIRTEEN presents a striking contrast. TWELVE was expansive. THIRTEEN is withdrawn. TWELVE was a lively member of the household. THIRTEEN remains as aloof from the household as possible. TWELVE was on an extremely positive beam of living. THIRTEEN is on the negative side.

The typical 13-year-old is described by his parents as thoughtful, inwardized, quiet, self-contained; and even in some cases as withdrawn, morbid, morose, moody, secretive, lethargic, indifferent, sullen, seclusive. Life is admittedly lived in a minor key.

Not only does boy or girl prefer the privacy of his or her own room, but even when in the company of others may remain aloof, having little—except maybe criticism—to contribute. As one typical 13-year-old expressed it, "Mother worries that we've lost the close relationship—but I don't want to be close with anyone."

14 Years

FOURTEEN, once again, is outgoing and energetic, joyous, enthusiastic and happy. As one parent put it "He's full of beans." The child of this age enjoys life and is friendly and positive in interpersonal relations, with friends and at school. (Home may be something else again, since parents can be a source of great embarrassment.)

FOURTEEN is expansive in ideas as well as in activity. He covers much ground with his body and often even more with his mind. Both emotional and intellectual appetites tend to be voracious—nothing seems too tremendous for him to undertake or imagine.

As Dr. Gesell has phrased it, "A full-blown 14-year-old is a spontaneous extrovert. He does not hold back and brood or feel sorry for himself. He is full of laughter, jokes, humor. He throws his voice around noisily and lets people know how he feels. He enjoys life."

15 Years

Here boy or girl pulls in again and life, much of the time, is lived in a minor key. This can be one of the most difficult ages for all concerned, since it is for many an age of withdrawal, indifference, surliness, hostility, rebelliousness, confusion, discontent, cynicism, and a marked need for almost total independence.

FIFTEEN may be at his best in the realm of friendship. Friendships can be intense. He is also good in the realm of intellect. Earlier, boy or girl perhaps cared most about the way people behaved. Now the concern is about what they *think*.

And for all his negative characteristics, one can say of the young person of this age that he is, much of the time, determined, self-confident, discriminating, and to quite an extent self-controlled.

FIFTEEN, especially at home, tends to be a somewhat private person. To insure this privacy he does not even need to withdraw to his own room as earlier. He can look right at you and still not see you.

16 Years

SIXTEEN is, perhaps predictably, back on a sunny beam again, highly reminiscent of the earlier positive ages of five and ten. One may say of the typical 16-year-old that he is outgoing, confident, and self-assured, friendly (even helpful), tolerant, on an even keel. Parents describe him as thoughtful, even-tempered, cooperative.

The emotional reaction to parents is much more tempered and much easier than it was just earlier. Boy or girl does not so much now fight for independence as merely *behaves* independently. And emotions in general are not only better in hand but on the whole gratifyingly positive.

These age descriptions from the three books in the so-called Gesell Trilogy[2,6,9] are all based on the concept that each age has its own individuality. These books are among Dr. Gesell's major publications, and are perhaps the most widely read and widely translated of any. But all three were written with the collaboration of his colleagues. It was the individuality of the *child*, not the individuality of the *age*, which throughout Dr. Gesell's professional life was to him the more vital concern.

Chapter 21

EMOTIONS

Though it was rather late in his career* that Dr. Gesell did any substantial writing on the subject of emotions, it is interesting to note that one of his very earliest publications, actually his doctoral dissertation,[1] published in 1906, dealt with the topic of jealousy. This work deals with the psychology of jealousy in animal and man. Among Dr. Gesell's conclusions are the following:

> Jealousy is interpreted as a self feeling, which depends for its content not only upon instinctive rivalry, but upon the influence of the social environment. . . . An analysis of jealousy as a mental state proves it to be peculiarly complex and variable, and perhaps the most painful of all emotions. . . . The scope of jealousy is shown to be much wider than is ordinarily recognized. (1, p. 494).

In spite of this rather promising beginning, in the next 25 years or so he wrote very little about emotions, in fact, published no papers on the subject. And until the publication of *The Child from Five*

---

* Though Dr. Gesell's first discussion of emotion appeared very early (1906), this subject did not thereafter appear substantially in his writings till much later, and was never a primary concern. Thus we chose not to begin this book with this topic.

to Ten,[2] book indexes either omit the word "emotions" entirely, or refer to it only briefly. Thus in books published between 1912 and 1940, we find the term in only four, as follows:

In *Guidance of Mental Growth in Infant and Child*,[3] "emotions" are mentioned at some length:

> Characteristics of mental health include wholesome habits of feeling. Mental hygiene is much concerned with the organization of emotional life. Happily, the feelings respond to training. It is quite wrong to consider that temper tantrums, morbid fears, timidity, jealousy, secretiveness, suspiciousness, and other unhealthy mental states are beyond control[3] (p. 151).

He then presents two cases of adoption. In one, the adopting mother feels an "exaggerated affection" for the child she has adopted. In the other, the mother feels "antagonism"[3] (pp. 211, 212).

A third discussion of emotions, in this same publication, is as follows:

> *Developmental Progressions in Emotional Behavior.* . . . The role of maturation in the control of emotional behavior has had scant recognition. The primary emotions have been discussed as though they were elementary stable phenomena subject only to the changes of social conditioning. This is the implication in much that has been written concerning the emotion of fear. It seems to us that the problem has been oversimplified. Fear may be an original tendency, but it is subject to the genetic alterations of organic growth as well as to organization by environmental conditioning. Such conditioning may determine the orientation and reference of fears, but the mode of fearing undergoes change as a result of maturation. Fear is neither more nor less of an abstraction than prehension. It is not a simple entity. It waxes and alters with growth. It is shaped by intrinsic maturation as well as by experience, certainly during the period of infancy.[3] (p. 289)

Dr. Gesell then discusses the changing reactions of infants aged 10, 20, and 30 weeks to being confined in a small enclosed space, concluding:

> Thus there are three gradations of response: first, no disquietude; second, mild disquietude; third, robust disquietude. Is

not this a genetic gradation of fear behavior which is based upon maturational sequence rather than upon an historical sequence of extrinsic conditioning factors? Such factors may account for specific aspects of fear behavior, but not for the organic pattern beneath such behavior. This pattern, we would suggest, is as much the product of organic growth as the various stages in the elaboration and perfection of prehension.

Incidentally, it may be said that the observation of duplicate twins will tend to substantiate the existence of maturational factors in the development of emotion. Although the tendency towards developmental divergence in identical twins is probably greater in the field of personality make-up than in any other sphere of behavior, there is, during infancy, an impressive tendency toward identity of emotional behavior. Our research subjects, Twins T and C, showed a highly significant degree of correspondence in their manifestations of initial timidity, in their responsiveness to social games, in their reactions to the mirror image, in their gestures of avoiding and refusing, in their seeking and begging gestures, in their laughter and crying. The relatively simultaneous and progressive nature of these changes in the field of emotional behavior suggests the influence of organic maturational factors as opposed to purely extrinsic factors in the determination of behavior pattern.[3] (pp. 290, 291)

In *Feeding Behavior of Infants,*[4] written in 1937, items indexed under "emotional" are *emotional apathy, losses in bottle feeding, reaction, tension.* No one of these references adds particularly to our understanding of emotions. Similarly, items indexed in *Biographies of Child Development*[5] in 1939 include only *attitudes, blocking, instability, maladjustment.* Again, no one of these references contributes a great deal to our understanding of emotions.

In *Developmental Diagnosis,*[6] Dr. Gesell discusses very briefly emotional behavior of the deaf child (tantrums, obstinacy, irritability at not being understood) and the emotional characteristic of the gifted infant. Of the latter he notes:

> Allowances must be made for their strength of will, their assertive craving for social experience, their strong drive to self-help or their extreme sensitivity as the case may be. Such infants do not always have the reputation of being "good babies," although usually their innate intelligence causes them to make good adjustments to requirements which are consistent with their welfare. Needless to say, temperamental traits as well as maturity level must be considered.[6] (p. 273)

In this book, he also briefly discusses[6] (p. 249) emotional signs suggestive of deafness in infants and young children.

From then on, we do not find "emotions" indexed in any book until the 1946 publication, *The Child from Five to Ten*.[2] His contribution in this book and in the two other books of his so-called Trilogy[7,8] will be discussed later.

During all these years, beginning as early as 1925, in his first presentation of the Gesell Developmental Examination, and in each subsequent revision of his norms, Dr. Gesell included one or two modest items having to do with emotional behavior. Thus in his first presentation of norms, in 1925, in *Mental Growth of the Preschool Child*[9] (pp. 137, 147) there are two items which have to do with emotions: "Shows affection" rates A at 18 months, B at 24. "Laughs aloud" rates B at 4 months.

In the 1934 edition of his norms, *Infant Behavior*[10] (p. 249), face brightening and smiling are listed as normative at 6 weeks, vocalizing small throaty sounds at 4 weeks, laughing at 16 weeks. Sobering at the sight of strangers is normative at 16 weeks.

In his 1940 book *The First Five Years of Life*, in listing interview questions to be asked of parents, under "Emotional Behavior" he lists: attitude toward strangers, amenability to control, and play with other children[11] (p. 349).

In his 1941 publication, *Developmental Diagnosis*[6] (pp. 31–79) there are a few more items dealing with emotions. Social smiling and facial social response are normative at 8 weeks of age; cooing, chuckling and "vocal-social response" at 12 weeks; spontaneous-social smile and laughing aloud at 16 weeks; smiling at own mirror image at 20 weeks; social vocalization and smiling and vocalizing at mirror image at 24 weeks; extends toy to person but no release at 44 weeks.

Through the years, in addition to the rather substantial treatment of emotional behavior to be found in the so-called Trilogy,[2,7,8] we find two minor and one major mention of emotions. In 1938 there is a brief "talk piece" on the subject.[12] Here Dr. Gesell points out that fear is not only natural but often "very wholesome," particularly in growing children. However, he gives a list for parents of ways to prevent "unnecessary" fears.

In 1945, there is a minor mention. In a picture book entitled *How a Baby Grows*,[13] he devotes two pages each (pictures and text) to crying and smiling. The brief text for each of these topics follows:

CRYING: THE BABY'S FIRST LANGUAGE. Crying is language. Respect it. Try to understand its meaning each time it occurs. Babies do not cry without cause. They cry on account of pain, hunger, fear, anger, anxiety, bodily discomfort (chafing and wetness), sudden changes, strangeness, solitude, fatigue, and constriction of movements by tight clothes.

Screaming, crying, fretting, frowning, whimpering, sobbing are forms of emotional expression. They all need sympathetic interpretation. Generally the Baby's crying is justified. It is very unwise to go to extremes in letting the Baby "cry it out." SMILING: EXPRESSES EMOTION, MOOD AND TEMPERA-MENT. As the Baby grows he gains in powers of expression. Crying comes first, smiling next, and laughter later. Social situations and pleasant surprise delight even the young baby. At 6 weeks his face brightens, at 8 weeks he smiles, at 12 weeks he chuckles, at 16 weeks he laughs aloud.

Smiling and laughter vary with temperament. Some babies are expressive and demonstrative. Others are reserved, self-possessed and sober. Respect these individual differences and do not stimulate laughing by excessive handling and tickling. The best smiles come naturally.

Every baby has a smile which is distinctive. As the baby grows his face moulds. As the expressive muscles of mouth, eyes, nose, and cheek mature, the smile takes on characteristic form.[13] (pp. 38, 40)

In 1949, in an article titled "Pediatrics and Child Psychiatry" Dr. Gesell discusses the question of whether or not pediatrics can deal with the complex field of emotions, "a field which psychiatry has made peculiarly its own"[14] (p. 672). As the following long, but important, quote makes clear, Dr. Gesell believes that psychiatry does not have a monopoly on the study of emotions:

Developmental Factor in Child Emotion

The question is sometimes raised whether pediatrics can undertake to deal with the complex field of emotions, a field which psychiatry has made peculiarly its own and which it investigates by elaborate therapeutic methods. The whole subject of emotions is admittedly in need of simplification. Alas, it yields reluctantly to dispassionate discussion. Emotions are realities, but they are not necessarily self-subsistent entities which move and motivate the individual. The individual is a complex action system which assumes constantly changing patterns of tension and equilibrium. These changes are determined by three major factors: maturity, life experiences and the constitutional make-up of the individual. All of these factors are accessible to pediatric approach, particularly if the diagnostic procedures are first of all directed to the underlying constitutional and maturational aspects of behavior.

The patterning of the child's emotional life changes with his perceptual insights and his personal-social adjustments, all of which have specific motor attitudinal manifestations and are fundamentally shaped by maturity factors. In this sense, there is no general emotion of fear, of anger, of jealousy, of insecurity. Emotions are formative phenomena which indicate the maturity and the developmental history of a growing action system. The influence of environment and of social experience is far reaching, but it is to a considerable degree delimited and defined by constitutional, developmental determinants traceable to species, racial stock and familial inheritance. The dynamics of the child's emotional behavior is inseparable from the dynamics of child development. The all-embracing dynamics of development therefore assume great importance in the clinical appraisal of human individuality.

Let me try to illustrate by a brief comparison of the developmental difference between an infant at 28 weeks and at 32 weeks of age. The 28 week old infant discriminates strangers but usually adapts well to them. He has himself well in hand. He seems to take in a total situation, and alternates with ease between self-directed and socially referred activity. At 32 weeks of age he is not so self-contained. His reactions are less forthright and his face often wears a questioning, half bewildered expression. He shows a greater sensitiveness in new situations and needs more time to adjust to them. Such sensitiveness combined with assimilativeness is part of the process of growth and it involves his visual functions which are developing in close correlation with his social attitudes.

I use this simple illustration to stress the fact that all psychologic developments including emotions are based on morphogenetic changes, changes which are just as real as the transformation of a limb bud into a fingered hand, and of an optic cup into lens and retina. *Psychogenic interpretations miss the mark whenever they fail to take into account the intrinsic developmental morphology of the growing action system.* Effects are sometimes ascribed to therapy when they are primarily due to inherent growth factors. Deep-seated maturational factors operate with special force throughout the preschool period.

Compare, for further illustration, the behavior traits of a normally developing child at 2½, at 3 and at 3½ years of age. Three is a nodal age. Normatively speaking, the child is then in a stage of relative equilibrium, whereas at 2½ and at 3½ he is in a transitional phase of less stable equilibrium. At 2½ he is more or less beset by conflicting opposites. Because of immaturity and inexperience, he chooses with difficulty between paired opposites—between yes and no, come and go, grab and throw, give and take, push and pull. He cannot modulate with facility between opposites. He does not automatically make a clear-cut distinction between spatial opposites, and is subject to amazing reversals in which he gets things wrong-side-to and upside down. His perversity, his perplexities and his ritualisms are often too readily ascribed to emotional factors as though emotions were the causative forces which determined his patterns of behavior. He has new difficulties in bladder control; he tends to over-hold and to over-release. It is well to note that comparable maturity traits pervade various aspects of his action system, and even his visual behavior, as registered in retino-cortical responses.

The 3½ year old child exhibits similar dynamic patterns, but at a higher level of reorganization. Compared with the 3 year old, he is sensitive and tentative. He is subject to a developmental kind of anxiety which has the quality of refined awareness rather than of primitive fear. He displays a pervasive incoordination manifested in faulty timing and poor modulation of movements. There is a definite increase of stumbling and fear of high places. The hands often are tremulous and awkward. Dominance in handedness undergoes shifts and confusions. Stuttering, tensional chewing, nail biting, nose picking, eye blinking appear transiently on the scene. And again the developmental dynamics of this maturity level manifests itself in changing patterns of visual behavior. . . .

All of this suggests that emotions are greatly influenced by an inherent dynamics of the action system. In the rapidly growing child emotional traits alter with age; but an underlying ground plan of growth is revealed in the recurring characteristicness with which the child reacts at ascending levels of the maturational spiral of development. A perceptive mother who knows her child can describe the characteristicness. A perceptive clinician can diagnose its distinctive trends even to the extent of predicting probable future manifestations.

This characteristicness is the core of individuality. It is accessible to clinical detection and will become more so with im-

proved technics. The pediatrician is already concerned with
symptoms of individuality as they show themselves in feeding
behavior, in nutritional peculiarities, in allergies, in the acquisition of sphincter controls, sleep characteristics, motor demea-
nors and numerous indicators open to observation and to interview. He is aware of the distinctive ways in which different
children meet and solve the universal problem of development.
A recognition of such normal individual differences is a prereq-
uisite for effective mental hygiene guidance.[14] (pp. 672, 673)

It was not until fairly late in his career that Dr. Gesell (and his
colleagues) extended the basic notion of reciprocal neuromotor
interweaving to the ages themselves.[7] As Chapter 20 of this book on
"Individuality of the Ages" explains in some detail, it appears that
ages characterized by relative equilibrium of behavior tend to alternate with ages of disequilibrium. Also ages at which behavior seems
to be somewhat inwardized alternate with ages when it appears to be
expansive.

These characteristics are described in words and are also illustrated by Figure 20-1. A further method of presenting this same
kind of information appears in Table 21-1, which shows what seems
to be the rather convincing information that a sequence of six
sharply different ways of behaving apparently repeats itself three
times between the ages of two and sixteen.

As will be seen even from these brief summaries (Figure 20-1
and Table 21-1), the descriptions of behavior which characterize the
several ages, it is emotional behavior which is strongly emphasized
and which to a large extent is the key to our understanding of the
age.

The treatment of emotional behavior was not particularly systematic in the first book of the so-called Trilogy which covered the
years from one through sixteen. In fact the word "emotion" was not
even indexed in this first book, *Infant and Child in the Culture of
Today*.[7]

Table 21-1.   A Repeating Cycle of Behavior Change

Smooth	Breakup	Balanced	Inwardized	Expansive	Troubled	Smooth
2 years	2½ years	3 years	3½ years	4 years	4½ years	5 years
5 years	5½–6 years	6½ years	7 years	8 years	9 years	10 years
10 years	11 years	12 years	13 years	14 years	15 years	16 years

However, in the second and third books of this series, *The Child from Five to Ten,*[2] and *Youth: The Years from Ten to Sixteen*[8] we come upon an embarrassment of riches which, were he to know of it, would surely confound Dr. Spock who complained that we did not "deal with" emotions. Since the material in each of these books is extensive enough to provide at least a small pamphlet in itself, we shall not attempt to reproduce it here but will merely describe it briefly.

In *The Child from Five to Ten,*[2] for every age level included, there is a detailed description of emotional behavior characteristic of that age. More than that, there is an entire 20-page chapter devoted to "Emotional Expression" of this whole age span. This chapter includes so-called gradients (tabular listings) covering age changes in *affective attitudes, crying and related behaviors,* and *assertion and anger.* A following chapter includes a gradient on *fears.*

In *Youth: The Years from Ten to Sixteen*[8] the treatment of emotions is even more comprehensive. Again, for every age level there is a detailed description of the emotional behavior characteristic of that age. There is also a 24-page chapter on the emotional behavior of this entire age range. This is, perhaps, the clearest and most comprehensive (and rather poetic) presentation of Dr. Gesell's feelings about emotions to be found in any of his writings.

As in the immediately preceding book,[2] the chapter includes gradients presenting age changes in different aspects of emotions; but here even more topics are included. One finds here gradients on *emotions in general, anger, worries and fears, humor, affectivity, self-assertion,* and *the expression of feelings.*

Aside from his basic theoretical idea that ages of equilibrium tended to alternate with ages of disequilibrium, and inwardized ages with outwardized ages, Dr. Gesell and his colleagues did not develop a comprehensive or systematic approach to the study of emotional behavior. Rather, he accepted the system of Constitutional Psychology provided by Dr. William Sheldon. This has already been referred to in Chapter 8 on Individuality.

We repeat here merely Sheldon's specific comments on emotions as summarized by Dr. Gesell in the book, *Youth: The Years from Ten to Sixteen*[8] (p. 29).

> In the area of emotions, for example, the endomorph tends to show his feelings easily at any age; other people are too important for him to withdraw very far, even in the most "with-

drawing phases." The mesomorph, at any age generally described as "less competitive" is non-competitive only in a
comparative sense—compared, that is, *with himself* at other ages.
The ectomorph is quicker to withdraw when troubled, takes
more pains to hide his feelings. He may show an alertness and
fast reaction, but in many areas he tends to show immaturities.
He seems to need more time to grow. Our observations indicate
that the gradients of growth take on added meaning when interpreted in the light of constitutional individuality.[8] (p. 29)

Thus, though it is true that in his early writings Dr. Gesell did
not highlight emotions as an area of behavior, in his later years the
emotional behaviors characteristic both of different kinds of children and characteristic of the various ages were dealt with by him in
fairly substantial detail.

Chapter 22

PRINCIPLES AND THEORIES
OF DEVELOPMENT

Dr. Gesell's basic theories of development obviously underlie nearly all of his clinical work, as well as his many publications. These theories will be fairly evident from earlier chapters in this book, even without a special chapter dealing with them. However, for the sake of clarity, we may here emphasize that the theory or philosophy underlying virtually all of his writings was that behavior in the human individual develops in a patterned, orderly manner, through stages which are highly similar if not identical from one human to another. This concept lay behind the development of his norms of infant and preschool behavior as well as his individual case studies.

However, though this concern was primary, two other considerations about human behavior were also of major importance. Thus though he did not develop this systematically, he consistently emphasized that each infant and child was an individual, different in many ways from every other, even from his identical twin.

A third consideration, in addition to the fact that behavior develops in a patterned way, through predictable stages, and that each person goes through these stages in a somewhat individual manner, was the fact that, rather obviously, behavior at any stage is at least to a certain extent influenced by environmental factors. The relationship between heredity and environmental factors is of major concern to all who deal with human behavior, and has been the subject of continuous and heated debate.

The first of these three factors, the patterned development of behavior, was, as noted, the subject of Dr. Gesell's well-known Developmental Norms. His interest in the second major factor, individuality, is described in Chapter 8.

As to the third major factor, the relationship between heredity and environment and the extent to which behavior is influenced by each, Dr. Gesell accorded considerable attention to what the environment could and should do to adapt both to the child's age and to his individuality. However, except for his twin studies, in which he altered the environment to the extent of training one twin in language, cube behavior, stair-climbing, etc., to see whether or not extra training substantially speeded up behavior (it did not), he did not conduct experiments to determine the effect of the environment on the individual. The relative weighting which he gave to each of these two factors—as he put it, since interaction was the heart of the matter, it was not useful to put too much emphasis on either or to argue about the relative contribution of each—has been discussed in detail in Chapter 18 on Heredity and Environment.

Thus the *outstanding* principle or theory which underlay all of Dr. Gesell's work was the so-called maturational approach, the belief that behavior in the human individual develops in a highly patterned way. The timing of behavior as mentioned just above might vary from child to child, but the sequence of stages remains largely inviolate.

The subprinciples which supported this major principle or concept are described by Dr. Gesell in Leonard Carmichael's *Manual of Child Psychology*[1] as follows:

1. The Principle of Developmental Direction:
Behavior in fetus and child develops in a cephalocaudad direction, that is, from the head to the foot. The head end of the body develops, physically and functionally, long before the tail end. Especially in crawling and creeping behavior we note that the arms are fully functional long before the legs.

Also, behavior develops in a proximo-distal direction. Thus gross movements of the whole arm precede movements from the forearm or wrist.

And it also develops in an ulnar radial direction. As the infant grasps, he first uses his whole hand in a pawlike manner. It is only toward the end of the first year that he can point with forefinger and grasp with pincer prehension, that is picking up objects between thumb and forefinger.

2. The Principle of Reciprocal Interweaving:

According to this principle, in any growing behavior, or area of behavior, it is possible to identify paired-but-opposed types of response that occur in repeated alternation until the behavior has reached its final or complete stage, spiralling upward as it progresses. Behavior does not simply develop in a straight-line direction, the immature gradually and without lapse giving way to the mature. Rather, if one of these opposites can be identified as immature and the other as mature (as is usually the case) we must anticipate repeated recurrences of the more immature behavior alternating with the more mature as the child grows older. In such an area as prone progression, where the chief alternating behaviors are flexion and extension, adduction and abduction, bilateral and unilateral movements, this principle is seen clearly.

In fact, it was largely through a study of prone progression that Dr. Gesell arrived at the principle of reciprocal interweaving. In the course of an investigation of this kind of behavior[2,3] it was determined that as the human infant lies on his stomach (that is, in prone) in the first year of life, he customarily goes through 23 rather well defined stages of behavior before he can stand upright and walk. This investigation was conducted partly by direct observation of infants and partly by cinemanalysis.

And here we were in for a surprise. Up to the time of this study of prone progression we had assumed that any given behavior in the human infant tended to develop in a straight-line direction, as from flexion to eventual extension, or from symmetric behavior to asymmetric behavior. However, early notes, dictated by Dr. Gesell in the course of numerous developmental examinations, frequently included such comments as "*Oddly enough* this 20-week-old infant seems to be more flexed than he was at 16 weeks of age."

Careful longitudinal observation of many infants as they developed eventually led to the conclusion that such "exceptions" were indeed the rule and not exceptions. It turned out to be the case that as the prone infant advanced in his behavior from week to week and from month to month, well-defined flexor stages were systematically followed by stages of extension, and that these in turn were followed by further stages of flexion.

Figure 22-1 tells the story of the sequential stages of prone progression and their rhythmic alternation between flexor and extensor stages of posture and activity. This figure is presented here because this finding, which Dr. Gesell, with his characteristic way with words titled "The Principle of Reciprocal Interweaving," turned out to

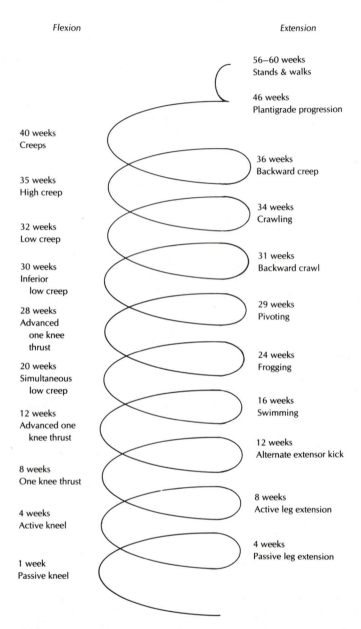

Figure 22-1. Alternating stages of flexion and extension in prone behavior illustrating the principle of reciprocal interweaving.

apply to, and to some extent to explain, behaviors far more complex than the relative simple patterns of prone progression. As elaborated in Chapter 20, on "The Individuality of the Ages," we find a similar kind of interweaving in the very ages themselves. The sequence of studies by Dr. Gesell and his colleagues (*Infant and Child in the Culture of Today*,[4] *The Child from Five to Ten*,[5] and *Youth: The Years from Ten to Sixteen*[5]) all suggested the hypothesis that as infant and child mature, stages when behavior, in general, is in a stage of equilibrium alternate rather rhythmically with stages of disequilibrium. And to quite an extent it was also found that stages of expansive behavior alternated with stages of inwardized behavior (See Figure 22-1). For the most part, ages of disequilibrium coincide with ages of somewhat inwardized behavior; ages of equilibrium, with ages in which behavior is more outwardized.

Thus, a finding of purely technical interest, that is, that in prone, stages of flexion alternated with stages of flexion, later yielded information of practical value. To the ordinary parent it matters little that his or her infant is in a stage of flexion *or* extension. It can matter a great deal to household harmony that any given child is in a stage of equilibrium or disequilibrium.

3. The Principle of Functional Asymmetry:

This is a special case of reciprocal interweaving that is really an exception to the rule. Here a behavior goes through a period of asymmetric or unbalanced development to enable the organism to achieve a measure of maturity at a later stage. A clear example of this is the so-called tonic neck reflex. This asymmetrical behavior is the precursor for the later development of symmetrical behavior. In fact, Dr. Gesell identified this later behavior, when it first appears, as the symmetro-tonic reflex.

4. The Principle of Individuating Maturation:

From the moment of fertilization, intrinsic and extrinsic factors cooperate in a unitary manner. But the original impulse of growth and the matrix of morphogenesis are endogenous rather than exogenous. The so-called environment, whether internal or external, does not generate the progressions of development. Environmental factors support, inflect, and modify but they do not engender the basic norms and sequences of ontogenesis.

Moreover, as a behavior develops, it tends to be a total body response to begin with. Then independent actions of the separate limbs separate themselves out. A total body behavior does not result from the combining of motions of the separate limbs, as some have argued.

5. *The Principle of Self-Regulatory Fluctuation:*
This in essence is somewhat similar to the principle of reciprocal interweaving. However, it was applied particularly to the infant's daily living—his periods of eating, sleeping, and waking. Dr. Gesell notes that the living system during the period of active growth is in a state of formative instability combined with a progressive movement toward stability. The so-called growth gains represent consolidations of stability. This opposition between two apparently opposing tendencies results in seesaw fluctuations. The maturing organism does not advance in a straight line, but oscillates along a "spiral" course between two self-limited poles.

Fluctuation is therefore a normal expression of the self-regulatory mechanisms of development. Superficially, fluctuations seem to be irregular and whimsical. Looked at in perspective, they prove to be expressions of a basic mechanism of adjustment. As the infant matures, the total duration of sleep per day and the number of feeding periods diminishes. The daily schedule becomes increasingly patterned and predictable. Progressive fluctuations, culminating in a more stable response, are characteristic of behavior development.

This so-called self-demand schedule for infants was offered by Drs. Gesell and Ilg in opposition to the rigid type schedule then in practice—that is, the idea of feeding the infant every 3 (or 4) hours regardless of his own preferences. Thus by following a strict schedule, one might feed the infant before he was hungry; or might keep him waiting an hour, crying for food, until the schedule said it was time to feed him.

The Gesell/Ilg experience with infants showed that if a parent followed the so-called self-demand and self-regulation schedule, eating and sleeping according to his own needs and demands, he would not only be more comfortable in his early weeks and months, but would quite soon settle down to a customary and (from the parents' point of view) desirable regular schedule of eating and sleeping.

This presentation of Dr. Gesell's main principles of development is given by him in fullest detail in the Carmichael volume.[1] It is summarized nicely by Neil J. Salkind in a 1985 book titled "Theories of Human Development."[8]

Salkind also discusses what he considers to be the leading theories of human development: The Maturational or Gesell Model, the Psychoanalytic Model, the Behavioral Model, the Cognitive-Developmental Model, and the Organismic Model. He summarizes the contrasting contributions of each of these models as follows:

> The cognitive-developmental and organismic theories share some of the same characteristics as the behavioral model in terms of inclusiveness. They are relatively content-free (they do deal with such areas as cognition and moral development), but they are best represented by the dual processes of organization and adaptation.
>
> In contrast to these two models, the psychoanalytic and maturational models tend to be highly content-specific. For example, the psychoanalytic model is a very comprehensive theory of human development, yet it is also the most highly content specific. It leaves little room for a distinction between the process of development and the outcomes that result from that process.
>
> For Gesell the case seems to be similar. The maturational model is highly content specific and more comprehensive than either the behavioral or organismic models. Gesell's description of development was less inclusive than that offered by the psychoanalytic model, because he concentrated primarily on physical development and only peripherally on such issues as emotional and social development. *Gesell's five principles of development were never applied to other dimensions of development* [Ital. ours], although the potential for such application exists. Those theories that are highly inclusive are not tied to specific content, but make statements about the general nature of behavior.[9] (p. 253)

Chapter 23

EVALUATIONS OF DR. GESELL'S WORK

In 1911 Arnold Gesell became assistant professor of education at Yale and Director of the Yale Clinic of Child Development, which he elevated to a position of international leadership. In 1915 he was appointed professor of child hygiene, a
field in which he retains undisputed leadership.[1] (p. 495)

This biographical description by the editor of *American Scientist* in-
troduced an article titled "Human Infancy and the Ontogenesis of
Behavior," a summation of material presented by Dr. Gesell in his
Sigma Xi National Lectureships given in March 1949. It fairly rep-
resented the attitude of much of the scientific world, both in the
United States and abroad, at that time.

Four years later, in 1953, in an article in *Postgraduate Medicine*,
Miriam Zeller Gross commented:

Dr. Arnold Gesell of New Haven, Connecticut will go down
in medical history as the individual who rescued "child development" from the limbo of empty abstractions. The result of his
more than 35 years of continuous research have enabled physicians to evaluate acutely the developmental patterns of both
normal and handicapped children.[2] (p. 179)

The June 1960 issue of *Child Development* was dedicated to Dr.
Gesell in honor of his work. This was the first time this magazine

had dedicated a volume to anyone. In the foreword, Dr. Benjamin Pasamanick, Professor of Psychiatry at the Columbus Psychiatric Institute and Hospital in Columbus, Ohio, and a former student of Dr. Gesell's, wrote:

> It is with profound pleasure that *Child Development* dedicates this issue to one of the great pioneers of child development, Arnold Gesell, on the occasion of his eightieth birthday, June 21, 1960. His life has been one incredibly concentrated and remarkably single-minded effort directed towards the scientific investigation and guidance of child behavior.
>
> The first generation of child psychologists included such great figures as Stanley Hall, Lightner Witmer, and John Dewey; the second, Terman, Goddard, Watson, and others. Arnold Gesell stems from the second generation.
>
> There are few areas Arnold Gesell did not help to enlighten—mental deficiency, handicapping conditions of all types of children, infant feeding, preventive medicine, and many others. No one has been more influential in shaping the modern practice of pediatrics.
>
> Dr. Gesell's contributions to science are as many and as long as his bibliography which consists of hundreds of monographs, papers and books. They have been incorporated into the living body of the life sciences, never to be lost.[3] (pp. 241, 242)

Comments and evaluations in the popular press were for the most part nearly as complimentary and uncritically admiring of Dr. Gesell's work, possibly more so than those of the psychological community in general. However, it seems fair to take the above valuations at face value. A few selections from the popular press will give the tone of respect for Dr. Gesell and his contributions which was customary.

In a significant evaluation of Yale's Institute of Human Relations at the time of its dissolution in 1939, *Time Magazine* made the telling summary:

> Some individual divisions, notably Dr. Gesell's, turned up much valuable data, but the Institute as a whole wandered all over creation.[4]

In 1952 in an unsigned piece in *Pageant Magazine*, we find a comment to the effect that "Dr. Arnold Gesell probably knows more about the growth and development of children than anyone in the world."[5]

In March 1954, in an article in *Parents Magazine* by Jack Harrison Pollack we read:

> Few men in history have influenced the rearing of children as profoundly as has Dr. Arnold Gesell. During the past half-century his pioneer studies have opened new horizons for millions of parents and helped shape the thinking of countless pediatricians, educators and others working with children.[6] (p. 80)

In March 1956, in a critical article in *Harper's Magazine*, Helen Puner observed:

> It is Gesell who has uniquely been draftsman of the architecture of the developing mind. . . . And it is Gesell himself who has presented the world with overall patterns and generalized chronological "norms" of behavior, against which the developing personalities of any and all children can—presumably—be assessed.[7] (p. 38)
>
> It may easily be that his aim—if not his point of view—has not been so much behind the (Freudian) times as ahead. For today it is he, and he alone, who has built up the only systematic body of observations on the development of human behavior and personality.[7] (p. 43)

In 1959 Sylvia Brody, in a review of the Gesell work published in *The Journal of Nursing Education,* concludes:

> Gesell's contribution towers over most others, I believe, because his theoretical framework always considered the functioning of the organism as a whole, and always was based upon direct observation of behavior.[8] (p. 13)

Lastly, in an obituary, the *New Haven Register* paid him a final tribute:

> In countless homes the name of Arnold Gesell was better known than that of the President of the United States. And to great numbers of occupants of those homes, Arnold Gesell was a far more important man than the occupant of the White House. . . . His work over many years in the field of pediatrics and child development paved the way to health and success for thousands,

mayhap millions. Dr. Gesell was a pioneer, one who traced uncharted paths to charted conclusions.[9]

Needless to say, Dr. Gesell was not without his critics. Among
the chief criticisms of his work were the following:

He did not pay enough attention to Freud and Freud's
work;

He did not pay enough attention to—did not "believe
in"—environment;

He did not use the term "interaction" as in "interaction
between heredity and environment";

He thought that children were all alike and did not respect individual differences;

His norms made parents anxious if their children did not
perform various activities at exactly the time he had
indicated.

The first of these criticisms is valid. Dr. Gesell was not the least
bit interested in the Freudian interpretation of human behavior. In
fact at the time that Eric Homburger (now known as Eric Erickson)
first came to Yale, Lawrence Frank, who administered the Macy
Foundation money, allegedly offered Dr. Gesell a grant if he would
study the behavior of nursery school children based on the notion
that whenever a child put one object into another (doll into carriage,
toy car into garage, pebble into pail) he was imitating the sex act. Dr.
Gesell declined the grant.

However, he *was* much interested in environment and in the
interaction between heredity and environment. This interest has
been discussed fully in Chapter 18 on Heredity and Environment. If
there was fault here it could have been that he did not mention this
relationship in every one of his writings. Nevertheless, any careful
student of his work will undoubtedly conclude that his numerous
statements about the relationship between heredity and environment do make it perfectly clear that he had full respect for environment and for the inevitable interaction between organism and environment.

As to the criticism that Dr. Gesell believed that all children were
alike and developed not only in rather much the same way but at the
same rate, any careful reading of his work would make it evident

that he did not believe that all infants and children were identical. Over and over he repeated the theme—"Infants are individuals."

As to any anxiety which his norms may have creaied in the minds of parents if their children did not match these norms, and the feeling on the part of some parents that all children *should* match and meet the Gesell norms, we can explain it this way. In his technical books in which the norms were first presented, books intended for use by professional persons, it seemed quite unnecessary to explain that norms are merely averages and that not every child should be expected to meet any given norm. In each of his later books written for parents (*Infant and Child in the Culture of Today*, *The Child from Five to Ten*, and *Youth: The Years from Ten to Sixteen*), he and his colleagues clearly warned early and often against misuse of norms:

> The reader is warned, in advance, however, that the age norms are not set up as standards and are designed only for orientation and interpretive purposes.[10] (p. 2)
>
> Norms of behavior development, as measures of maturity, must be applied with even greater caution (than height and weight norms). The lay person should not attempt to make a diagnosis on the basis of such norms. . . . It is not intended that a single age profile should be used to determine whether a given child is bright or dull, good or bad. Individual deviations are almost as normal as they are numerous.[10] (p. 70)

In the second book of this series, *The Child from Five to Ten*, he notes:

> For convenience, each gradient consists of a series of levels arranged by weeks, months or years. This does NOT mean that the itemized gradient levels should be regarded as statistical age norms. The parent who reads a gradient should never say "My child ought to be at this particular level of the gradient because he is old enough." The child may well be younger or older than the age assigned by the gradient. It is more important to find the gradient level which approximately describes the stage of maturity which he has actually attained. The gradients are intended to show the overall developmental *sequences* of behavior rather than rigid standards of expectancy. Individual differences are too great to permit rigid standards rigidly applied.

Generous allowance should be made for age variations.[11] (pp. 222, 223)

Similar cautions appear in the third book of this series for parents, *Youth: The Years from Ten to Sixteen*:

> Any gradients of growth, however, have their limitations. They must be interpreted judiciously, because of a wide diversity of individual variations. The gradients do not constitute a psychometric scale; but they do afford a useful indication of how the growth process trends toward its goals. . .[12] (p. xiv)
>
> Clearly, these growth gradients and maturity profiles are not psychometric norms. They do not measure specific abilities. They are not to be construed as normative standards nor as diagnostic criteria, except under clinical auspices and safeguards. However, they constitute a kind of "comparator"—an instrument for comparing something with a like thing. They are orientational devices which permit us to identify and assess levels of maturity.
>
> The overruling emphasis is on the sequences and patterns of maturity rather than on age assignments. Our research interest was to gain a better understanding of the *dynamic trends of the growth process* operating over a period of time.
>
> With all these cautions and reservations we hope that the reader will look upon the growth gradients as convenient tabular summaries, which suggest how behavior characteristics may change with advancing stages of maturity. Common sense will protect the gradients from misinterpretation and misuse.[12] (pp. xiv, 24)

Aside from evaluative comments in the scientific and popular press, there have been numerous reviews that describe Dr. Gesell's body of work and also include a certain amount of evaluation, too long for inclusion here. But we list them in chronological order and include comments from each.

Probably the most comprehensive presentation of Dr. Gesell's life and work is to be found in *Arnold Lucius Gesell, 1880–1961: A Biographical Memoir*, by Walter R. Miles.[13] Dr. Miles assembled a comprehensive biography of Dr. Gesell's life and work—the only such body of information, aside from Dr. Gesell's own autobiographical sketch which he contributed to *A History of Psychology in Autobiography*.[14] In addition to the bibliographic section of Dr. Miles's memoir was a full bibliography of all Dr. Gesell's writings.*

Dr. Miles's contribution combined factual information about Dr. Gesell's life and work with a modest amount of evaluation of that work. Brief quotes from his *Biographical Memoir* follow:

> Dr. Gesell founded the Clinic of Child Development at Yale in 1911 and was its director until 1948, when he became professor emeritus. This clinic functioned primarily as a research center by operating as a service organization. It thus won the confidence of many parents and achieved fame in the greater New Haven area. . . . Ten years later . . . the effort to study objectively human infant growth had taken on man-size proportions and was exerting nationwide influence. . . .[13] (p. 55)
>
> Dr. Gesell was a potent leader in making clear the important relationships that may exist between medicine and psychology and he did much to establish the point of view that psychology is comparable to physiology as a fundamental or partner of medical science. The developing human body is subject to profound laws of growth and an adequate clinical science must be founded upon good principles and methods of developmental diagnosis. It was cheering to Dr. Gesell that in 1935 the American Board of Pediatrics established the field of Growth and Development as a basic requirement for specialty certification. By the Gesell type of persistent study, research and publication, the evolution of preventive medicine moves forward in its service to man.
>
> By the late 1940s there had developed a demand for postgraduate training in the methods of developmental diagnosis. . . . Dr. Gesell and his staff organized a systematic two-year course that involved cinema studies and full-time clinical observations and reports and was designed as a standard requirement for specialization in this field. A number of externs from the United States and abroad were so trained. Widening of the horizon for responsible departments of pediatrics may be considered the crown of Dr. Gesell's life work. Through his tireless efforts he had brought new light, careful surveys, and some

---

* Readers who are interested in a full listing of all Dr. Gesell's published works are referred to this memoir by Dr. Miles.

systematic understanding to what had formerly been a vague and rather dark no man's land. He had promoted a strong campaign to educate doctors, teachers, parents and the public in the science of human development.[13] (p. 71)

The traditional life calendar rules for academic retirement operated at Yale as elsewhere. Dr. Gesell reached this descending stairway at the end of June 1948, but he knew where to go and what to do and had the physical and mental vigor to carry on. Fortunately, others were aware of this and he was invited to become a research associate in the Harvard Pediatric Study under the director, Dr. Francis McDonald. . . . And there was a second opportunity that came to this Emeritus Professor who had demonstrated his ability to see where others had groped for light. This was a two-year research grant labeled "For the investigation of the developmental aspects of child vision."[13] (p. 72)

How can such a man as Arnold Gesell, whose thinking, work and vision were always projected forward, reach a life's terminal? The best ending is to see others take up the course. And so it was that in 1950 former staff associates of the Yale Clinic brought about an independent organization, The Gesell Institute of Child Development, incorporated to continue this field of endeavor, and found a location on Prospect Street, New Haven. Here Dr. Gesell, who for twenty years was Attending Pediatrician at the New Haven Hospital, gave of his counsel to the end of his days.[13] (p. 73)

In 1965 Professor William Kessen of Yale offered his own thoughtful evaluation of Dr. Gesell's contributions:

Terman made no important theoretical statement about the nature of intelligence or about human development. The promulgation of general principles of ontogenesis and the use of tests as a polemical device become the duty of Terman's friend and colleagues at Los Angeles State Normal School, Arnold Gesell. . . .

During his medical training at Yale, he established the clinic of child development that was to be a center of research and rhetoric on the child for over thirty years. Gesell stands in the near distance of our history—far enough away to have attained the status of legend and symbol, too close to see with a scholarly indifferent eye. The ambiguity arises in part because Gesell's

doctrinal heirs continue his work forcefully and with great influence, partly because Gesell became, for the behaviorists interested in children, the bugbear hereditarian. His refusals to be
moved as psychology became more often defined by its studies
of learning, and his surprising indifference to the progress of
psychoanalysis combined to make Gesell fair game for many
hunters. The importance of his contribution can be seen only
through the still-settling dust of contention, but there can be no
doubt that Gesell continued, with remarkable equanimity, the
traditions of Darwin, Galton, and Hall.[15] (p. 209)

The clinical goal toward which Gesell was directed throughout his career was the diagnosis of developmental pathology;
his interest in the abnormal child is shown in a number of his
papers and books. But it was as the most articulate spokesman
for maturation as the central concept of developmental psychology that Gesell takes his place in the history of child study. In
many places, he laid out the principles of his view of man and,
although the elegance of his language sometimes fogs the message, Gesell's opinions cannot be doubted. They can be put in
catechismal form. What is the principle of development? Maturation is the necessary condition of developmental change.
What is the role of the environment? Although the environment
provides a setting for growth and may on occasion direct the
particular shape of development, the contribution of environmental variation to variation in development is relatively slight.
What determines growth? Within wide limits of variation in experience—typically, those limits which permit life to continue
—the child will grow as his germ plasm directs.[15] (pp. 210, 211)

Gesell was an ethologist of human behavior at a time uncon-
genial to the notion that the major dimensions of one's development were determined at the conceptual union. In the present
climate of child psychology, sympathetic to behavioral cata-
loguing by the ethologists and willing once more to admit the
claims of heredity, Gesell's theory of man seems far less extrav-
agant than it did when it was written.[15] (p. 211)

Kessen continues, apparently in rather strong support of the
Gesell position:

It appears, then, in summary, that there is a profound in-
terdependency between "heredity" and "environment" in the

control of development. These terms, from tradition, are dualistic in connotation, but growth itself is integrative and resolves the antithesis. The ancient antinomy of determinism versus freedom likewise seems inapplicable to the facts of growth. All growth is lawful and in that sense determined. The intrinsic determiners of development work in conformance to genetic laws, the extrinsic factors work in similar and coordinated conformance. The spheres of intrinsic and extrinsic influences are not separate but interpenetrate, and scientifically, if not metaphysically, it is impossible to assign a unique and absolute autonomy to any factor which enters into the growth complex.[15] (p. 225)

All things considered, the inevitableness and surety of maturation are the most impressive characteristics of early development. It is the hereditary ballast which conserves and stabilizes the growth of each individual infant. It is indigenous in its impulsion, but we may well be grateful for this degree of determinism. If it did not exist, the infant would be a victim of a flaccid malleability which is sometimes romantically ascribed to him. His mind, his spirit, his personality would fall a ready prey to disease, to starvation, to malnutrition, and worst of all to misguided management. As it is, the inborn tendency toward optimum development is so inveterate that he benefits liberally from what is good in our practice, and suffers less than he logically would from our unenlightenment. Only if we give respect to this inner core of inheritance can we respect the important individual difference which distinguish infants as well as men.[15] (p. 227)

Kessen concludes:

In 1928, Gesell was in mid-career; for another two decades he would continue his work of measurement and diagnosis, changing his attitudes toward the child hardly at all in the interval but adding steadily to our knowledge of man developing. The stability of the Gesellian position is even more noteworthy in consideration of the turmoil—or better, the several turmoils—through which psychology passed between the award of his Ph.D. in 1906 and his retirement from Yale in 1948.[15] (p. 228)

The next substantial evaluation of Dr. Gesell's contributions appeared some years later, in 1980. This review was by William C. Crain in a book titled *Theories of Development: Concepts and Applications.*[16]

The person who most thoroughly applied the embryological model to the study of child development was Arnold Gesell (1880–1961). In his 50 years at the Yale Clinic of Child Development, he and his colleagues engaged in incredibly extensive and detailed studies of the neuromotor development of babies and children. They developed behavior norms which are so complete that they still serve as a primary source of information for pediatricians and psychologists. Gesell also developed one of the first tests of infant intelligence and was one of the first researchers to make extensive use of film observation.

Gesell also wrote on child-rearing, advocating a child-centered approach. He was the best known "baby doctor" in the early 1940s, until Spock published his own famous book. Nevertheless, Spock was partly influenced by Gesell. . .[16] (p. 21)

In spite of his emphasis on maturation, Gesell considered the environment important. He pointed out that specific environmental conditions are necessary for normal growth, as we can observe when there is damage to the organism.[16] (p. 23)

Gesell's most important research was on early motor development, but he believed that maturation governs every aspect of growth. He said, for example[10] (p. 11) "The child's nervous system matures by stages and natural sequences. He sits before he stands; he babbles before he talks . . . he is selfish before he is altruistic; he is dependent on others before he achieves the laws of growth.[16] (p. 24)

Gesell strongly believed in the uniqueness of each child. Unfortunately, however, his position was obscured by the way in which he summarized his findings. . . . His actual position was that normal children all go through the same *sequences*, but they vary in their *rates* of growth.[16] (p. 27)

In Gesell's hands Rousseau's ideas of an inner developmental force became the guiding principle behind extensive scholarship and research. Gesell showed how the maturational mechanism, while still hidden, manifests itself in intricate developmental sequences and self-regulatory processes. . . . (Though) most contemporary psychologists would consider Gesell's maturational position too extreme . . . still it is largely because of Gesell's work that even the most ardent learning theorists take some notice of inner maturational process.

The most frequently voiced criticisms of Gesell center on his manner of presenting age norms. . . . Nevertheless, Gesell's norms, particularly with respect to infant development, are extremely valuable. His observations were so careful and detailed that they are still useful to pediatricians, educators and psychologists working with children. . . . Gesell also provided a coherent philosphy of child-rearing. We should not, he said, try to force children into predetermined designs, but should follow their cues as they express basic biological forces of growth. . . . And there is some evidence . . . that things can go very wrong when Gesell's principles are excessively violated.[16] (p. 31)

Perhaps philosophies such as Gesell's will never be completely proven or refuted by empirical evidence alone; too much may depend on one's own values. All the same, it would seem that we have much to gain by listening to Gesell. For while it is true that we must control, direct and instruct our children to some extent, we usually seem to be in quite a hurry to do these things. What seems more difficult for us is to take the time to watch, enjoy, and appreciate our children as we give them a chance to do their own growing.[16] (p. 32)

Even more recently Sandra Scarr, formerly of Yale, in her lively book *Mother Care, Other Care*,[17] has this to say about Dr. Gesell's basic position:

Gesell's child is not so much malleable as to be thrown off course by parents' "miscalculated management," because she has internal direction. Gesell's child is shaped by nature to grow up without much fuss by the parents. Child development is in fact so predictable that Gesell was able to publish norms or standards for behavioral development, much like those for physical growth —height, weight and head circumference.[17] (p. 63)

Gesell's descriptions of normal development were so successful that they formed the basis for his developmental test, which is still used today. *The Bayley Tests of Mental and Motor Development*, and the *Denver Developmental Screening Test*, used by nearly all pediatricians, follow Gesell's ideas closely and even use many of his items. The tests serve well to identify at early ages children who lag seriously behind 90 or 95 percent of their age-mates.

Gesell recognized and respected individual differences. His norms were meant to convey a description of average development. Children within a normal range but ahead or behind their peers are not necessarily advantaged or disadvantaged. . . .

Children have different developmental patterns that deserve respect from parents and others.[17] (p. 64)

More Gesellian psychologists, such as Edward Zigler and I, stress the importance of the child's biological organization and the individual differences in developmental patterns that determine most of the ways children develop, as long as they have reasonable environments. We argue that parents can and do have important effects on their children but that most middle-class families provide adequate care for their children to develop normally, even optimally.[17] (p. 78)

The most thorough review of Dr. Gesell's position and contribution appears in Neil Salkind's *Theories of Human Development*.[18] He observes:

> Arnold Gesell, the foremost maturationalist in developmental psychology, represents a unique approach to the study of human development. A physician, Gesell believed that the sequence of development is determined by the biological and evolutionary history of the species. In other words, development of the organism is essentially under the control of biological systems and the process of maturation. Although the environment is of some importance, it acts only in a supportive role and does not provide any impetus for change. . . .
>
> Gesell believed that the most important influences on the growth and development of the human organism were biological directives. He summarized the theory in five distinct principles of development, which he later applied to behavior. All these principles assume that the formation of *structures* is necessary before any event outside the organism can have an influence on development. Interestingly, the notion that "function follows structure" was pursued not only by Gesell, but designers, architects, and engineers have also found a great deal of truth in these words as well.
>
> Gesell also believed that behavior at different stages of development has different degrees of balance or stability. . . . He believed that development is cyclical in nature, swinging from one extreme to another, and that by means of these swings, the child develops and uses new structures.[18] (pp. 11, 13)
>
> Unquestionably, Gesell's greatest contribution has been to the understanding of the development of the "normal" child. His detailed cinematic records, their analyses, and their translation into books for the popular press have influenced child-rearing patterns in this country as much as that of the famous

Dr. Spock (who incorporates many of Gesell's principles into his philosophy).

Gesell's ideas and theoretical approach never entered the mainstream of current thought about developmental psychology. Perhaps this is because much of his work was seen as too biological in nature and not sufficiently theoretical. Both from a historical and applied perspective, however, his contribution was and still is an outstanding one.[18] (p. 14)

Since Gesell was well versed in many different fields, he could speak knowledgeably to different constituencies. In addition, because he wrote for scientific, professional and popular audiences, his impact was widespread. Even though this impact is still apparent today, many practitioners who reflect his influence are not directly familiar with Gesell's contribution.[18] (p. 42)

Thousands of pediatricians, teachers, and parents have been influenced by Gesell's philosophy that time (or the process of maturation) takes care of most problems in behavioral development. . . . Arnold Gesell's legacy has been significant and large. His basic contributions in the area of how to study development (methodology) and accumulated information (data) will always stand as a significant advance in the area of developmental psychology.[18] (p. 55)

One final evaluation which speaks for itself is one which appeared in the Newsletter of the APA Division on Developmental Psychology in the spring of 1983.[1] We reproduce it here:

MODERN CLASSICS IN CHILD DEVELOPMENT
J. D. Hogan and M. A. Vahey
St. John's University, New York

In any discipline, it is difficult to know which works will survive the test of time. Those writings of apparent value today may be seen as faddish or of limited worth tomorrow. It is worthwhile, therefore, to ask if there are works of years past that still have relevance to the contemporary scene.

The present survey sought to identify "modern classics" in child development.

Fourteen contemporary textbooks in child development (published since 1978) were inspected. They were first examined for all references dated 1941 to 1960. Recurrent contributions were noted and tallied. In addition, those authors appearing most frequently in that time period were noted.

Eleven publications were cited in 6 or more of the textbooks. Beyond that there was little agreement; the next closest publication was cited in three textbooks. (In some cases, there were different publication dates for essentially the same work because of revisions, translations and so on. If any work appeared in any version within the appropriate time span, all references to it were included.)

Following is a list of the most common citations, that is, the eleven "modern classics." The number preceding each author represents the number of texts in which the reference appeared.

(13) Erickson, E. H. Childhood and society. New York: Norton, 1963. (Originally published 1950).

(12) Sears, R. R., Maccoby, E. E., and Levin, H. Patterns of child rearing. Evanston, Ill.: Row, Peterson, 1957.

(11) Piaget, J. The origins of intelligence in children (trans. by M. Cook). New York: International Universities Press, 1952.

(11) Aries, P. Centuries of childhood (trans. by R. Baldick). New York: Knopf, 1960.

(10) Piaget, J. Play, dreams and imitation in childhood. New York: W. W. Norton, 1951.

(10) Skinner, B. F. Verbal behavior. New York: Appleton-Century-Crofts, 1957.

(9) Piaget, J. The construction of reality in the child. New York: Basic Books, 1954.

(7) Lorenz, K. Z. King Solomon's ring. New York: Crowell, 1952.

(6) Gesell, A. Developmental diagnosis: Normal and abnormal child development. New York: Hoeber, 1941.

(6) Harlow, H. F. The nature of love. American Psychologist, 1957, 12, 673–685.

(6) Harlow, H. F. and Zimmerman, R. R. Affectional responses in the infant monkey. Science, 1959, 130, 421–432.

Authors with referenced publications in the years between 1941 and 1960 who were cited in the most texts are the following (the number following the name indicates the number of different texts in which they were cited at least once.) J. Piaget (14), E. Erikson (13), A. Gesell (12), H. Harlow (12). R. Sears (12), R. Spitz (12), P. Aries (11), K. Lorenz (11), S. Freud (10), B. F. Skinner (19), N. Chomsky (9), W. Dennis (9), B. Inhelder (9), A. Kinsey (9), H. Rheingold (9), N. Bayley (8), J. Bowlby (8), E. Gibson (8), J. P. Guilford (8), M. Honzik (8), M. C. Jones (8), and P. Mussen (8).

These names are not surprising. The list reads like an honor roll of contributors to child development.

Chapter 24

DR. GESELL AND OTHERS—HISTORICAL

As is true of everyone, Dr. Gesell was influenced both by contemporaries and by those who had gone before. Also, like others, he was sometimes not influenced by some whose names were at least on occasion linked with his. From among the many individuals who might be mentioned, we have chosen to comment on his relationship with the following.

First of all, in the present chapter, we mention two of his historical forebears—Pestalozzi and Froebel, to both of whom he often gave courteous recognition. In this same chapter we discuss Dr. Gesell's attitude toward three further historic figures—one of whom, Charles Darwin, he knew only through writings and reputation; the second, G. Stanley Hall, who was his professor and mentor at Clark University. A third, rather removed from the other two, but a man he admired vastly—Abraham Lincoln.

In the following chapter we include six of his contemporaries —Piaget, Mead, Montessori, Spock, Freud, and Coghill. Though these six may seem an ill-assorted group, we combine them here because they are perhaps those about whom people ask most: what was their influence on, or their relationship to, Dr. Gesell. (Interestingly enough, none of the six had a strong influence on, and with the exception of Margaret Mead and, more significantly, George Coghill, any substantial relationship with Dr. Gesell.)

PESTALOZZI, FROEBEL, DARWIN, HALL, AND LINCOLN

Pestalozzi

Dr. Gesell's several references to Pestalozzi are made perhaps more out of deference to his historic role than because Gesell himself was particularly influenced in his own work by anything that Pestalozzi had to say.

The first such reference was made in 1912, the year after Dr. Gesell came to Yale. His comment at that time was as follows:

> A specific and focalized interest in the child is of very recent date. In 1775 Pestalozzi began his quaint diary of a father, which contains random observations and a few naive experiments on his son, Jacobli. The entries are often emotional and prayerful and yet they contain a view of empiricism which links them to the later systematic studies of children.[1] (p. 21)

In 1923 we find further reference to Pestalozzi. In discussing this scholar and home education, Gesell notes:

> It is interesting and instructive to consider Pestalozzi, who is regarded as a leading educational reformer, and who spent most of his life among a peasant people, in an agricultural age, before the industrial revolution had got fairly under way . . . His whole career was an effort to exalt and to reconstruct the home. He believed that social reform and educational reform could come through the home alone.
>
> His very first educational treatise—and he was a voluminous writer and pamphleteer—contained these two aphorisms: "A man's domestic relations are the first and most important of his nature. The home is the true basis of the education of humanity." He recommended that the ideal mother teacher should "make her house a temple of the living God, and win heaven for her husband and her children."[2] (pp. 152, 153)

In 1925 Gesell comments briefly that the observational biographical methods is the oldest and most widely used method of studying children:

> In the following chronological list are found some of the names which are associated with this type of child psychology:

> Pestalozzi, 1774; Tiedman, 1787; Perez, 1787; Froebel, 1826;
> Mme. Necker de Saussure, 1893; Moore, 1896; Major, 1906;
> Dearborn, 1910.
> Pestalozzi, who heads the list, was a picturesque educational
> reformer, whose diary of his little son, Jacobli, is full of quaint
> and pious entries but with many suggestions of modern atti-
> tude.[3] (p. 27)

Any further references to Pestalozzi which occur in Dr. Gesell's writings do not go far beyond such courteous acknowledgments. However, we should mention specially a brief paper on "Pestalozzi and the Parent-Child Relationship," contributed by Dr. Gesell, who is described by the Pestalozzi Foundation as "a fellow-member of the Pestalozzi Foundation and, we believe, America's outstanding authority on Child Development." This paper was reprinted from *Amerikanische Schweizer Zeitung*, October 9, 1946:

The two paragraphs referring specifically to Pestalozzi, somewhat repetitious of earlier mentions, read:

> The world wars have demonstrated beyond doubt that
> home is the most fundamental unit of a democratic culture.
> Pestalozzi, without the aid of world catastrophe, saw the truth of
> this proposition, which he summed up in a few words: "A man's
> domestic relations are the first and most important of his nature
> . . . The home is the true basis of the education of humanity."
> For most of his life, by means of speeches, pamphlets,
> books, and by demonstration, Pestalozzi exalted the home as
> an educational agency. Many of his writings were directly ad-
> dressed to parents. His exhortations were so zealous and so sim-
> ple, that they seem somewhat quaint when reread today. But
> behind their ardor there lies deep truth, which can be readily
> restated in modern terms.[4]

A final Pestalozzi item in Dr. Gesell's bibliography[5] is not available in our files and seems in all likelihood merely a reprint of the above.

Froebel

Comments about Froebel, as well, chiefly acknowledge his historical importance. Gesell's first reference to Froebel, as to Pestalozzi, appeared in 1912:

In 1826 appeared Froebel's wonderful book "The Education of Man." Miss Shinn, herself the author of an important
work on the mental development of the child, has half-humor-
ously suggested that Froebel's works are like the Koran, and that
our subsequent child study is like the Alexandrian Library: "If
child study agrees with Froebel, it is of no use, burn it; if it does
not, it deserves only to be burned." Froebel undoubtedly ranks
among the deepest interpreters of childhood. He appreciated
the value of play, and his writings are pervaded with the concepts of growth and development. But these concepts were derived from a half-mystical, philosophical view; they are pro-
phetic and intuitive rather than biological. Darwinism had not
yet come. Froebel's theories present a curious admixture of the
logical and the genetic points of view, and in the light of present
knowledge they need correction at many places. Much of the
meaning that lies only vaguely hidden in Froebel has been made
explicit by recent child study, so it would not be wise to burn the
latter.[1] (pp. 21, 22)

In 1923 Gesell suggested:

There are good reasons for believing that the kindergarten
originated with Froebel as a movement for nursery reform.
Although he never adhered as tenaciously as did Pestalozzi to
the view that the home was the chief agency for early education,
there is evidence that he approved the idea and wished to make
the kindergarten consistent with it. He had a sort of education
of parents in mind when he started the kindergarten. The desti-
nation of nations lies far more in the hands of women—the
mothers—than in the possesors of power, or of those innovators
who for the most part do not understand themselves. We must
cultivate women who are the educators of the human race, else
the new generation cannot accomplish its task. There is little
hope for improvement until mothers begin to educate themselves. Let them attend kindergarten and study the system themselves.

Gesell concludes:

We have quoted these views of Froebel, not so much for
their intrinsic worth, but as an answer to those of his followers
who would confine the organization and operation of the kindergarten to a narrow circle painted on the floor of a schoolroom.
The problems of the hygiene and education of the preschool

child cannot be separated from those of home and parenthood. The kindergarten cannot realize its full objectives unless some form of parental training and cooperation is incorporated into its program.[2] (pp. 154–156)

Froebel, along with Pestalozzi, is listed among early leaders in the field of child behavior.[3] And a further mention of his ideas is given in 1930 when Gesell notes[6] that Froebel, as a pedagogist, drew upon horticulture and crystallography for some of his insights.

Charles Darwin

There is no question that of all those who came before him, Charles Darwin was the scientist who influenced Dr. Gesell most, and whom he most admired. References to Darwin were frequent in Gesell's writings, voluminous, and invariably highly laudatory.

Gesell first mentioned Darwin in 1912:

> After all has been said, the most profoundly revolutionary and productive event in the history of biological thought was the publication, in 1859, of Darwin's "Origin of Species." Everything in nature has a pedigree, a history. An organism is really not understood even when anatomy, physiology, and histology combine to explain its structure and mechanism in minute detail. There always remains the great historical question of origin and development. This was Darwin's problem, and to its solution he consecrated his genius.
>
> As the fossil remains of extinct creatures came to be better known, the idea of the fixity of species became more and more untenable. Buffon, Erasmus, Darwin, and Goethe all doubted such fixity.
>
> Charles Darwin, after twenty-five years of quiet, patient study, presented an explanation of the way in which species originate and are transformed in his epoch-making book. His explanation was the principle of natural selection, which Romanes calls the most important idea ever conceived by man. This principle, like a telescope, freed man from the narrow horizon of the present and the recent, and allowed him to glimpse down the deep perspective of the geologic past . . . So extensively was the intelligence of the age affected that the nineteenth century has even been called Darwin's century.[1] (pp. 17, 18)

Dr. Gesell's next mention of Darwin, in 1923, was brief:

The major figures in the historical development of the fundamental biological and medical sciences were Harvey in physiology, Versalius in anatomy, Pasteur in bacteriology, Mendel in genetics, Darwin in biology, Leibig in chemistry, Jenner in medicine.[2] (p. 17)

In 1930 Dr. Gesell repeats his earlier comment that the nineteenth century has sometimes been called Darwin's century, and then he continues:

> Not without some justification, for Darwin contributed profoundly to the developmental outlook upon nature and man, which was one of the most significant achievements of his century. Darwin was not, of course, alone responsible for the genetic interpretations which came to prevail in all departments of thought.
> However, when in the closing decades of the nineteenth century the philosophy of child life was increasingly permeated by secular, biological modes of thinking, Darwin's impress became more and more apparent. Not only through his publications but by personal correspondence he influenced his contemporaries.[6] (pp. 34, 42)

Next, in 1938, comes the commentary:

> Noah's Ark was still far from a metaphor to large sections of the population who fumed or laughed at Charles Darwin, author, in 1859, of that shocking, green-covered volume entitled "The Origin of Species."
> As early as 1840, Darwin had made a diary record of the development of his newborn son, William. The diary made special notes relating to anger, fear, left-handedness, affection, reason, moral sense and communication. Even before this, the young father had been interested in "expression of the emotions," convinced of the *gradual and natural origin* of every form of human and animal expression.
> In this genetic point of view, in this perception of gradual origins, lay Darwin's contribution to the intellectual thought of his own century and of the present century. The developmental outlook upon nature and upon the human species led to profound revisions in the interpretation of childhood. The concept of evolution with all its corollaries induced a new and humanizing kind of relativity. Even New England divines, still wrestling with Calvinistic and Augustinian ideas of original sin, softened

their doctrines of infant baptism. The new naturalism proved to be a solvent of the gloomier beliefs in fixity and fate. *So pervading was Darwin's influence that it has even been said that he won for men absolute freedom in the study of the laws of nature* [Italics ours].

Without that freedom it would be impossible to penetrate into the meaning of infancy and into the nature of child development. So we can scarcely err in paying our first tribute to Charles Darwin, remover of trammels, even though we realize that science in its most organic sense is a social phenomenon, a cultural product. He, more than any other single individual, initiated the genetic and rationalistic trends which characterize present-day interpretations of childhood.[7] (pp. 36, 37)

In 1939 came Dr. Gesell's longest and strongest accolade to Charles Darwin, in a six-page article in the *Scientific Monthly*.[8] We give only excerpts from this comprehensive commentary:

"Without doubt the first three!" This was the emphatic answer which Charles Darwin gave when as an old man he was asked which years of life he considered the most "subject to incubative impressions." There is much evidence that he was deeply intrigued by the phenomena of human infancy.

Darwin's mind ranged over all natural phenomena—geology, infancy, zoology, anthropology. The same passionate inquisitiveness as to the genesis of things which caused him to spend years of exacting study on his "beloved barnacles" led him also to set down abundant notes on the behavior of babies. . . .

Darwin's perplexities were those of a naturalist. His mind had a scientist's "naked need for ideological order." This order he sought tirelessly. . . . He converted the enigma of infancy into one more touchstone for understanding the origin of species. . . .

Darwin's approach to the problem of child behavior is comparative. He is equally interested in the pouting of the European child, of Kafir, Fingo, Malay, Abyssinian, orang and chimpanzee. . . . For Darwin, the naturalist, comparative psychology was more capacious; it was truly comparative.

Darwin was not a psychologist, but he had already inaugurated concepts of life and growth which were to revolutionize the psychological formulations of child development. . . .

The most concrete contribution which Darwin made to the embryonic science of child psychology was embodied in his volume on "Expression of Emotions." Here he deployed his genius as a naturalist with the same penetration which he brought to bear on barnacles, coral atolls, orchids and earthworms. He did not set himself up as a psychologist; indeed, he never entirely escaped a certain naive dualism in his views of the human mind. But it was as a naturalist that he addressed himself to the far-reaching problems of fear, rage, and affection. He attacked them with a boldness, objectivity and freshness which make much present-day discussion of similar subjects seem somewhat anemic in comparison. We may well go back to Darwin for vitalization of outlook and even of method. . . .

So pervading was Darwin's influence that it has been said that he won for man absolute freedom in the study of the laws of nature.[8] (pp. 548–555)

G. Stanley Hall

Of all of Dr. Gesell's teachers, the individual whose thinking influenced him most was the pioneering child psychologist, G. Stanley Hall, head of the department at Clark University where Dr. Gesell did his graduate work. His references to Hall were numerous and laudatory. The first appeared in 1912:

The child is a part of living nature. The greatest modern student of the child is G. Stanley Hall. When the history of science is seriously recorded, his name will be linked with that of Charles Darwin. Both are large-visioned interpreters of nature, combining scientific methods with a philosophic temper. Darwin applied his genius to the great genetic problems of biology. *Hall is the Darwin of Psychology.* Both have gleaned the fields of paleontology, geology, anthropology, botany and zoology to set forth illuminating interpretations concerning the development and expression of life. In many fields their studies overlap.

Indeed, the psychology of Hall is biological; he has brought these two sciences into intimate and fruitful union. Darwin could limit himself, rather strictly, to measurable, verifiable data, in his studies of the plant and animal kingdom. Hall's labors lie in the much less tangible kingdom of soul, and in this difficult, submerged field he has manifested intuition and suggestiveness characteristic of genius. He has collected his data from every possible source—from biography, and great quantities of confessions and *questionnaire* returns; from prisons, insane wards, medicine, superstition, myths, folklore—all for the purpose of restoring to our appreciation the extinct phases of the life of the soul. For he believes that our present consciousness is but a species, a stage in evolution; that its history began with the origin of organic life, if indeed not earlier, and that it inherits as instincts, latencies, rudiments, recapitulatory nascencies, or unconscious impulses, the prehuman features of its development.

G. Stanley Hall is at once the foremost leader of genetic psychology and of the child-study movement. No one has so clearly and consistently held that the child is a worthy center of unity for a new synthesis of all the knowledge bearing on physical and mental development. He has not stood aloof from the popular and practical phases of such a movement, but has encouraged a harmony of psychology and pedagogy, of science and all sociological endeavor which concerns the child. Such a specific and focalized interest in the child is of very recent date. Modern studies of children began with Preyer in Germany and with G. Stanley Hall in America.

The "Study of the Contents of Children's Minds on Entering School" by Hall is the first landmark in the child study of this country. This interesting census revealed a most wonderful amount of error and ignorance in the primary child's information, and showed the practical usefulness as well as scientific interest of inquiry into his characteristics.

We can only make a compressed summary of the subsequent development of child study. G. Stanley Hall, with an enthusiastic group of coworkers and students at Clark University, has been the chief leader of this development. He founded the *Pedagogical Seminary* and the *American Journal of Psychology* for the publication of child-study investigations. His monumental work "Adolescence" ranks as the most important contribution to child-study literature. This work embodies an incredible amount of study in the varied fields of physiology, anthropology, sociology, sex, crime, religion, and education, and furnishes new insight into a most baffling and vital problem. He has just completed an equally monumental work entitled "Educational Problems."[1] (pp. 20–23)

In 1925[3] (p. 28) Dr. Gesell notes that Hall made good use of the "observational biographical method of studying child behavior" and that for a time the questionnaire method was "a major device in the hands of G. Stanley Hall and his school."

In 1930, we find the following mention of Hall in relation to the beginning of the Child Study Movement[6] (pp. 44, 45):

In the Gay Nineties of the nineteenth century the interest in child psychology reached popular and nationwide proportions. America became the scene of a child-study movement which embraced hamlets and cities; schoolteachers, parents, and university professors; parlors and laboratories. G. Stanley Hall was the leader of this movement. He was a pupil of Wundt, but still more, he was the exponent of Darwin in the interpretation of mental development in the child and the race. It is easy to smile at the errors and miscarriages of this late Victorian child-study movement; but in spite of its shortcomings, it accomplished an extensive humanization of outlook. It opposed the same old tenacious doctrines of child depravity and adult prerogatives which Charles Dickens combatted by fiction; but used the methods of popularized and of technical science. A simple investigation in 1880 made by G. Stanley Hall with the aid of kindergartners, entitled "The Contents of Children's Minds on Entering School" was the forerunner of a fast-expanding literature on child nature.

Again writing about the beginnings of the Child Study movement in America, in 1938, Dr. Gesell noted[7] (p. 35) that Hall's paper on the contents of children's minds, referred to above, was a legitimate landmark since it was a "firsthand, inductive study." He adds:

> G. Stanley Hall was a powerful exponent of Darwinism. With fertile suggestiveness and comprehensiveness he applied the concepts of evolution to the mind of the child and the race. He became the leader of the popular child study movement of the nineties which accomplished an extensive humanization of outlook.

In 1948, Dr. Gesell had this to say:

> Darwin was not a psychologist, but he had already inaugurated concepts of life and growth which were to revolutionize the psychological formulations of child development. He profoundly influenced G. Stanley Hall, a young scientist who became a powerful exponent of Darwinism in America. Hall applied the concepts of evolution to the mind of the child and of the race. He also became the father of a nationwide child study movement which liberalized elementary education and led to scientific advances in the study of child development.[9] (p. 40)

And a final comment in 1952:

> As a Clark man, I would like to formulate my specific indebtedness to each and all of the distinguished group of profes-

sors who still remained there after the hegira to the University of Chicago. Burnham had a carefully wrought and sympathetic historical approach to problems of child hygiene; Chamberlin, in anthropology, was notable for his warm and catholic protagonisms; Hodge for his informal, leisurely interpretations of ecology; Sanford in experimental psychology, was an exemplar of precise thinking, joined with an attractive personality. The venerable psychiatrist, Dr. Edward Cowles, conducted impressive demonstrations of psychotic patients.

G. Stanley Hall was the acknowledged genius of the group at Clark. Although the term genius is often overused, we can safely apply it to his intellect. True genius may be regarded as a creative developmental thrust of the human action system into the unknown. Hall embodied such bursts, almost inveterately, in his thinking and in his teaching. He had, in addition, an empathetic propensity to revive within himself the thought processes and the feelings of other thinkers. This same projective trait enabled him to penetrate into the mental life of children, of defectives, of primitive peoples, of animals, of extinct stages of evolution.[10] (p. 126)

There is clearly no question as to the respect with which Gesell viewed Hall's work, and his role in helping to establish the study of child development in this country.

DR. GESELL AND ABRAHAM LINCOLN

One person, definitely outside his own field, whom Dr. Gesell admired vastly was Abraham Lincoln. To the best of our knowledge, Gesell was a Democrat politically, and yet this outstanding Republican was definitely an object of his admiration. Though mention of Lincoln was sparing in his work, he did mention this historic figure on occasion, and was an avid collector of Lincoln memorabilia. And his final publication was a brief tribute to Lincoln in his youth.

Dr. Gesell's first published mention of Lincoln appeared in 1930 in his book *The Guidance of Mental Growth in Infant and Child.*

It is natural that genius should be characterized by acceleration of growth on the one hand and prolongation of growth capacity on the other. The superior person manifests the gift of growth. This trait is very clear, for example, in the writing and utterances of Abraham Lincoln. Sandburg has given a vivid impression of the psychological process of ripening which steadily seasons Lincoln's thought and character.[6] (p. 131)

Further mention of Lincoln's genius was made in a Lecture to the Laity given at the New York Academy of Medicine in February 1942.

> Genius is a growth phenomenon. . . . Genius implies gestation, whether we think of specific acts of creation or the longer reaches of the life cycle. In some persons it is the total life career rather more than individual accomplishments which denotes their genius. Such a person was Abraham Lincoln. His career is a striking example of the configuring forces of a slow and steady growth. He was slow-minded, retarded in repartee, not distinguished for inspired feats of brilliance. As a tall, blue-chinned youth, he was an irresistibly funny talker. In his early maturity his poetry was doggerel, his lectures ornate, his speeches somewhat bombastic. Not until he was in his forty-sixth year did his public utterance rise to the dignity, breadth, and sympathy which came to characterize his diction. His Springfield speech of 1854 was the prelude to the Gettysburg Address, the Bixby letter, and the exalted cadences of the Second Inaugural. The evolution of his literary style reflects the development of his genius. He was slowly seasoned by the times which he himself did so much to create. In perspective, his life career takes on the dimensions and the design of a myth, because there was a profound correspondence between his peculiar genius and the culture in which he grew.
>
> Cultures like individuals seem to obey laws of growth and to have their periods of bloom, of birth and rebirth. Lincoln's great Springfield speech belonged to that golden half-decade between 1850 and 1855 which marked the American Renaissance and saw the appearance in succession of Emerson's essay, *Representative Men*, Hawthorne's *Scarlet Letter*, Melville's *Moby-Dick*, Thoreau's *Walden*, and Whitman's *Leaves of Grass*.[11] (pp. 152–153)

A passing reference, of no great significance except to show that Dr. Gesell did, in varied contexts, have Lincoln in mind, appeared in 1948:

> On the fourth day of February 1864, the very month in which he called for 500,000 volunteers, Abraham Lincoln for-

mulated a remarkable sentence in behalf of a widowed mother
who sought his help. He wrote this sentence in his own clear
hand on the back of a folded letter:

> If oath shall be made by this lady & the gentleman accom-
> panying her that she is a widow with four small children,
> & no person to assist her unless it be the son in the Army,
> let that son be discharged.

> Here we have a poignant reminder of the inescapable prob-
> lem of child care which confront a nation at war; and by similar
> token, a nation at peace. For the wartime needs of children are
> the needs of peacetime. Children always require food and shel-
> ter, affection and protection, understanding and guidance.
> These three kinds of need, physical, personal, developmental,
> are so profoundly joined that there is only one institution in our
> culture which can fully satisfy them. That institution is the
> home.[9] (p. 214)

Interestingly enough, and perhaps more significant for timing
than for its content, is the fact that Dr. Gesell's final publication
dealt entirely with Abraham Lincoln. This publication was the introduction to a book entitled *Lincoln's Youth: Indiana Years—Seven to
Twenty-One—1816–1830*, by Louis A. Warren.
    We quote briefly from this introduction:

> Abraham Lincoln ranks as one of the most remarkable
> figures of modern times. His extensive writings assembled in
> chronological order, and a vast body of Lincoln literature which
> pertains to them, have created and continue to create a social
> heritage. In countless ways Lincoln's image has entered the folk
> consciousness of America. After thirty years of pioneering study
> of his life career, Ida Tarbell (in 1924) considered that "There's
> no man in American history with whom the people so desire
> intimate acquaintance as they do with Abraham Lincoln."
>   However, when Dr. Louis A. Warren left New England and
> became editor of the *Larue County Herald* in Hodgenville, Ken-
> tucky, he found even the local folklore extremely unreliable and
> often contradictory.
>   Thomas and Nancy Lincoln lived in the very center of bitter
> slavery controversy. Abraham and Sarah heard the heated ser-
> mons of emancipator preachers. The little Lincoln family of
> four crossed the broad Ohio River in the autumn of 1816; the
> Indiana period extends from 1816 to 1830.

The fourteen Indiana years have a strategic position in the life cycle. They comprise one full fourth of Abraham Lincoln's allotted life span of 56 years. . . . Growth is a key concept for understanding Lincoln as an exceptionally great man who was both simple and elusively complex. He came by his mind as he came by his body, through deep-seated mechanisms of growth. Such mechanisms operated throughout his total life cycle from before birth to his final year. Although he was moved and moulded by the events of the world into which he was born, he was an end product of the vast universal forces of evolution which determine the primary growth potentials of each and every individual. Lincoln was uniquely endowed with patterns and innate capabilities of growth which came to consistent and discernible manifestations in his public career. Were they not also present in the more private and limited career of his un-recorded childhood and youth?

A great universal idea had its germ in this boy at twelve years. Abraham was a book-loving boy. At twelve he was beginning to read at a level of conceptual thinking with a growing interest in broad principles of government. Later he sought for these principles in the current newspapers as well. By one definition genius is an idea of youth developed in maturity. In Lincoln this was a slow and steady development. It took the form of recurring periods of sheer meditation. It was part of the process of growing up.

His life career tends to take on the dimensions and the design of a myth because there was a profound correspondence between his peculiar genius and the pioneer culture in which he grew.[12] (pp. xx, xxi)

Chapter 25

DR. GESELL AND OTHERS—
CONTEMPORARY

Piaget, Mead, Montessori, Spock, Freud, and Coghill

ARNOLD GESELL AND JEAN PIAGET

Perhaps suprisingly, there is very little mention of Piaget in Dr. Gesell's writings. (It seems also very likely that there is little mention of Gesell in Piaget's books and papers.)

Five of Piaget's early books were reviewed briefly by Gesell, and we find two further mentions of Piaget by Gesell. Though Piaget's books were in Gesell's library and thus available to students, Piaget was not listed in the required readings recommended by Gesell for his section of the Yale Pro-Seminar course required of all students in the Psychology Department.

Correspondence between the two men is virtually nonexistent and their meetings appear to have been few and brief. The first meeting between the two occurred on September 4, 1929 when both appeared on a program on child behavior apparently sponsored by the "International Committee" and chaired by John Anderson of the University of Minnesota.

Following that, on June 26, 1930, Dr. Gesell did write to Piaget to introduce one of his staff members, John McGinnis, who wished to visit in Geneva. A second, not particularly revealing, letter from Gesell to Piaget was dated March 9, 1931, and is reproduced here:

Professor Jean Piaget
Director of the Institute Rousseau
Geneva, Switzerland

Knowing your interest in the humor as well as philosophy of language development in children, I am transcribing below a dialogue between two boys, age approximately four and five years.

4 years: "I know that Pontius Pilate is a tree."
5 years: "No, Pontius is not a tree at all."
4 years: "Yes, it was a tree because it says 'He suffered *under* Pontius Pilate' so it must have been a tree."
5 years: "No, I am sure Pontius Pilate was a person and not a tree."
4 years: "I know he was a tree, because he suffered under a tree—a big tree."
5 years: "No, he was a person, but he was a very pontius person."

I have read with much interest your last volume on *The Child's Conception of Physical Causality.*
Don't trouble to acknowledge this note.
With cordial greetings and best wishes for your work.

Yours sincerely, Arnold Gesell

On April 13, Dr. Gesell again wrote to Piaget to introduce a colleague, Dr. Ruth Washburn, who wished to visit him. This letter was acknowledged by Piaget by a letter dated April 28, 1937. This, too, is reproduced:

Monsieur le Professeur Arnold GESELL
Directeur de la Clinique of Child Development
YALE UNIVERSITY The School of Medicine
NEW HAVEN (Connecticut)
14 Davenport Avenue

Mon cher Professeur Gesell,

J'ai reçu avec grand plaisir la lettre que vous avez bien voulu m'envoyer concernant Miss Washburn. J'ai beaucoup regrette, au mois de Septembre, de vous voir si brièvement à Harvard et espérais pourir m'arrêter à Yale University lors de mon retour, mais j'ai eu des occupations si nombreuses que ce plaisir n'a pas été possible.

Vous savez quel souvenir inappréciable je garde de votre

charmant accueil à Yale lors du Congrès de Psychologie. Je n'oublierai jamais la grande impression que m'a faite votre Clinique ainsi que le contact personnel que nous avons pu acquérir (malgré le langage!) Alors de vos réceptions et excursions. J' espère vous recevoir un jour à Genève de la même manière.

Je recevrai, avec grand plaisir, Prof. Washburn et mé ré jouis de travailler avec elle. D'un autre côté, je me permets de vous recommander Miss Edith Damos qui vient de passer une année dans notre Institut et qui a fait preuve d'un grand zèle et d'une grande bonne volonté. C'est encore une débutante mais elle a fait de grand progrès et parviendra certainement à un bon rendement si elle peut travailler dans votre Université.

Merci encore, et croyez mon cher Professeur Gesell, à mes sentiments cordialement dévoués.

Un Directeur:
(Jean Piaget)

A letter dated 28 III 53 and penned on stationery of the Hotel Taft in New Haven is virtually undecipherable, but appears—suffering both from faintness of copy and our translation from the French—to give the following message. It appears to say that Piaget was touched to receive Dr. Gesell's "aimable lettre" which he received after "le conférence." Unfortunately, he said, someone was coming for him by automobile and he must leave directly after lunch. He much regretted that the two of them would not be able to get together.

He went on to say that he remembered vividly his visit to Dr. Gesell's clinic in 1929 and the ride they had in Dr. Gesell's automobile. He then asked Dr. Gesell to accept his cordial sentiments.

Thus the two men apparently met briefly in New Haven in 1929 and again briefly at Harvard apparently in September 1936. That seems to have been it. There is no indication that Dr. Gesell ever visited Piaget in Geneva.

The first of Dr. Gesell's two specific references to Piaget appeared in 1933, as follows:

> Piaget has made extensive psychological studies of the child's language, early forms of reasoning, articulate concepts of physical causality and cosmology, and the nature of moral judgment. His approach upon the problem is at once philosophical, clinical and generic, and in his last work he has made correlations with the literature of theoretical sociology. In his interpretations he uses biological concepts only to a limited extent and it

therefore becomes interesting to inquire into his views concerning the interaction of the individual and environment.

We quote a few passages *which in spite of a certain abstruseness indicate the lines of his interpretation*: "This concordance of our results with those of historico-critical or logical-sociological analysis brings us to a second point: the parallelism existing between moral and intellectual development. Everyone is aware of the kinship between logical and ethical norms. Logic is the morality of thought just as morality is the logic of action. . . . One may say, to begin with, that in a certain sense neither logical nor moral norms are innate in the individual mind. . . .

"This does not mean that everything in the *a priori* view is to be rejected. Of course the *a priori* never manifests itself in the form of ready-made innate mechanism. The *a priori* is the obligatory element, and the necessary connections only impose themselves little by little, as evolution proceeds. Yet to speak of directed evolution and asymptotic advance towards a necessary ideal is to recognize the existence of a something which acts from the first in the direction of this evolution." (Etc.)

The foregoing interpretation, *although too mentalistic to be brought into a biological discussion*, indicates the presence of "a priori" factors which may be envisaged in terms of maturation. These factors become somewhat less mystical if they are ascribed to the growth characteristics of a total action system whose elementary mechanisms have been studied by direct approach[1] (pp. 225–226).

A second very similar comment, made in the following year gives Gesell's opinion that:

> Piaget has made extensive psychological studies of the child's language, early forms of reasoning, articulate concepts of physical causality, and of cosmology, and the nature of moral judgment. His approach upon the problems is at once philosophical, clinical, and genetic, and in his last work he has made correlations with the literature of theoretical sociology. In his interpretations *he uses biological concepts only to a limited extent* and it therefore becomes interesting to inquire into his views concerning the interaction of the individual and environment. We quote a few passages which in spite of a certain abstruseness indicate the lines of his interpretation.[2] (pp. 312–313)

(Since this quote does not add to our knowledge of Dr. Gesell's feelings about Piaget and his work, it will not be reproduced here.)

Gesell's main comments about Piaget's writings are to be found in his reviews of five of Piaget's books.[3,4,5,6,7] Two of these[5,6] are unavailable. Excerpts from the other three are reproduced herewith. Since all of these reviews are more reportorial than evaluative, they will not be quoted in full.

The first of these three reviews Piaget's book *The Language and Thought of the Child*. It reads in part:

> This book deals with the ordinary subject of childish conversation, but approaches it with such clinical directness and insight that the findings become of great value for genetic psychology. The author combines the equipment of a naturalist, a zoologist, a philosopher versed in logic and epistemology, and a psychologist who has familiarized himself with the outlook of James, Dewey, Janet, Stanley Hall, and J. Mark Baldwin.
>
> Jean Piaget conducted his observations at the Maison des Petits of the Institute J. J. Rousseau, Geneva, and used the simple expedient of recording verbatim the spontaneous conversation of young children at work and play, and of inducing them to take the lead in their speech. This method is similar to the free-association device frequently employed by psychiatrists in working with adults.
>
> Clinical method has sometimes been criticized as being too subjective and too uncontrolled for scientific research; but Piaget has demonstrated that it can be made very fruitful, that it has experimental and quantitative values.
>
> The fruitfulness of the results, however, lies mainly in the author's penetration. He succeeds remarkably in divesting himself of adult preconceptions when he analyzes his data. He does not assume that the child means what he says, as though words were coins, which have equal value whether offered in the realm of child or of grownups. On the contrary, Piaget asks, What are the *needs* which a child tends to satisfy when he talks? . . .
>
> He believes that the age at which a child really begins to communicate his thought is probably between seven and eight, for then the proportion of egocentric remarks fall to about twenty-five percent. These age figures cannot be taken without qualification. The conclusions rest upon a small number of cases, intensively studied, and the author has not perhaps sufficiently recognized the influence of native intelligence, to say nothing of personality makeup. He has, however, shown that the functional, the psychological essence of language, is profoundly influenced by age and experience. The age levels considered range from two to eleven years, and embrace the func-

tions of language, understanding, and verbal explanation, and the types of *Whys* a child will ask—the *Whys* of explanation, of motivation, and of justification.

Piaget's book is an important scientific contribution because it undermines the inveterate intellectualism which the adult so naturally ascribes to the less sophisticated logic, but it is different from the adult's. This difference is well worth understanding for reasons of education as well as of genetic psychology. The present volume is to be followed by another on "Judgment and Reason in the Child." Together these two volumes will make a significant survey of the psychological foundations of Child Logic. (p. 72)

Dr. Gesell's second review of a Piaget book covers Piaget's *Judgment and Reasoning in the Child*,[4] and is quoted at length:

Professor Piaget has provided us with a valuable sequal to his earlier volume entitled "Language and Thought of the Child." Together these two volumes constitute what is in a sense the first systematic outline of the logic of childhood. The author approaches his subject in the spirit of a naturalist and of a clinical observer. The pages are crowded with dialogues and soliloquies, interspersed with statistics and specimens of childish conversation elicited under both spontaneous and experimental conditions. Eight children from three to seven years of age furnished 10,000 recorded remarks for analytic study. Scores of children from four to twelve years were individually examined with numerous questions and test situations, to determine their ability to distinguish between right and left, to detect absurdities and contradictions, to introspect, to define, to judge and reason about simple mechanical and physical problems.

The result of these patient studies is a mass of verbatim data which wears a superficial guise of familiarity and even of triviality. But Piaget comments on this "obvious" material with such penetrating analysis that we are afforded definitely new glimpses into the dynamics of the child's reasoning.

The very intimacy of our ordinary acquaintance with children tends to blur perception of their true nature. There is an inveterate tendency to regard the child as a miniature adult, merely reduced in dimensions but identical in organization. It is the business of genetic psychology to dispel this error. We place such naive interpretation on the language and thought of the child that systematic study of their peculiar mechanism is a scientific, and ultimately, a practical necessity.

For one thing we shall not understand much of the "lying" of young children until we appreciate the frailties of early logic, which up to the age of eight years make the child's thought literally teeming with contradictions. . . . Logical reasoning proper is a fruit of long and slow growth.

In discussing the stages of development, the author utilizes psychoanalytic concepts and perhaps places undue explanatory stress upon the egocentricness of the child. . . . Although the text requires close reading, it is far from dull and is so contributive both in content and suggestion that it will have a stimulating effect on many students.[4] (p. 208)

Dr. Gesell's next two reviews of Piaget work, his discussion of *The Child's Concept of the World*[5] and of *The Child's Concept of Physical Causality*[6] are not available in our own files or in libraries to which we have access, and thus cannot be excerpted here. But we do have copy for his review of *The Moral Judgment of the Child*,[7] which reads in part as follows:

This present study explores the child's morality, and demonstrates important parallelisms between moral and intellectual development. In their entirety, Piaget's five related volumes constitute a notable and scholarly contribution, distinctly European in flavor, to a genetic understanding of the subjective life of the child, and of the antecedents of adult mentality.

The pyramid of Professor Piaget's writings rests on a broad base. He is well grounded in philosophical literature including epistemology and logic; he has had training in natural science; he is experimentally interested in problems of early education represented in the activities of the Geneva Institute; he has observed his own children, and hundreds of others with the assistance of his institute co-workers, seven of whom collaborated in the writing of the new volume on moral judgment. His work is marked by a correlation of what might be called philosophical clinical, and genetic aspects of child psychology. Indeed, in the present instance he has extended the correlation into the fields of theoretical sociology and of social ethics. He would hold that a critical interpretation of cultural and societal organization is dependent upon a more realistic insight into the developing process whereby the child attains moral stature.

And how does Piaget scientifically seek to penetrate a realm so subjective and subtle as the maturing of a child's moral judgment? He uses the same methods previously applied to exploring the child's ideas of the physical world and of causation, namely, the "clinical interrogatory" or the method of analytic conversations with individual children from three to fourteen years of age.

Piaget believes that it is futile to ask the child to introspect and to report his introspections directly to the psychologist; but even the young child when given a series of stories relating different kinds or degrees of lying, stealing, and injustice, gives answers which prove very revealing as to the nature of his moral judgment. Piaget also brings clumsiness within the scope of his inquiry into objective responsibility and immanent justice.

His analysis of the children's conversations concerning the consequences of clumsiness is highly suggestive. It reveals moreover how blind (and clumsy!) is the adult attitude which places sole reliance on authority, but is on a unilateral respect, as the source of morality.

Piaget's conclusions are not readily summarized and his discussions sometimes seem over-detailed and recondite, but he has quite justified the modest hope that his present book "may supply a scaffolding which those living with children and observing their spontaneous reactions can use in erecting the actual edifice."[7] (p. 168)

Taken together, these quotes suggest a certain ambivalence in Dr. Gesell's feelings about Piaget's writings. A courteous acknowledgment of their value is in many instances balanced by at least mild criticism.

Thus in his first comment about Piaget's work he notes that:

The foregoing interpretation, although too mentalistic to be brought into a biological discussion, indicates the presence of "a priori" factors which may be envisaged in terms of maturation.[1] (p. 226)

Faint praise indeed! In his next reference he comments:

In his (Piaget's) interpretations he uses biological concepts only to a limited extent and it therefore becomes interesting to inquire into his views concerning the interaction of the individual and the environment. We quote a few passages which in spite of a certain abstruseness indicate the lines of his interpretation.[2] (p. 312)

In the three book reviews which are available, Gesell's remarks become somewhat more complimentary. Thus in his review of *The Language and Thought of the Child*, he notes:

This book deals with the ordinary subject of a childish conversation, but approaches it with such clinical directness and
insight that the findings become of great value for genetic Psychology. . . . Piaget's book is an important scientific contribution.[3] (p. 72)

A further positive comment occurs in Gesell's review of *Judgment and Reasoning in the Child*:

Professor Piaget has provided us with a valuable sequel to
his earlier volume, *Language and Thought in the Child*. Together
these two volumes constitute what is in a sense the first systematic outline of logic in childhood. . . . In discussing the stages of
development, the author utilizes psychoanalytic concepts and
perhaps places undue explanatory stress upon the egocentricness of child. . . . Although the text requires close reading, it is
far from dull and is so contributive both in current and suggestion that it will have a stimulating effect on many students.[4] (p.
208)

In his final review of Piaget's *The Moral Judgment of the Child*
Gesell remarks as already noted:

In their entirety, Piaget's five related volumes constitute a
notable and scholarly contribution, distinctly European in flavor,
to a genetic understanding of the subjective life of the child, and
of the antecedents of adult mentality. The pyramid of Professor
Piaget's writings rests on a broad base. . . .
Piaget's conclusions are not readily summarized and his
discussions sometimes seem over-detailed and recondite, but he
has quite justified the modest hope that his present book "may
supply a scaffolding which those living with children and observing their spontaneous reactions can use in erecting the actual
edifice."[7] (p. 168)

A certain light is thrown on Dr. Gesell's somewhat lukewarm
praise of Piaget by comments made by Jerome Kagan in his book,
The Nature of the Child, published in 1984:

Finally, it remains a puzzle why Piaget minimized the role
of maturation in early intellectual growth. Even though he acknowledged that the child is born with important sensory-motor

actions and processes, making a purely environmental interpretation of intellectual development impossible, he wanted to award to biology as little fixed influence as possible. "Hereditary transmission," he wrote late in life, "seems to play only a limited role in the development of cognitive functions."

A similar assumption is present in a debate the twenty-year-old Piaget had with a Polish taxonomist regarding the bases for variation among species of freshwater snail. In sharp disagreement with his older colleague, Piaget minimized mutation and maximized the influence of the environment by proposing that the structures of the snail are transformed gradually through their interaction with the environment.[8] (pp. 194, 195)

This minimization of maturation and of the contribution of biology to human behavior, conspicuous throughout the work of Piaget, seems reason enough that neither Gesell nor Piaget was ever totally appreciative of the work of the other.

ARNOLD GESELL AND MARGARET MEAD

In contrast to the contact between Gesell and Piaget, an interesting and substantive relationship did develop between Dr. Gesell and Margaret Mead. Needless to say, their points of view and approaches to human behavior were in rather sharp distinction. Margaret Mead, like most anthropologists, emphasized the role of society in determining human behavior. Gesell emphasized the role of the individual in determining the customs of society.

Though respectful of Margaret Mead and her work, Dr. Gesell did not find it useful in supplementing or supporting his own, and no references to her appear in his writings. Mead, on the other hand, though she did not particularly agree with Gesell, referred to him in her own works and on one notable occasion used his theories in a substantial way in one of her own major undertakings.[9]

Margaret Mead's first contact with any of the Gesell group was in meeting Dr. Ilg at Vassar in 1945. She describes her reaction to this meeting and her subsequent interest in the Gesell work as follows:

In 1945, at the Vassar Summer Institute, I was a colleague of Dr. Frances Ilg and had an opportunity to hear her present

studies of different "ages" in which she described, so vividly that
my fingertips tingled, the motor-kinesthetic patterns peculiar to
different stages of development. As I came to understand the
spiral concept of development, how it supplements the concepts
of epigenesis of Erik Erikson and reorders many of the observations on children's behavior that had been classified as regression, and how the development of a series of spiral models
would give us a device for examining cultural specializations in
terms of timing of learning, I felt that I had found something I
had been looking for for the last ten years—a research device
that would make it possible to explore the nexus between the
rhythms of given temperaments and the way in which a culture
institutionalizes these rhythms so that all individuals born within
the culture, at varying cost, are also subjected to the same pattern of learning. But it seemed clear that in order to use this
Gesell-Ilg approach, ages were absolutely necessary, and much
more comparable situations would also be essential, so I assumed that any use of the method would have to wait upon
more field work.

In early 1946 I read a paper at the Viking Fund, "On the
Implications for Anthropology of the Gesell-Ilg Approach to
Maturation," [10] which Dr. Ilg discussed. My first personal contact with Dr. Gesell was when he and I delivered papers together
at a meeting of the New York Neurological Society, January 8,
1946, where it was possible to discuss some of the implications of
the symmetro-tonic stages of the spiral, in particular the ease
with which a seven-month-old child is able to repeat a symmetrical prayer gesture.

In the spring of 1946 I met Frances Macgregor in connection with her search for comparative cross-cultural material on
attitudes toward bodily disfigurement, and discussed with her
her hope of using photography as a tool in anthropological
work. . . . In the course of this discussion it first occurred to me
. . . to do at least an exploratory study of the Gesell-Ilg hypothe-
ses by using the existing collection of Balinese photographs. [9]
(pp. 198, 199)

It was presumably as a result of her 1945 meeting with Dr. Ilg
and this introduction to the Gesell point of view that Mead published her 1947 paper, "On the Implications for Anthropology of
the Gesell-Ilg Approach to Maturation". [10]

The message of this paper is a little hard to decipher but,
roughly, what she seems to be saying is this:

In selecting the developmental point of view, especially
some of the recent aspects of the Gesell-Ilg approach to the

study of maturation, for discussion in an anthropological context, I have done so because I believe that certain of the concepts emerging from this approach may be of the very greatest
importance to the field worker, especially the field worker who
is concerned with child development.[10] (p. 70)

The Gesell-Ilg findings can be of the very greatest significance if we recognize that their observations provide us with a
model, a basic way of thinking about the maturation of the individual, in terms of which any given culture's expectations and
demands can be calibrated. . . . For research purposes we can
use these descriptions which, properly abstracted from the cultural matrix, give us a picture of the pattern of human growth,
as a means of *studying* cultural developmental mechanisms
without necessarily evaluating them. . . .

Gesell and Ilg use the spiral as a mechanical model, which,
provides for the concept of continuous growth that nevertheless
contains both upward and downward gradients, and allows for
the systematic inclusion of repetitions of behavior characteristic
of previous stages, *as part of growth rather than as regression.*

The Gesell-Ilg method makes it possible to follow through
the development of special bodily emphases, or special emphases on segments of the body, as on arm movements, leg movements, or the importance of the head, as these reappear in different stages in the maturation sequence.[10] (p. 71)

If it were found—from the examination of Gesell's data
and other similar types of data—that types of innate maturation
style could be distinguished, these differences could be counter-
poised against detailed records of cultural expectations, and we
would be able to study these cultures which had come to special-
ize in exactly hitting a natural rhythm, peculiar to one constitutional type, and also those cultures where child-rearing practices
tend toward smoothing out the differences by superimposing
patterns specifically congenial to no type, or intermediate patterns which blur the distinction between types.[10] (p. 76)

The meaning of all this is not entirely clear to us, but undoubtedly was to Margaret Mead. At any rate, from this initial paper she
progressed to suggesting that Dr. Gesell and his staff collaborate
with her on the investigation which ended up as her book, *Growth
and Culture.*[9]

In using the Gesell work in the preparation of this book, Mead
notes:

We have drawn on Gesell's research in two ways: by an
initial use of the published materials, especially *The Atlas of In-*

fant Behavior, to organize our materials in a form suitable for communication with the members of the Gesell group, and by invoking the experiences of Dr. Gesell, Dr. Ilg, and Dr. Ames, through having them examine intensively the series of photographs, which were successively organized in response to their comments, so as to invoke further comment.[9] (p. x)

Margaret Mead and Frances Macgregor spent two days in New Haven in November, 1947, going over their material with Gesell, Ilg, and Ames. Though both Gesell films and Mead films of child behavior were available, they did not seem to add substantially to what could be done with still photos. And so it was decided that the project would be based on still photos alone.

From November to March, Frances Macgregor worked on the Balinese photographs again, arranging them in accordance with the "new insights" that had developed in the conferences with the Gesell group. This rearrangement was then presented to Dr. Ilg and Dr. Ames in a conference in New York in March 1948.

As we at Gesell interpreted our contribution to this project, we were shown unmarked still photos of Balinese babies of different ages and in different postures. Then we attempted to determine the exact ages of these infants. If we could determine, from postures alone, the correct ages of the babies (working from our knowledge of postures of American babies at different ages) it would be assumed that the two groups of infants, from two very different cultures, developed in very much the same way.

A quite graphic description by Mead of our collaborative efforts notes that, in relating to the Balinese photographs:

> The Gesell group could respond quickly, comparatively, the first response often being a postural one, as Dr. Gesell lightly threw his shoulders into an amazing imitation of a Balinese child's dancing posture, Louise Ames experimented with what difference it would make to extend the knees in the Balinese frogging position, and Frances Ilg tested the complexities of touching the middle of the back with an outwardly rotated arm.[9] (p. 56)

Following the second conference, Mead and Macgregor:

> . . . presented the Gesell group with our materials arranged in their categories and also in what seemed to Frances Macgregor

to be "different." To this they responded by refinement within their categories, by reacting to what was new in our material, and by their comments and discussion . . . Very rapid and satisfactory communication was established.[9] (p. 204)

In February 1951 the Mead plates were pasted up and again taken to the Gesell group.

> In this conference, although no new insights were developed, the final phrasing as given in the conclusions was clarified and the order of the plates was rearranged . . . but no new material was added. . . . With slides of these plates, Ilg and Ames presented at the Viking Fund, April 2, 1951, a paper on "How Knowledge of Child Development in Our Culture Can Be Useful to Anthropologists."[9] (p. 205)

The results of this entire undertaking were not spectacular, though Mead comments on

> . . . the greater ease with which it is possible to communicate when both approaches are systematic, so that working with the Gesell group proved much easier than working with some other specialists.[9] (p. 208)

Mead did feel that:

> The results have not contributed heavily to our knowledge of the way in which the Gesell spiral can be used to interpret Balinese material, or of the way in which the Balinese material can contribute to the spiral model.[9] (p. 207)

However, from our point of view, results were somewhat impressive. In the majority of instances we could identify the age of the Balinese babies from the unmarked photographs within a week or two of their actual ages. This led to the conclusion that Balinese babies did develop in a manner very similar to that characteristic of American babies. One major difference noted was the unusual postural flexibility of the Balinese. For them, any posture that was physically possible might very often occur. In American babies there are many postures which *could* be assumed which simply are very seldom seen.

Thus from the Gesell point of view, one might explain the kind of dancing which comes so easily to the Balinese, young and old, as having resulted, to begin with, from the fact that the postures they assume in dancing are natural and comfortable for them, and not merely because young Balinese have the opportunity of seeing the older Balinese as they assume such postures.

Though a mountain may seem to have labored to bring forth a mouse, this collaborative effort between Mead and Gesell and his staff was of great interest to both groups and certainly seemed worthwhile.

For all her personal friendliness to Dr. Gesell and his colleagues, and despite the fact that it was she, not we, who suggested that we work together, Margaret Mead did definitely have reservations about the usefulness of the body of the Gesell work, especially as it related to writings for parents.

Thus in her book, *Growth and Culture*[9] (pp. 19–22), she elaborates on what she calls *misunderstandings* of the Gesell point of view. She points out that as new research develops in the field of human relationships, there is a tendency to use it to counter some other tendency that has gone too far.

She seems to see Dr. Gesell's work as a contrast to an earlier environmental approach. She feels, however, that instead of understanding what Gesell was saying, many parents interpreted his norms as meaning that all children "ought" to develop at the same rate. Thus she concludes that:

> By a painful irony, the work of Dr. Gesell, the impassioned champion of the right of children to grow at their own pace . . . has often been transformed instead into an instrument through which mothers rob their children of this very right. Books that were designed as guides to help the mother know what to expect, so that she might take care not to hurry her child on the one hand, and to take full advantage of the need for new experiences on the other, are used instead as ways of comparing one's child with other children, simply to establish how well one is doing as a mother.[9] (p. 20)

At any rate, a relationship with Margaret Mead continued through most of her lifetime and in the mid-1950s she generously agreed to become a member of the Scientific Advisory Board of the Gesell Institute. Though they approached the study of human behavior from almost diametrically opposed points of view, the relationship between Mead and Gesell was both respectful and cordial. She, like William Sheldon, added a good deal of liveliness to the Gesell work and the Gesell Institute.

ARNOLD GESELL AND MARIE MONTESSORI

We find only two references to Montessori in Dr. Gesell's writings—one in 1912, and another in 1923. Both were courteous and extremely guarded. We reproduce them here at some length.

The first of these references appeared in an appendix to Dr. Gesell's *The Normal Child and Primary Education* as follows:

> We add this appendix with some hesitation. After our book was ready for press, we became interested in the accounts of Dr. Marie Montessori's work and the American reception of her much-heralded methods. *There is the usual danger that such methods, because they have taken a concrete form in merchantable apparatus, will be taken over in an ill-considered and half-considered manner.*
>
> While the Montessori Kindergarten, with its social features and its modern expressions of Froebel's philosophy and of Seguin's pedagogy, must surely have something to teach us, *a precipitous adoption of the didactic apparatus all out of its natural setting and needed support will have possibilities of harm as well as of good. The Montessori ideas should at least go through a period of slow, adaptive naturalization instead of being welcomed with an emotional readiness that promises to make Montessorianism a new cult.*[11] (p. 323)

Dr. Gesell gives a brief history of the Montessori movement, and then comments:

> Her experience was first with the abnormal, and her conceptions of education bear the stamp of medicine and physiology, and of experimental rather than genetic psychology.[11] (p. 326) . . . The Montessori system is an eight-hour nursery-kindergarten-school, and not a set of purchasable didactic apparatus.[11] (p. 329) . . . Teaching the kindergarten children to write has been called "the most striking and impressive of Montessori's achievements." . . . Nearly all the pupils learn penmanship at four, and usually it takes only a month or six weeks before they "burst forth into writing." Unthinking people seize upon this achievement as the most important contribution of the Montessori education. It has been overadvertised and so "over-

heralded" that we are left with the impression that American
children can learn to write with ease and economy only by the
Montessori devices. Does this necessarily follow?

In the first place, Montessori makes penmanship a kindergarten operation. A few years ago we were advised, on hygienic
grounds, that children should not be taught reading and writing
until the age of ten . . . (And) there is nothing new in the Montessori method of teaching reading. However, it is still a question when the technique shall be taught.[11] (p. 330)

Dr. Gesell points out especially:

There is no need of teaching the American primary child as
though he were blind. . . . A word of caution is in order with
respect to the general tendency to take over, without criticism,
the findings from experience with subnormal children and to
transfer them to the normal child. Especially is this true of the
learning process. . . . The fact that methods of sensorial training
have proved useful with sense defective and those mentally deficient must therefore be used with caution.[11] (p. 333)

Our school system does not need special devices, technical
apparatus, graduated and systematized processes. . . . Moreover,
the moment that one insists upon elaborate didactic material,
the natural relation of the child to life is in danger.[11] (p. 335)

It is believed by some that this rather negative evaluation of
the Montessori method slowed down, or helped to slow down, the
American acceptance of Montessori by several decades.

Dr. Gesell's second and, to the best of our knowledge, only
other reference to Montessori came in 1923 when he commented:

The much heralded "Houses of Childhood" were a venture
into the field of nursery education. They originated as nursery
schools, established as part of a model tenement enterprise in
Rome, in 1907. These schools kept their children eight hours or
more each day under the socialized maternal control of professional trained directresses, with physicians and caretakers as-
sisting. The daily program included so-called exercises of practical life, such as washing, dressing, dusting, sweeping; gymnastic
exercises, singing, dancing, rhythm work, speech training, serving luncheon, playing in the garden, and sleeping. With the aid
of some 1100 pieces of autosensorial didactic apparatus, children from four to five years old learned to write and read and

cipher with the facility of children of the second and third grades.

This graded sensory and didactic material captured the attention of the public, and was adopted in different countries the world over. In many minds, it became synonymous with "the Montessori Method," although actually the Montessori idea was a socialized type of pedagogical nursery, which could be adopted only by making fundamental social and architectural adjustments such as characterized the original *Casa dei Bambini*. The didactic apparatus was sold in large quantities, both in this country and England, and was introduced into existing kindergartens and infant schools; but without fundamentally altering either their organization or policy. Many of the so-called Montessori schools which opened in the United States were merely more or less progressive kindergartens, with the additional paraphernalia of Montessori apparatus, and with a partial application of her pedagogy; only rarely were they true nursery schools.[12] (pp. 48, 49)

DR. ARNOLD GESELL AND DR. BENJAMIN SPOCK

We include a brief commentary about the relationship, or non-relationship, between Drs. Gesell and Spock because the two men had certain things in common and are often considered more or less together in the public mind. Both were pediatricians, both advised parents, and both were prominent at national and international levels.

Their differences, however, were much greater than their similarities. Though Dr. Gesell did indeed write for parents, he contributed most seriously as a careful scientist. Spock went from the practice of pediatrics to writing for the public, teaching, and administration. Dr. Gesell was an exceedingly private person even after he became well-known. Spock was a much more flamboyant personality who apparently relished publicity.

At any rate, the first and only reference to Spock which we find in Dr. Gesell's writings appeared in 1946, shortly after the publication of Dr. Spock's now famous book which appeared some 3 years after Dr. Gesell's *Infant and Child in the Culture of Today*. We reproduce this review of Spock's book as it appeared in the *New Haven Register* during the month of June 1946:

> Readers of *The Register* will turn with special interest to this book, for its author was born and bred in New Haven. They will

not be disappointed for this is a very valuable and readable volume, crammed with information and practical guidance. The guidance deals chiefly with problems of so-called "physical care;" but Dr. Spock makes it clear that such care is closely bound up with the psychological attitudes and the actions of the parents.

Drawing on his extensive experience as a practising pediatrician, he talks to parents in a friendly, conversational manner which reinforces the usefulness of his hints and counsels. Over five hundred different subjects, listed by number, are concretely considered—subjects which range from abscesses, allergy and air bubbles to worms, wounds and zweiback.

Practical problems of diet and feeding get the lion's share of attention: (about half of the entire volume)—a priority to which the babies themselves would doubtless subscribe. For if parents (and doctors) show common sense in the regulation and methods of feeding, they promote at once mental as well as physical welfare.

In line with the best trends of the day, Dr. Spock encourages breast-feeding and points out the simple measures which would enable many more mothers to nurse their children. He does not favor rigid feeding schedules, but thinks that the baby, through his own language of crying, of gesture, of appetite and preference, should have some voice in the matter.

However, Dr. Spock never waxes dogmatic; so he closes his discussion of self-demand schedules with this calming conclusion: "I don't think it's very important whether a baby is fed purely according to his own demand or whether the mother is working toward a regular schedule—just as long as she is willing to be flexible and adjust to the baby's needs and happiness."

This statement is characteristic of the tone and temper of other sections of the book which deal briefly but sensibly with such topics as illnesses, accidents, infections, stomachaches and upsets, thin children and fat children, glands and posture. Danger signs are pointed out, but not in a manner to unduly worry the reader. Page one carries the caution that the book is not a substitute for the doctor: "Parents who are able to get medical advice by visit and by telephone should always turn to their doctor, not only when a child is not doing well, but for all specific directions about formulas, vitamins, etc."

A final word about the jolly pen-and-ink illustrations by Dorothea Fox. They are delightfully done and they invite you to "Love and enjoy your child, for what he is, for what he looks like, for what he has done, and forget about the qualities that he doesn't have." [13]

There is, however, a postscript to this story. A further relationship, not so much between Spock and Gesell as between Spock and the Gesell Institute developed in 1950. Shortly after our founding (in 1950), we assembled a Scientific Advisory Board. This board consisted of the following members: Drs. Wendell Bennett, Leonard Carmichael, Freddy Homburger, Arthur Jersild, Clarence Cook Little, Margaret Mead, Benjamin Pasamanick, William H. Sheldon, Benjamin Spock, and Helen Thompson.

Dr. Spock, who was an acquaintance of Dr. Frances L. Ilg, joined this board at her invitation. We were extremely appreciative of his acceptance, since our prospects at that time were not at their brightest, and certainly Dr. Spock had nothing to gain by his brief alliance with our group.

He did, then, in the early 1950s, attend one of our Board meetings, at which time he confessed to Dr. Ilg that he just did not "get" age levels. After perhaps a 3-year-term on our Board he asked to be excused because, in his opinion, we did not deal adequately with "emotional factors" in child behavior.

Preceding this relationship of ours with Dr. Spock through his taking part in our Scientific Advisory Board was a request from Spock to Ilg, conveyed in an undated (probably 1944) handwritten letter:

Dear Dr. Ilg:

I would like very much to have you read the manuscript of my baby and child care book, specifically to see if you think that what developmental data is in it is correct, but also for your general suggestions.

As you can see there is relatively little on neuromuscular development, mostly because I don't know enough, but also because, cramming and cutting to get everything in, I have in general kept to topics which have an immediate practicality. It is heavily weighted in the direction of trying to prevent all the common disturbances that I have been constantly dealing with in practice.

If you can do it will you say yes on the postcard. Don't feel that you have to read the whole thing, only the parts that interest you.

Sincerely,
Ben Spock

114 East 9th Street
New York

Dr. Ilg accepted this invitation, read the manuscript, and gave it a favorable rating. However, LBA, whom Dr. Ilg asked to read it, gave (privately) a less favorable estimate. Her evaluation was that "There's nothing here that everybody doesn't know, and he is very weak after two years of age. But it *might* sell."

Arnold Gesell and Sigmund Freud

One has to search diligently to find any mention of Freud in the writings of Arnold Gesell. In 1923, in the index of his book *The Preschool Child*, we find this item: "Freud, Dr. S., p. 120." The reference itself, commenting that someone named Rows has described the case of a mentally ill woman in whom the germ of a serious breakdown 30 years later was laid in her fifth or sixth year, continues:

> In somewhat the same strain, Freud has said: "The little human being is frequently a finished product in his fourth or fifth year and only reveals gradually, in later years, what has long been ready within him."[12] (p. 120)

In 1930 Gesell comments that psychiatry, in its quest for the causes of disorder, carries the interpretations of maladjustment back to adolescence, childhood, infancy, and even to the prenatal period. He then again quotes the above statement from Freud.[14] (p. 315)

In 1938, Gesell, in a discussion of Darwin, observes:

> Sigmund Freud, also in the nineties, approached the broad problem of the origins of the human mind through the avenue of psychopathology and of cultural anthropology. His great contemporary, Pavlov, approached the same problem through the salivary glands of the dog. Both men reinforced the trend toward scientific determinism.[15] (p. 37)

From 1938 on, no reference to Freud appears in the index of any of Dr. Gesell's numerous books. In Gesell's alphabetical card index of topics and people, the name "Freud" does not appear; and there is no evidence of any correspondence between the two men. It seems very safe to say that Dr. Gesell was not influenced by the work of Sigmund Freud.

DR. GESELL AND GEORGE E. COGHILL

Of the numerous scientists whom Dr. Gesell mentioned from time to time, probably the one who influenced him most was George E. Coghill, whose work was first quoted, at length, in Gesell's early (1928) book, *Infancy and Human Growth*.[1] Coghill was not mentioned more than a dozen or so times by Gesell, but the relative infrequency of reference does not diminish his importance. In the 25 years years following 1928, Gesell leaned heavily on Coghill for support and confirmation of his own finding and interpretation that the innate maturation of the nervous system determined its primary structure and that separate reflexes do not grow independently, to be later combined into a total unity but arise by a process of individuation within a primarily integrated total pattern.

Coghill's ideas are so basic to Dr. Gesell's principal work on the patterned development of behavior that we quote this first (1928) reference in full:

> The general problem of maturation has been investigated in great detail by G. E. Coghill in his "Correlated Anatomical and Physiological Studies of the Growth of the Nervous System in Amphibia."* The studies were based on numerous systematic sections of the nervous system, and cell count delineations of the neurones at different levels and stages.
>
> Coghill found that the innate maturation of the nervous system determined its primary structure, and that function or exercise did not even hasten the various types of reaction. He infers that the specificity of nervous structures in terms of behavior is "determined by laws of growth in which the behavior values of the patterns of response have no part."

But he also notes that mere maturation results in stereotyped performance, that even in such a function as swimming "the early growth of association neurones into the motor mechanism introduces unpredictable elements in behavior." This progressive, adap-

---

* Six of these studies have appeared in Volumes 24, 26, 37, 40 and 41 of *The Journal of Comparative Neurology*. The last of these deals with "The Mechanism of Integration in Amblystoma Punctatum." See also G. E. Coghill: "The Growth of Functional Neurones and its Relation to the Development of Behavior." Published in *The Proceedings of the American Philosophical Society*, Vol. 65, no. 1, 1926.

tive mechanization of the association systems is equivalent neuro-embryologically to habituation and conditioning of reflexes.

Although the development of the nervous system of vertebrates does not proceed in a homogeneous manner, it appears from the beginning to maintain the integration of the individual. Separate reflexes do not grow independently to be later combined into a total unity; but "arise by a process of individuation within a primarily integrated total pattern." It is quite conceivable that the integrity of the infant as well as amblystoma is preserved in the same manner. There is no suggestion that the growing complex of infant behavior can be accounted for by a combination of smaller behavior units.

The following conclusion is of such fundamental import for the theoretical interpretation of behavior development, that it should be quoted in full from the author's monograph.*

"The form of the behavior pattern in Amblystoma up to and including locomotion is determined by specific neural counterparts that acquire their specificity in functional value through laws of growth in the nervous system. There is evidence also that mechanisms that condition the performance of such a behavior pattern as locomotion in mammals are determined in the same manner. It is important, therefore, to know how far growth, in the sense of the differentiation of new functional parts of cells, is projected into the life-history of the vertebrate, for so long as it continues it must participate in the function of the nervous system as a whole and, therefore, in the development of the behavior pattern."

Here we glimpse the meaning of growth as opposed to learning in the traditional and somewhat mechanical sense.

> It appears that through growth, experience becomes incorporated into the maturing nervous system. Tanxi and Cajal suggested that function or exercise activated the growth of nerve cells. Coghill holds that the nerve cells grow by their own intrinsic potentiality, and that while growing the nervous mechanisms acquire their behavior specificity.
>
> Not the least value of this conception of the growth of neurones in relation to behavior lies in the constructive effect which it has on the nature versus nurture antithesis. Original growth potency is realized in no foreordained detail. Experience and milieu enter into the very process of growth.[16] (pp. 360–365)

* P. 136, *Journal of Comparative Neurology*, Vol. 41, No. 1, August, 1926. The Wistar Institute Press, Philadelphia, Pa.

A second strong reference to Coghill occurs in 1933.

> In the notable investigations of G. E. Coghill the embryonic development of the nervous system of the salamander (*Amblystoma punctatum*) has been charted in minute detail. These studies have correlated the anatomical and physiological aspects of growth in a way which throws light on the most general principles of behavior patterning. A major conclusion is formulated as follows:

> > "Behavior develops from the beginning through the progressive expansion of a perfectly integrated total pattern and the individuation within it of partial patterns which acquire various degress of discreteness. The mechanism of the total behavior pattern is a growing thing."

> The function of the nervous system is to maintain the integrity of the organism. The nervous system grows according to its own intrinsic pattern and thereby establishes the primary forms of behavior. These forms are not determined by stimulation from the outside world. Experience has nothing specifically to do with them. Coghill has shown that the primary nervous mechanism of walking (in the Amblystoma) is laid down before the animal can at all respond to its environment. Similarly, the sense-organs are the last elements of the vestibular system to maturate:

> > It is possible also that conditioning processes are registered in structural counterparts in the sense that neural mechanisms acquire functional specificity with reference to the experience. In the counterpart of the form of the pattern, the specificity of function is fixed by the relations into which the elements grow. In the counterpart of experience, on the other hand, specificity of function is established by interaction of growth and excitation; that is to say, excitation fixes upon the growing terminals of neurones its own mode of activation.[1] (pp. 213–215)

In 1938, Dr. Gesell gives the following short summary of Coghill's work:

> The work and the career of George E. Coghill furnish solid evidence of the scientific significance of the neuro-physiological approach. His primary interest was psychological, but even as a

graduate student he says, "I became aware that the natural approach to the kind of psychological information I wanted lay through the physiology of the nervous system. Obviously, also, the physiology of the nervous system must be approached through its anatomy, about which I knew nothing." So for thirty years or more he has been making minute studies of the genetic and functional histology of *Amblystoma*, a mere mud puppy. Did he go astray?

Although Coghill has not made a single experiment in psychology, in the orthodox sense, he has already had a profound influence on the biological interpretation of psychological problems. His three lectures on "Anatomy and the Problem of Behavior," delivered in London, bid fair to become classic. The thin volume which contains them belongs on a five foot shelf.[17] (p. 8)

Numerous glancing references to Coghill and his work occur from time to time in Dr. Gesell's writings. Thus in 1939 he notes that:

In discussing the growth of a localized center in a relatively equipotential nervous organ, Coghill has called attention to the fact that structural development agrees in principle with the development of behavior.* We may envisage reciprocal neuromotor interweaving as a spiral kind of organization which applies with equal force to somatic and functional end-products.[18] (p. 179)

However, this and other such references do not add substantially to the basic credit given in the initial 1928–1938 references.

In the following year (1940), in a study—with Ames—on prone progression, Dr. Gesell leans heavily on Coghill, as he points out that:

Coghill, on the basis of observations of Amblystoma, has pointed out that limbs act together under dominance of the trunk before they are ready to act independently of their own accord. He refers particularly to the early stages of locomotion.[19] (p. 257)

In 1941 he noted that:

* Coghill, G. E. Growth of a localized functional center in a relatively equipotential nervous organ. *Archives of Neurol. and Psychiatry*, 1933, vol. *30*, pp. 1086–1091.

Coghill's life work has been devoted to correlated anatomical and physiological studies of the growth of the nervous system in amphibia. His monumental studies are summarized in three London lectures under the title, *Anatomy and the Problem of Behavior,** a slender volume which bids fair to becoming a classic.[20] (p. 185)

Repeated references to Coghill are found in Gesell and Amabruda's *Embryology of Behavior*. Among the more important of these are the following:

Our own indebtedness to Coghill is great. He merged in his remarkable career the labor and the outlook of an anatomist, a neurologist, an embryologist and a philosophical psychologist. Although his lifelong subject was the lowly Amblystoma, his classic volume on anatomy and the problem of behavior has for-reaching implications for the study of mankind. (xi)

The most basic laws of development have wide application. This has been demonstrated by the remarkable researches of George E. Coghill. . . . With the same indomitable tenacity which marked the labors of Darwin, Coghill charted the development of behavior in Amblystoma, particularly in the field of locomotion. These intensive data, interpreted with philosophic insight, led to a concept of integration and individuation which has important implications for the embryology of behavior in higher as well as lower organisms.[21] (pp. 7, 8)

As Coghill has so ably insisted, the organization of behavior expresses itself in both integration and individuation. The two processes are reciprocal. Each implies the other. By individuation, a part of the organism can acquire a degree of individuality in its behavior. The individuality may be so highly localized as to produce what is called a reflex act. But this is not an absolute, unchangeable, fixed condition. It is a fluid, variable, and even reversible condition, for the reflex "can instantaneously *return* to the complete dominance of the individual as a whole and become blended (fused) with the total pattern." We italicize the word *return* to remind us that from an embryological if not a physiological standpoint, the individuated behavior was born without a total growing system.[21] (p. 36)

The embryo, as Coghill's studies of Amblystoma have shown, is perfectly integrated before it has a nervous system.

* Coghill, G. E. *Anatomy and the Problem of Behavior*, Cambridge, England: Cambridge University Press, 1929, pp. xii + 113.

Indeed, there are directing forces, such as gradients of electric potential and external limiting membranes, which guide the growth of the nerve cells under a preneural system of integration.[21] (p. 39)

As Coghill put it, growth *is* the creative function of the nervous system.[21] (p. 189)

In 1946 there is another brief mention of Coghill as Gesell points out that the individual is a member of a species and that his most fundamental behavior characteristics are those which are common to the species as a whole. His specific comment is that:

> The lowly Amblystoma embodies generic patterns of locomotion. This primitive vertebrate in the hands of Coghill has become a touchstone for elucidating problems of human behavior.[22] (p. 295)

A further reference to Coghill ties up Dr. Gesell's acknowledgments to this scientist whose work he found so extremely supportive. This reference will not be quoted since it is substantially the same comment made in his 1938 summary of Coghill and his book, published in 1929. He repeated his accolade: "This thin volume— *Coghill's Anatomy and the Problem of Behavior*—belongs on a five-foot shelf."[23] (p. 50)

It seems altogether possible that this book may have influenced Dr. Gesell, in his thinking and in his work, more than any other single volume. A final reference, in Dr. Gesell's own autobiography, expresses very directly his feelings about Coghill:

> George E. Coghill was to determine the significance of the neurophysiological approach for developmental psychology. His Cambridge lectures are gathered in a thin volume entitled *Anatomy and the Problem of Behavior* which bids fair to become classic. I was a great admirer of Coghill's work. We found common strands of interest in Amblystoma and in the human infant.[24] (p. 134)

Chapter 26

HISTORY OF THE GESELL INSTITUTE

The Gesell Institute of Human Development saw its start in 1911, when Dr. Arnold Gesell, a new (1906) Ph.D. from Clark University accepted an invitation from Professor E. C. Moore, head of the recently formed Department of Education at Yale, to join that department as an Assistant Professor of Education. Dr. Gesell's chief interest at that time was the study of retarded children. Dr. George Blumer, Dean of the Medical School, provided him with a room* in the New Haven Dispensary on Congress Avenue and appointed him Director of what was then called the Juvenile Psycho Clinic. He had one assistant, Margaret Cobb Rogers.

Problems of mental defect and handicap were for Dr. Gesell an early and strong concern. He was firmly intent on bringing these problems to the attention of both public and professional, his thesis being that it is the responsibility of the public to help schools and families with the care and education of those with less than normal endowment. Twenty-three of the 64 publications that he authored between 1913 and 1926 dealt with these topics.

Having started medical school at the University of Wisconsin in 1910–1911, Dr. Gesell continued his medical studies and received

* A modest beginning for work which would one day be known around the world.

his M.D. from Yale in 1915. Shortly after this he was promoted to a full professorship in the Yale Graduate School with the condition that he devote part of his time to serving as school psychologist for the State Board of Education of Connecticut. Dr. Gesell was the first school psychologist in the United States.

In 1918, he undertook a mental survey of the elementary schools in New Haven and wrote a report entitled "Exceptional Children and Public School Policy" which had much to do with the development of an excellent system of special classes in this city. He also prepared a manual titled "What Can the Teacher Do for the Deficient Child?"

Gesell's work with and his interest in defect and deviation continued and, very early, found a new interest in charting the infant and childhood behavior of presumably normal infants. As he often put it, in his office at the New Haven Dispensary, he was "in auditory communication, at least" with infants in the Well Baby Clinic. He believed very firmly that human behavior develops in a patterned, predictable way and it was his purpose to provide norms of human behavior which could be used in the diagnosis of normal, deviant, and defective behavior. He soon came to the conclusion that such studies should begin in infancy. He thus began to follow a trail which continued throughout his lifetime.

However, his interests and activities were always multifold. During these early years, from 1911 to 1920, he worked in the public schools, did what he could to improve the understanding and conditions of the retarded, offered courses in the Yale graduate school, pursued a clinical practice, and began his research in the development of infant and preschool behavior.

In 1920, Dr. Gesell moved the base of his operations to 28 Hillhouse Avenue and the title of his clinic was shortened to (Yale) Psycho Clinic. His staff seems still to have been extremely small. Our records note that in 1922 "Elizabeth Evans Lord replaced Margaret E. Cobb." His publications continued to deal chiefly with defect, but also reflected a beginning interest in twins. In the year 1923–1924 he saw 581 clinical cases in addition to his research work and public service.

A big year for Dr. Gesell's Clinic was 1925. A second assistant, Dr. Ruth W. Washburn, was added to his staff, and his first normative publication, *The Mental Growth of the Preschool Child*, appeared. This volume was amply illustrated with photographs—a strong interest in photography having preceded his later vigorous interest in the use of the cinema. His publications in 1925 numbered 17. Clinical and teaching work continued.

In 1926 the Psycho Clinic moved once again, this time to attractive and commodious quarters at 52 Hillhouse Avenue. Due to a generous grant from the Laura Spelman Rockefeller Fund, money was made available for photograph research. This led to the building of a photographic laboratory at the clinic, a laboratory which eventually provided miles of film which became the basis for photographic research for years to come and also later provided the data for the two *Photographic Atlases of Infant Behavior*.

In 1927 nearly a thousand clinical cases were seen, another major book publication, *Infancy and Human Growth*, was published, and Dr. Gesell's staff had grown to nine, including Drs. Castner, Halverson, and Thompson, who remained as active staff members until 1940. By 1928 the staff had increased to 12, and the following year Dr. Catherine Strunk Amatruda joined the group. A Nursery School was begun under the direction of Anne Jennings.

In 1930 came another major move. Dr. Gesell and his clinic, now named the Yale Clinic of Child Development, moved from 52 Hillhouse Avenue to one wing of the Institute of Human Relations at 14 Davenport Avenue. This setting provided elegant and extensive quarters for the now expanded clinic. Dr. Gesell himself occupied an entire floor which included an office for him, offices for his research assistant and private secretary, a conference room and a library and lounge. On the floor above was a "sun nursery," for research and photography, and a so-called residence suite (a small apartment) where children being studied, and their caretakers, could live. On the four floors below were offices for a staff of 31, the famous Photographic Dome, examining rooms, an attractive and commodious nursery school, and work rooms where films were developed, stored, analyzed, and edited. This physical setting was, indeed, rather splendid, though Dr. Gesell always emphasized that one by no means needs a large or elegant setting to carry on developmental examining and/or research.

The setting was not only elegant but also formal and business-like. Dr. Gesell at one time, as he left for a lecture tour, warned his staff that there was to be "no informality" at the Clinic while he was gone. Staff all worked hard and Dr. Gesell the hardest of all. He now gave numerous course to the graduate students; continued his research, writing, and film making; served on numerous state and national committees and boards as well as on editorial boards of journals; and supervised the work of staff, gradute students, and fellows. (In 1932 Dr. Frances L. Ilg joined the group as a fellow, and in 1933 Louise Bates Ames arrived as a graduate student and research assistant.) By the end of 1934 Dr. Gesell's publications numbered close to 200—some already in translation.

Areas of research interest by now included: A further refinement of developmental norms, twinning, defect, and deviation, cinemanalysis, individuality, theoretical considerations of the interaction between heredity and environment, the pediatrician's role in evaluating development, school behavior with special emphasis on the preschool, mental hygiene, parent guidance, adoption, fetal behavior.

All went smoothly for the next years, until 1940, when Yale's Institute of Human Relations more or less went out of business. Its epitaph was written by a *Time* reporter, whose summary was to the effect that the Institute, "under pipesmoking Mark May" had spent 10 years and $10 million, but that with the exception of Dr. Gesell's Clinic of Child Development and Robert M. Yerkes's Department of Primate Biology, had wandered all over the place and come up with very little of any value.

This Institute, then, whose premature aim had been to bring together and integrate the work of the various disciplines dealing with human behavior, collapsed, and with it its supporting funds. This meant that those departments which were continued had to be absorbed by other departments. We, fortunately, were absorbed by the Medical School. Thus our basic work was actually not interrupted, though Dr. Gesell was forced to dispense with the service of most of the psychologists on the staff—Professor Halverson, Dr. Castner, and Dr. Helen Thompson. The major staff, from 1940 to 1948, then consisted of Gesell, Ilg, Amatruda, and Ames, plus Janet Learned, and a fairly large nursery school and secretarial staff, as well as graduate students and bursary students. Richard N. Walker joined our group during these years as a bursary student.

In spite of the smaller staff, work flourished. Dr. Gesell's publications in those years amounted to well over 100, including such major books as *The First Five Years of Life, Wolf Child and Human Child, Developmental Diagnosis, Infant and Child in the Culture of Today, How a Baby Grows, The Child from Five to Ten, Vision: Its Development in Infant and Child,* and over half-a-dozen films.

Two of these books, *Infant and Child,* and *The Child from Five to Ten,* reflect an entirely new turn which the Gesell work, due to the inspiration of Dr. Ilg, had taken. It was her suggestion that not only individual human beings but actually the ages themselves each have their own characteristic personality or individuality.

All in all, it would be fair to say that during these years we were on top of the world (except for a scare one afternoon when it was thought that German warplanes were about to attack). So far as we knew, we had few rivals. Visitors came in large numbers from all over the world. In the year 1946–1947 we had 1,060 visitors; in 1947–1948, 1,049. In that latter year people came from, among other countries. South Africa, South America, China, India, Canada, Hawaii, the Philippines, Austria, Belgium, Czechoslovakia, , Denmark, France, Holland, Italy, Poland, Norway, Sweden. Our books were translated into some 20 or more languages.

Though Dr. Gesell was extremely cautious about publicity—he tended to shun it rather than to seek it—his work attracted a good deal of attention. In fact former Mayor Richard E. Lee of New Haven (at that time Director of Publicity for Yale) once commented that Dr. Gesell turned down more publicity than he (Lee) could attract for Yale. *Life, Time, Readers' Digest, Colliers* and many other popular magazines featured his work. *The American Scientist*, in October 1949, commented of Dr. Gesell: "In 1915 he was appointed Professor of Child Hygiene at Yale, a field in which he retains undisputed leadership."

We were, of course, fully aware that by 1948 Dr. Gesell would be required, by custom, to resign his position at Yale. We assumed that our new Director would be someone of impressive stature, exciting to work with and, needless to say, one who admired and respected the Gesell work. We thus did not believe the rumors, spread by secretaries and janitors, that Yale was going to get rid of our Clinic.

The rumor, unfortunately, turned out to be true. The University formed a committee on Child Development—consisting of Grover Powers, Neal Miller, Mark May, Professor Hill from Education, and one or two others, to "decide what Yale would do about Child Development." What they decided to do was, indeed, to get rid of us. Dr. Milton J. E. Senn was engaged to direct this dismemberment.

We *were* permitted 2 "transition years," financially supported by a grant of close to $100,000 from the American Optical Company to underwrite a new interest of Dr. Gesell's—the study of the development of vision in infant and child. This special work was carried out

Figure 26-1. Three locations of Gesell's work. (Top) Yale Clinic of Child Development, 52 Hillhouse, New Haven, Connecticut. (Bottom) YCCD at 14 Davenport, New Haven, Connecticut. (Right) Gesell Institute, 310 Prospect, New Haven, Connecticut.

by Drs. Gesell and Ilg, assisted by Glenna Bullis and Dr. Richard Apell, who joined our staff at this time. Some fragments of the Gesell work continued briefly at our old location, renamed the Yale Child Study Center. Dr. Catherine Amatruda remained there for a year, until her sudden death in the Fall of 1949; and LBA remained for one year and during a second year was relocated in the Medical School Library as Curator of the Yale Films of Child Development. Janet Learned was retained as head of the Nursery School.

By the spring of 1950 our 2 years of grace were approaching their termination and the Gesell staff were forced to make a decision about the future—would we accept individual jobs wherever they were offered or would we try to stay together as a group. Yale suggested, through Dean Long, that we go to California. We decided to stay in New Haven, partly for personal reasons and partly because we wished to remain with our basic research group of boys and girls, now most of them eleven years of age and being followed for inclusion in a forthcoming study of adolescents.

Through the generosity of Dr. Ilg we were able to buy the land

and building at 310 Prospect Street and there in March 1950, Drs. Ilg and Ames, and Janet Learned founded the Gesell Institute in honor of Dr. Gesell, who joined our group as Research Consultant. Dr. Richard J. Apell came with us as Staff Optometrist. A Nursery School was begun after the acquisition, the following year, of the property at 314 Prospect Street. Since there were no funds available (and none forthcoming) most of the staff worked for the first two years without salaries.

But the work continued as before. Our special areas of interest at this time were the continuation of our longitudinal study of age differences which culminated, in 1956, in the publication *Youth: The Years from Ten to Sixteen*; a beginning study of projective techniques which yielded three books on the Rorschach and one on the Lowenfeld Mosaic Test; a beginning study of Constitutional Psychology, undertaken with the help of Dr. William H. Sheldon; a clinical approach to the study of vision; research into the developmental aspects of aging; and perhaps most significant of all, research in the general area of school readiness. Our clinical service accepted children from infancy through the teens.

Financial support finally appeared (and in the nick of time) in the spring of 1952 when Robert M. Hall, President of the Post-Hall Syndicate, invited us to write a syndicated daily newspaper column. This column was an immediate success. We started with 30 newspapers and fairly soon were writing for 65 of the major papers in the country, including *The New York World Telegram, Washington Post, Boston Globe, Philadelphia Bulletin, Pittsburgh Post-Gazette, New Orleans Times-Picayune, Los Angeles Times, New Haven Register,* and the *San Francisco Chronicle.* Our papers spanned the country from Portland, Maine to Portland, Oregon and we had literally millions of daily readers.

The newspaper column soon spread to television when, through the support of the *Boston Globe* we began a live weekly broadcast over Station WBZ in Boston. The earnings from column and television kept us going until the clinical service caught on and funds became available from other sources, including the Old Dominion and Ford Foundations.

Richard N. Walker returned from graduate school; the Vision Department attracted interns and students; research assistants abounded. In addition, in 1966 Clyde Gillespie joined the Staff and in 1969, Jackie Haines.

The years from 1950 to 1972, when Dr. Ilg retired and Ames

and Apell took over as co-directors were wild and wonderful—exciting, demanding, rewarding, and cliff-hanging. (The full story of these years may be told later, in some other context.) Money, or the lack of it, was always a prime concern. However, the work went on uninterrupted. During these fruitful years we saw a full schedule of clinical cases, ran a busy nursery school, published our daily newspaper column, produced a weekly syndicated TV series from Station WEWS in Cleveland, lectured extensively, produced nine major books and over 100 scientific articles, and expanded our work on school readiness through workshops.

Special mention should be made of the firm support we received during all of these years from our Scientific Advisory and Corporate Boards, which included, among others, such individuals as Freddy Homburger, John I. Taylor, John Fedoruk, Felix Drury, G. Harold Welch, Jr., Frank Logue, Jan Stolwijk, Howard Kahn, and Drs. William H. Sheldon, Margaret Mead, and Benjamin Spock.

From 1972 on, we undertook a vigorous search for a new Director. It was our good fortune that such an individual came our way in the person of Dr. Sidney M. Baker. On March 28, 1978, the Corporate Board voted to appoint Dr. Baker Executive Director of the Institute, a position which he held from 1978 to 1987. Dr. Baker currently holds the position of Director of Medical Research. He was succeeded briefly as Director of the Institute by Dr. Erik Esselstyn. In 1988 he was succeeded by Frank Logue, former Mayor of New Haven and our present Director.

We have closed our nursery school and modernized that building. It now houses the nationwide Seminar and Workshop Division of the Developmental Department. The Developmental, clinical, visual, pediatric, nutritional, and research staffs are now housed in the newly renovated building at 310 Prospect Street, our original home since we left the University.

REFERENCES

Chapter 1

1. Gesell, A. Mental hygiene and the public school. *Mental Hygiene*, 1919, *3*, 4–10.
2. Gesell, A. Kindergarten control of school entrance. *School and Society*, 1921, *14*, no. 364, 559–565.
3. Gesell, A. *The Preschool child from the standpoint of public hygiene and education.* New York: Houghton Mifflin, 1923, vii + 264.
4. Gesell, A. The preschool age and school entrance. *School Health Studies*, 1924, *8*, 6–8.
5. Gesell, A., & Gesell, B. *The normal child and primary education.* New York: Ginn & Company, 1912, viii + 342.
6. Gesell, A. The special province of child hygiene in the public school. *The Child*, January, 1913, 1–6.
7. Ilg, F. L. & Ames, L. B. *School readiness.* New York: Harper & Row, 1964, xv + 396.

Chapter 2

1. Miles, W. R. *Arnold Lucius Gesell 1880–1961. A biographical memoir.* Reprint from *Biographical Memoirs*, xxxvii, New York: Columbia University Press, 1964, 55–96.

2. Gesell, A. The village of a thousand souls. *The American Magazine,* 1913, *76,* 11–16.

3. Gesell, A. The university in relation to the problems of mental deficiency and child hygiene. *Transactions of 4th International Congress of School Hygiene,* 1913, *5,* 613–621.

4. Gesell, A. *What can the teacher do for the deficient child? A manual for teachers in rural and graded schools.* Conn. School Document No. 5, Whole No. 425, 1918, 1–47.

5. Gesell, A. Feebleminded children in the country home schools of Connecticut. *Connecticut Bulletin, 72,* Series 1917–1918 pp. 3–11.

6. Gesell, A. A follow-up study of one hundred mentally deficient school children. *Connecticut State Board of Education Bulletin, 26,* Series 1918–1919.

7. Gesell, A. Special provisions for exceptional school children. *Connecticut School Document,* February, 1919, 1–76.

8. Gesell, A. *Announcement of a one-month course for the training of teachers of backward and deficient children at New Haven, Connecticut.* April 28 to May 24, 1919.

9. Gesell, A. Mental diagnosis and special education. *University State of New York Bulletin, No. 702,* January 15, 1920, 73–79.

10. Gesell, A. The problem of mental subnormality. *Bulletin Child Welfare,* 1920, May 24, *no. 1.*

11. Gesell, A. Review, H. H. Goddard, Psychology of the normal and subnormal. *Psychology Bulletin.* 1920, *4,* 131–133.

12. Gesell, A. Vocational probation for subnormal youth. *Mental Hygiene,* 1921, *2,* 321–326.

13. Gesell, A. Public school provision for exceptional children. *Annals American Academy Political and Social Science,* 1921, *98,* 73–80.

14. Gesell, A. *Exceptional children and public school policy, including a mental survey of the New Haven elementary schools.* New Haven: Yale University Press, 1921, 1–66.

15. Gesell, A. Report of the Commission on Child Welfare to the Governor: Handicapped children in school and court. *State of Connecticut Public Document.* Hartford, Conn., 1921, Chapter 355, Public Acts of the State of Connecticut.

16. Gesell, A. Hemihypertrophy and mental defect. *Archives Neurology & Psychiatry,* 1921, *6,* 400–423.

17. Gesell, A. The pre-school hygiene of handicapped children. *Pedagogical Seminary,* 1922, *3,* 232–236.

18. Gesell, A. Feeble-mindedness: state policy of control. *Nation's Health,* 1923, *3,* 1–3.

19. Gesell, A. The exceptional child. *Kindergarten and First Grade Magazine*, 1925, *46*, 5, p. 46.

20. Gesell, A. The early diagnosis of mental deficiency. *The National Review of Reviews*, 1925, *4*, 192–194.

21. Gesell, A. Developmental diagnosis in infancy. *Boston Medical and Surgical Journal*, 1925, *192*, 1058–1064.

22. Gesell, A. *The retarded child: How to help him.* Bloomington, Ill.: Public School Publishing Co., 1925, 1–100.

23. Gesell, A. *The mental growth of the preschool child.* New York: Macmillan, 1925, x + 477.

24. Gesell, A. The influence of Puberty Praecox upon mental growth. *Genetic Psychology Monographs*, 1926, *1*, 6, 511–539.

25. Gesell, A. Precocious puberty and mental maturation. *Twenty-seventh Yearbook of the National Society for the Study of Education*, 1928, *Part 1*. Bloomington, Ill.: The Public School Publishing Co., 299–409.

26. Gesell, A. Precocious pubescence and mental growth. *Journal American Medical Association*, March 1928, *90*, 840–841.

27. Gesell, A., Thoms H., Hartman, F. G., & Thompson, H. Mental and physical growth in pubertas praecox. *Archives of Neurology & Psychiatry*, April 1939, *41*, 755–722.

28. Gesell, A. et al. *Biographies of child development.* New York: Hoeber, 1939, xvii + 312.

29. Gesell, A., & Amatruda, S. *Developmental diagnosis.* New York: Hoeber, 1941, xii + 447.

30. Gesell, A., & Amatruda, S. Hemihypertrophy and twinning: A further study of the nature of hemihypertrophy with report of a new case. *American Journal Medical Science*, 1927, *173*, 542–555.

31. Gesell, A., & Amatruda, S. Clinical mongolism in colored races, with report of a case of Negro mongolism. *Journal American Medical Association*, 1936, *106*, 1146–1150.

32. Gesell, A., & Amatruda, S. A comparative study of six infant cretins under treatment: Influence of thyroid on mental growth. *American Journal Dis. Child.*, 1936, *51*, 1236–1242.

33. Gesell, A., Amatruda, Catherine, S., & Culotta, C. S. Effect of thyroid therpy on the mental and physical growth of cretinous infants. *American Journal Diseases Child*, 1936, *52*, 1117–1138.

34. Gesell, A. et al. Motor disability and mental growth: The psychological effects of cerebral birth palsy. *Psychological Record*, 1937, *1*, 87–94.

35. Gesell, A. , & Zimmerman, H. Correlations of behavior and neuropathology in a case of cerebral palsy from birth injury. *American Journal of Psychiatry*, 1937, *94*, 505–536.

36. Gesell, A. A behavior study of birth injury. A correlation of psychological and neurological findings in a case of cerebral palsy with double athetosis. *Journal of Psycho-asthenics*, 1937, *43*, 37–43.

37. Gesell, A. Developmental diagnosis and guidance for the palsied child. *The Physical Therapy Review*, 1948, *28*, 128–129.

38. Gesell, A. Cerebral palsy research and the preschool years. *Postgraduate Medicine*, 1954, *15*, 104–108.

39. Gesell, A. Foreword to *Proceedings of the Annual Meeting of the American Academy for Cerebral Palsy*. Fort Worth, Texas, Oct. 30, 31, 1953.

40. Gesell, A. Diagnosis and supervision of mental growth in infancy. Chapter IX, in Vol. 1 *Brennemann, practice of pediatrics*. Hagerstown, Maryland: W. F. Prior Co., Inc., 1936, 3419.

41. Knobloch, H., & Pasamanick, B., (Eds.) *Gesell & Amatruda, developmental diagnosis*. (3rd Ed.) New York: Harper & Row, 1974.

42. Knobloch, H., Stevens, F., & Malone, A. F. *Manual of developmental diagnosis*. New York: Harper & Row, 1980, xiii + 286.

43. Gesell, A. Introduction, H. M. Smith, *Management of the handicapped child*. New York: Grune & Stratton, 1957.

44. Gesell, A. Early diagnosis of behavior defects and deviations. From Symposium on Behavior Problems in Children. *Journal Connecticut State Medical Society*, 1939, *3*, 1–4.

45. Gesell, A. The differential diagnosis of mental deficiency in infancy. *Clinics*, 1943, *2*, 294–308.

46. Gesell, A. Differential diagnosis of mental deficiency in infancy. *The Nebraska State Medical Journal*, 1947, *32*, 304–307.

47. Gesell, A. The clinical supervision of child development. *Centaur* (Menasha), 1948, *53*, 139–144.

48. Gesell, A. Introduction, H. M. Smith, *Management of the handicapped child*, New York: Grune & Stratton, 1957.

CHAPTER 3

1. Gesell, A., & Gesell, B. *The normal child and primary education*. New York: Ginn & Co., 1912, x + 342.

2. Gesell, A. Mental hygiene and the public school. *Mental Hygiene*, 1919, *3*, 1, 4–7.

3. Gesell, A. *Exceptional children and public school policy, Including a mental survey of the New Haven public schools*. New Haven, Conn.: Yale University Press, 1921, 66 pp.

4. Gesell, A. The significance of the pre-school age for school hygiene.

Proceedings of the Thirteenth Congress of the American School Hygiene Association, 1921, *9*, 24–31.

5. Gesell, A. A mental hygiene service for pre-school children. *American Journal of Public Health*, 1922, *12*, 1030–1034.

6. Gesell, A. *The preschool child.* Boston: Houghton Mifflin, 1923, xv + 264.

7. Burnham, W. H. *The normal mind.* New York: D. Appleton & Co., 1924, xviii + 702

8. Beers, C. *The mind that found itself.* New York: Longmans, Green, 1908.

9. Gesell, A. The nursery school movement. *School and society*, 1924, *517*, 9, 644–652.

10. Gesell, A. The importance of considering the mental hygiene of the pre-school child. *Western Hospital and Nurses' Review*, 1925, *6*, 1, pp. 19, 26.

11. Gesell, A. *The mental growth of the pre-school child.* New York: Macmillan, 1925, x + 447.

12. Gesell, A. The kindergarten as a mental-hygiene agency. *Mental Hygiene*, 1926, *10*, 1, 27–37.

13. Gesell, A. Mental hygiene measures for pre-school children. *The Child*, 1926, *16*, 7, 193–197.

14. Gesell, A. Normal growth as a public health concept. *Public Health Nurse*, 1926, *18*, 394–399.

15. Gesell, A. Child mental welfare paramount. *Michigan Education Journal*, 1929, *7*, 164–165.

16. Gesell, A. A decade of progress in the mental hygiene of the preschool child. *Annals of the American Academy of Political and Social Science*, 1930, Pub. # 2428, *151*, 143–148.

17. Gesell, A. Announcement: The First International Congress on Mental Hygiene Held at the Yale Clinic of Child Development at Yale University, May 9, 1930.

18. Gesell, A. Mental hygiene and the public school system. *Bulletin Assoc. School Boards and Trustees State of New York*, 1930, 2, 7–9.

19. Gesell, A. *The guidance of mental growth in infant and child.* New York: Macmillan, 1930, xi + 322.

20. Gesell, A. *Letter* to Dr. Welch re. Clifford Beers, Feb. 17, 1933.

21. Gesell, A. The mental welfare of normal infants. *Public Health Nursing*, 1934, *25*, 5, 229–232.

22. Gesell, A. The day nursery as a mental hygiene agency. *Day Nursery*, 1940, *1*, 1–3.

23. Gesell, A. et al. *The first five years of life.* New York: Harper, 1940, xiii + 393.

24. Gesell, A., & Amatruda, C. S. *Developmental diagnosis.* New York: Hoeber, 1941, xiii + 447.

25. Gesell, A. The protection of early mental growth. *American Journal of Orthopsychiatry,* 1941, *11*, 3, 498–502.

26. Gesell, A., Ilg, F. L., Ames, L. B., & Learned, J. *Infant and child in the culture of today.* New York: Harper, 1943, xii + 399.

27. Gesell, A. Pediatrics and child psychiatry. *Pediatrics,* 1949, *4*, 670–676.

28. Burnham, W. H. Mental hygiene for normal children. *Mental Hygiene,* 1918, *2*, 19–22.

29. Taft, J. Supervision of the feebleminded in the community. *Mental Hygiene,* 1918, *2*, 434–442.

30. Berence, L. The mental hygiene of the educator. *Mental Hygiene,* 1954, *38*, 426–433.

CHAPTER 4

1. Gesell, A., & Gesell, B. *The normal child and primary education.* Boston: Ginn & Co., 1912, x + 342.

2. Gesell, A. The special province of child hygiene in the primary school. *The Child,* 1913, *6*, 1–6.

3. Gesell, A. Mental hygiene and the public school. *Mental Hygiene,* 1919, *1*, 4–10.

4. Gesell, A. *The preschool child from the standpoint of public hygiene and education,* Boston: Houghton Mifflin, 1923, xi + 264.

5. Gesell, A. A decade of progress in the mental hygiene of the preschool child. *The Annals of the American Academy of Political and Social Science,* 1930, Pub. No. 2428, *151*, 143–148.

6. Gesell, A. The mental welfare of normal infants. *Public Health Nursing,* 1934, *5*, 229–232.

7. Gesell, A. The protection of early mental growth. *American Journal Orthopsychiatry,* 1941, *11*, 498–502.

8. Gesell, A. The significance of the preschool age for school hygiene. *Proc. 13th Congress of American School Hygiene Association,* 1921, *9*, 24–31.

9. Gesell, A., & Abbott, J. W. The kindergarten and health. *Health Education,* 1923, 14, 1–37.

10. Gesell, A. The preschool child as a health problem. *American Journal of Nursing,* 1923, 1–4.

11. Gesell, A. Mental development in infancy: its measurement and hygiene. New York Times, Sunday, January 21, 1923.

12. Gesell, A. The preschool age and school entrance. Dept. of Interior, *Bureau of Education Publication*, 1924, 6–8.

13. Gesell, A. The baby in the house of health. *Childhood Education*, 1926, August, 1–32.

14. Gesell, A., & Ilg, F. L. *Feeding behavior of infants.* Philadelphia: Lippincott, 1937, ix + 201.

15. Gesell, A., & Amatruda, C. S. *Developmental diagnosis.* New York: Hoeber, 1941, xii + 447.

16. Gesell, A., Ilg, F. L., Ames, L. B., & Learned, J. *Infant and child in the culture of today.* New York: Harper, 1943, xii + 388.

17. Gesell, A., & Ilg, F. L. In collaboration with Louise Bates Ames and Glenna Bullis. *The child from five to ten.* (rev. Ed.) New York: Harper & Row, 1974, xviii + 460.

18. Gesell, A., Ilg, F. L., & Ames, L. B. *Youth: The years from ten to sixteen.* New York: Harper, 1956, xvi + 542.

CHAPTER 5

1. Gesell, A., Ilg, F. L., & Bullis, G. E. *Vision: Its development in infant and child.* New York: Paul B. Hoeber, Inc., 1949, xvi + 329.

2. Gesell, A., & Gesell, B. C. *The normal child and primary education.* Boston: Ginn & Co., x + 342.

3. Gesell, A. The special province of child hygiene in the primary school. *The Child*, 1913, *6*, 1–6.

4. Gesell, A. Public school provision for exceptional children. *Annals of the American Academy*, 1921, *98*, 73–80.

5. Gesell, A. The preschool hygiene of handicapped children. The *Pedagogical Seminary and Journal of Genetic Psychology*, 1922, *29*, 232–246.

6. Gesell, A. *The preschool child from the standpoint of public hygiene and education.* Boston: Houghton Mifflin, 1923, xv + 264.

7. Gesell, A. Monthly increments of development in infancy. *The Pedagogical Seminary and Journal of Genetic Psychology*, 1925, *32*, 203–208.

8. Gesell, A. *The mental growth of the preschool child.* New York: Macmillan 1925, x + 447.

9. Gesell, A., & Thompson, H. *Infant behavior: Its genesis and growth.* New York: McGraw Hill, 1934, viii + 343.

10. Gesell, A., & Thompson, H. *The psychology of early growth.* New York: Macmillan, 1938, ix + 290.

11. Gesell, A., & Blake, E. Twinning and ocular pathology. *Archives of Ophthalmology*, 1930, *15*, 1050–1071.

12. Gesell, A., & Zimmerman, H. M. Correlations of behavior and neuropathology in a case of cerebral palsy from birth injury. *American Journal of Psychiatry*, 1927, *94*, 505–536.

13. Gesell, A. et al. *Biographies of child development.* New York: Paul B. Hoeber, 1939, xvii + 328.

14. Gesell, A. et al. *The first five years of life.* New York: Harper, 1940, xiii + 393.

15. McGinnis, J. Eye movements and optic nystagmus in early infancy. *Genetic Psychological Monographs*, 1930, *8*, 321–430.

16. Gesell, A., & Amatruda, C. S. *Developmental diagnosis.* New York: Paul B. Hoeber, 1941, xii + 447.

17. Gesell, A., Ilg, F. L., Ames, L. B., & Learned, J. *Infant and child in the culture of today.* New York: Harper, 1943, xii + 399.

18. Gesell, A., Ilg, F. L., Ames, L. B., & Bullis, G. E. *The child from five to ten.* New York: Harper, 1946, viii + 492.

19. Gesell, A., Ilg, F. L., & Ames, L. B. *Youth: The years from ten to sixteen.* New York: Harper, 1956, xv + 542.

20. Gesell, A. *How a baby grows: A story in pictures.* New York: Harper, 1945, 78 pp.

21. Gesell, A. *The embryology of behavior.* New York: Harper, 1945, xix + 289.

22. Gesell, A., & Ames, L. B. *Self discovery in the mirror.* A 400 foot 16 mm. film distributed by Encyclopaedia Britannica, 1947.

23. Gesell, A., & Ames, L. B. The infant's reaction to his mirror image. *Journal Genetic Psychology*, 1947, *70*, 155–175.

24. Gesell, A. The developmental aspect of vision. *Science*, 1949, *109*, p. 342.

25. Gesell, A. The developmental aspect of child vision. *Journal of Pediatrics*, 1949, *35*, 310–316.

26. Gesell, A. Development of vision in childhood. *Modern Medicine*, 1949, *18*, 80–83.

27. Gesell, A., et al. *The embryology of human behavior.* A 30-minute 16 mm. sound film (in color). Chicago: Medical Film Institute of American Medical Colleges in cooperation with the Bureau of Medicine and Surgery and Office of Naval Research, 1950.

28. ` Gesell, A. Infant vision. *Scientific American*, 1950, *182*, 20–22.

29. Gesell, A. Child vision and developmental optics. *L'Anneé psychologique*, 1951, *50*, 379–395.

30. Gesell, A. *Infant development: The embryology of early human behavior.* New York: Harper, 1952, xi + 108.

31. Gesell, A. Development of the infant with retrolental fibroplastic blindness. *The Field of Vision.* New York: Harcourt Brace, 1953, ix, + 1–2.
32. Ames, L. B., Streff, J. W., & Gillespie, C. *Stop School Failure* (rev ed.). Flemington, New Jersey: Programs for Education, 1985.

CHAPTER 6

1. Gesell, A. Mental hygiene and the public school. *Mental Hygiene,* January, 1919, *3*, 1, p. 4–10.
2. Gesell, A. Kindergarten control of school entrance. *School and Society,* 1921, no. 364, p. 559–565.
3. Gesell, A. *The Preschool Child.* Boston: Houghton Mifflin, 1923, xv + 264.
4. Gesell, A., & Abbott, J. W. *The Kindergarten and Health.* Washington, D.C. Department of the Interior, Bureau of Education, 1923, pp. 24–29.
5. Gesell, A. The nursery school movement. *School and Society,* 1924, November 22, *20*, no. 517, p. 644–652.
6. Gesell, A. The downward extension of the kindergarten: A unified policy for early education. *Childhood Education,* October, 1925, *2*, 2, pp. 53–59.
7. Gesell, A. The kindergarten as a mental hygiene agency. *Mental Hygiene,* January 1926, *10*, 1, pp. 27–37.
8. Gesell, A., & Washburn, R. Special guidance for exceptional kindergarten children. *Childhood Education,* February 1926, *2*, 6. pp. 261–268.
9. Gesell, A. *Mental hygiene and the public school system.* Bulletin of the Associated School Boards and Trustees of the State of New York. Mt. Vernon, New York: November, 1930, *11*, 4, pp. 7–9.
10. Gesell, A. The American kindergarten. *N.E.A. Journal,* "after September 12, 1932."
11. Gesell, A. Looking backward: to a demonstration kindergarten, 1876. *Childhood Education,* January 1934, *10*, 4, pp. 171, 172.
12. Gesell, A., & Ilg, F. L. *The child from five to ten.* New York: Harper & Row, 1946, xii + 473.

CHAPTER 7

1. Gesell, A. Hemihypertrophy and mental defect. *Archives of Neurology and Psychiatry,* 1921, *6*, 400–423 (Reprint page numbers 1–24).

2. Gesell, A. Hemihypertrophy and twinning: A further study of the nature of hemihypertrophy with report of a new case. *American Journal Medical Science*, 1927, *173*, 5, 542–555.

3. Gesell, A. et al. *Biographies of child development: The mental growth careers of eighty-four infants and children.* New York: Hoeber, 1939, xvii + 312.

4. Gesell, A. Mental and physical correspondence in twins. *The Scientific Monthly*, 1922, *xiv*, Nos. 4 & 5, 305–344.

5. Gesell, A. A psychological comparison of superior duplicate twins. Abstract of paper given at the Thirtieth Annual Meeting of the American Psychological Association. *Psychological Bulletin*, 1922, *19*, 3.

6. Gesell, A. Twins again. *The Scientific Monthly*, 1922, *13*, 93–96.

7. Gesell, A. Every man his own twin. *Literary Digest*, May 20, 1922, p. 21.

8. Gesell, A., & Thompson, H. Learning and growth in identical infant twins. Abstract of paper given at the Thirty-seventh Annual Meeting of the American Psychological Association. *Psychological Bulletin*, 1929, *26*.

9. Gesell, A., & Thompson, H. Learning and growth in identical twins. *Genetic Psychology Monographs*, 1929, *6*, 1, 1–124.

10. Gesell, A., & Thompson, H. Twins T and C from infancy to adolescence: A biogenetic study of individual differences by the method of co-twin control. *Genetic Psychology Monographs*, 1941, *24*, 3–121

11. Strayer, L. C. Language and growth: The relative efficacy of early and deferred language training studied by the method of co-twin control. *Genetic Psychology Monographs*, 1930, *8*, 249–359.

12. Hilgard, J. The effect of early and delayed practice on memory and motor performance studied by the method of co-twin control. *Genetic Psychology Monographs*, 1933, *14*, 493–567.

13. Gesell, A. The developmental psychology of twins. In Murchison, C. *A Handbook of Child Psychology*. Worcester, Mass.: Clark University Press, 1931, pages 158–203.

14. Gesell, A., & Thompson, H. Learning and maturation in identical infant twins: An experimental analysis by the method of co-twin control. In Barker, Kounin. & Wright. *Child behavior and development*. New York: McGraw Hill, 1943, 209–227.

15. Gesell, A., & Ames, L. B. *Twins T and C: Similarities of behavior.* Films distributed by Encyclopaedia Britannica, 1941.

16. Gesell, A., & Ames, L. B. *Twins T and C: Differences of behavior.* Film distributed by Encyclopaedia Britannica, 1941.

17. Gesell, A. The method of co-twin control. *Science*, 1942, 94, 446–448.

18. Gesell, A. The method of co-twin control in conjunction with the

method of cinemanalysis. *Acta Geneticae Medicae et Gemellologiae*, 1952, *1*, 25–28.

CHAPTER 8

1. Gesell, A. Mental and physical correspondence in twins. *Scientific Monthly*, 1922, *14*, 305–344.
2. Gesell, A. The nursery school movement. *School and Society*, 1924, *20*, 644–652.
3. Gesell, A. The ontogenetic patterning of infant behavior: a psychomorphological approach to the problem of constitution and type. In *The biology of the individual*. Baltimore: Williams & Wilkins, 1933, 68–80.
4. Gesell, A. Child development and individuality. In P. Kaufman (Ed.), *Understanding ourselves*. U.S. Dept. Agriculture, 1938, 11–20.
5. Gesell, A. et al. *Biographies of child development*. New York: Hoeber, 1939, xvii + 328.
6. Watson, J. B. *Psychological care of infant and child*. New York: Norton, 1928.
7. Gesell, A. The teacher-pupil relationship in a democracy. *School and Society*. 1940, *51*, 193–198.
8. Gesell, A. et al. *The first five years of life*. New York: Harper, 1940, xiii + 393.
9. Gesell, A., Ilg, F. L., Ames, L. B., & Learned, J. *Infant and child in the culture of today*. New York: Harper, 1943, xii + 399.
10. Gesell, A. What makes for likenesses and differences in children? *Childhood Education*, 1945, *21*, 195–196.
11. Gesell, A. *How a baby grows*. New York: Harper, 1945, vii + 78.
12. Gesell, A., assisted by L. B. Ames. Early evidences of individuality in the human infant. *The Scientific Monthly*, 1937, xiv, 217–225.
13. Gesell, A., & Thompson, H. Twins T and C from infancy to adolescence. A biogenetic study of individual differences by the method of co-twin control. *Genetic Psychology Monographs*, 1941, *24*, 3–121.
14. Sheldon, W. H. *Varieties of human physique*. New York: Harper, 1940, xii + 347.
15. Gesell, A., Ilg, F. L., Ames, L. B., & Bullis, G. *The child from five to ten*. New York: Harper, 1946, xii + 475.
16. Gesell, A., Ilg, F. L., & Ames, L. B. *Youth: The years from ten to sixteen*. New York: Harper, 1956, xv + 542.
17. Gesell, A. The development of personality: Moulding your child's character. *The Delineator*, April 1925, 3–8.

18. Gesell, A. *Infancy and human growth.* New York: Macmillan, 1928, xvii + 418.

CHAPTER 9

1. Gesell, A. A clinical preschool psychology. *Mother and Child,* 1923, *2,* 64–66.
2. Gesell, A. Mental development in infancy: Its measurement and hygiene. New York Times, January 21, 1923.
3. Gesell, A. The nursery school movement. *School and Society,* 1924, *517,* 644–652.
4. Gesell, A. The early diagnosis of mental deficiency. *The Medical Review of Reviews,* 1925, *4,* 192–194.
5. Gesell, A. Developmental diagnosis in infancy. *Boston Medical and Surgical Journal,* 1925, *192,* 1058–1060.
6. Gesell, A. Monthly increments of development in infancy. *Pedagogical Seminary and Journal Genetic Psychology,* 1925, *32,* 203–208.
7. Gesell, A. A comparative method for demonstration of normal development in infancy. *Journal American Medical Association,* 1926, *86,* 1277–1281.
8. Gesell, A. *The mental growth of the pre-school child: A psychological outline of normal development from birth to the sixth year, including a system of developmental diagnosis.* New York: Macmillan, 1925, x + 447.
9. Gesell, A., Thompson, H., & Amatruda, C. S. *Infant behavior: Its genesis and growth.* New York: McGraw-Hill, 1934, viii + 343.
10. Gesell, A., Thompson, H., & Amatruda, C. S. *An atlas of infant behavior: Normative series.* New Haven, Conn: Yale University Press, 1934, 1–524.
11. Gesell, A., & Thompson, H. *The psychology of early growth, including norms of infant behavior and a method of genetic analysis.* New York: Macmillan, 1938, ix + 290.
12. Gesell, A. et al. *The first five years of life. A guide to the study of the preschool child.* New York: Harper, 1940, xiii + 393.
13. Gesell, A., & Amatruda, C. S. *Developmental diagnosis: A manual of clinical methods and applications designed for the use of students and practitioners of medicine.* New York: Paul S. Hoeber, Inc., Medical Book Department of Harper & Row, 1941, xiii + 447.
14. Gesell, A., & Amatruda, C. S. *Developmental diagnosis.* Knobloch, Hilda and Pasamanick, Benjamin (Eds.) New York: Medical Department of Harper & Row, 1974., xxv + 538.

15. Knobloch, H., Stevens, F., & Malone, A. F. *Manual of developmental diagnosis.* New York: Harper & Row, 1980, xiii + 286.

16. Ilg, F. L., & Ames, L. B. *School readiness: Behavior tests used at the Gesell Institute.* New York: Harper & Row, 1964, xv + 396.

17. Ames, L. B., Gillespie, C., Haines, J., & Ilg, F. L. *The Gesell Institute's child from one to six: Evaluating the behavior of the preschool child.* New York: Harper & Row, 1979, xi + 228.

18. Haines, J., Ames, L. B., & Gillespie, C. *The Gesell preschool test manual.* Lumberville, Pa.: Modern Learning Press, 1980, 1–70.

CHAPTER 10

1. Gesell, A. *The preschool child.* New York: Houghton Mifflin, 1923, xvi + 264.

2. Gesell, A. *The mental growth of the preschool child.* New York: Harper, 1925, x + 447.

3. Gesell, A. Psychological guidance in child adoption. *A pamphlet for the Children's Bureau,* U.S. Dept. of Labor, Washington, D.C.: Government Printing Office, 1926, 1–12.

4. Gesell, A. Reducing the risks of child adoption. *Bulletin Child Welfare League of American,* 1927, vol. *6,* no. 6, 1–2.

5. Gesell, A. *Infancy and human growth.* New York: Macmillan, 1928, xvii + 418.

6. Gesell, A. *The guidance of mental growth in infant and child.* New York: Macmillan, 1930, xi + 322.

7. Gesell, A. et al. *Biographies of child development.* New York: Hoeber, 1939, xvii + 328.

8. Gesell, A., & Amatruda, C. S. *Developmental diagnosis.* New York: Hoeber, 1941, xiii + 447.

9. Gesell, A. Pediatrics and the clinical protection of child development. *Journal of Pediatrics,* December 1941, *19,* 6, 755–761.

10. Gesell, A. *Child adoption in Connecticut.* New Haven, Conn.: Child Welfare Association, 1943, pp. 1–9.

11. Dr. Gesell of Yale tells why Senate Bill 117, eliminating compulsory investigation prior to adoption should not pass. In *Under the Golden Dome,* vol. *5,* no. 11, March 17, 1947, New Haven Conn.: Connecticut Child Welfare Association, March 17, 1947, 1–4.

12. Gesell, A. *Studies in child development.* New York: Harper, 1948, x + 224.

13. Knoblock, H., & Pasamanick, B. *Gesell and Amatruda's Developmental Diagnosis* (3rd. ed.) Hagerstown: Harper & Row, 1974.

CHAPTER 11

1. Gesell, A. The significance of the pre-school age for school hygiene. *Proceedings of the 12th American Congress of the American School Hygiene Association*, 1921, *9*, 24–31.

2. Gesell, A. *The preschool child from the standpoint of public hygiene and education*. Boston: Houghton Mifflin Co., 1923, vii + 264.

3. Gesell, A. The preschool child as a health problem. In Harriet Wedgewood (Ed.), *School health supervision*, Washington, D.C.: Department of the Interior, Bureau of Education, 1924, 6–8.

4. Gesell, A. Preschool development and education. *The Annals of the American Academy of Political and Social Science. New Values in Child Welfare*, 1925, *121*, 146–150.

5. Gesell, A. The nursery school movement and home economics. *Journal of Home Economics*, 1925, *17*, 7, 369–371.

6. Gesell, A. The preschool child and the present-day parent. *Proceedings of the Midwest Conference on Parent Education*, March, 1926, 332–334.

7. Gesell, A. Normal growth as a public health concept. *Public Health Nurse*, 1926, *18*, 394–399.

8. Gesell, A. The organization of child guidance and developmental supervision. *Mental Hygiene*, 1929, *13*, 4, 780–787.

9. Gesell, A. Child mental welfare paramount. *Michigan Education Journal*, 1929, *7*, 164–165.

10. Gesell, A. A decade of progress in the mental hygiene of the preschool child. *Annals of the American Academy of Political and Social Science*, 1930, *151*, 143–148.

11. Gesell, A. *The guidance of mental growth in infant and child*. New York: Macmillan, 1930, xi + 322.

12. Gesell, A. The educational status of the preschool child. *School and Society*, 1934, *39*, 495–500.

13. Gesell, A. Cinema as an instrument for parent education. *Parent Education*, 1935, *2*, 8, 9.

14. Gesell, A. Pediatrics and the clinical protection of child development. *Journal of Pediatrics*, 1941, *19*, 755–761.

15. Gesell, A. *A handbook for the Yale Films of Child Development*, privately printed, 1934, 15 pp.

16. Gesell, A. et al. *The first five years of life*. New York: Harper, 1940, xiii + 393.

17. Gesell, A., Ilg, F. L., Ames, L. B., & Learned, J. *Infant and child in the culture of today*. New York: Harper, 1943, xi + 399.

18. Gesell, A. *How a baby grows: A story in pictures*. New York: Harper, 1945, vii + 78.

19. Gesell, A., Ilg, F. L., Ames, L. B., & Bullis, G. *The child from five to ten.* New York: Harper, 1946, xii + 475.
20. Gesell, A., Ilg, F. L., & Ames, L. B. *Youth: The years from ten to sixteen.* New York: Harper, 1956, xv + 542.
21. Ames, L. B. *Child care and development.* Philadelphia: Lippincott, 1970, xii + 426.
22. Gesell, A. The nursery school movement and home economics. *Journal Home Economics*, 1925, *7*, 369–371.

CHAPTER 12

1. Gesell, A. The nursery school movement. *School and Society*, 1924, *20*, 644–652.
2. Gesell, A. The significance of the pre-school age for school hygiene. *Proceedings of the 13th Congress of American School Hygiene Association*, 1921, *9*, 24–31.
3. Gesell, A. The preschool child: His social significance. *The Annals of the American Academy Political and Social Science.* January 1923, *105*, 277–280.
4. Gesell, A. The pre-school child as a health problem. *American Journal of Nursing*, 1923, 1–4.
5. Gesell, A. The pre-school age and school entrance. *Department of the Interior, Bureau of Education*, 1924, 6–8.
6. Gesell, A. Preschool development and education. *The Annals of the American Academy of Political and Social Science. New Values in Child Welfare.* September 1925, *121*, 148–150.
7. Gesell, A. The downward extension of the kindergarten: A unified policy for early education. *Childhood Education*, October 1945, *11*, 53–59.
8. Gesell, A. The nursery school movement and home economics. *Journal of Home Economics*, July 1925, *17*, 369–371.
9. Gesell, A., & Lord, E. E. A psychological comparison of nursery school children from homes of low and high economic status. *Pedagogical Seminary Journal of Genetic Psychology*, September 1927, *34*, 339–356.
10. Gesell, A. The guidance nursery of the Yale Psycho-Clinic. *Journal National Education Association*, April 1929, *18*, 105–106.
11. Gesell, A. A decade of progress in the mental hygiene of the preschool child. *The Annals of the American Academy of Political and Social Sciences*, 1930, *151*, 143–148.
12. Gesell, A. The New Haven Child Care Center: An account of its origins and organization. *Childhood Education*, April 1943, *19*, 366–370.

13. Gesell, A., Ilg, F. L., Ames, L. B., & Rodell, J. L. *Infant and child in the culture of today: The Guidance of Development in Home and Nursery School.* New York: 1943. (Rev. ed., 1974), xii + 420.

14. Pitcher, E. G., & Ames, L. B. *The guidance nursery school: A Gesell Institute book for teachers and parents.* New York: Harper, 1946 (Rev ed., 1975), xii + 319.

Chapter 13

1. Gesell, A. *The preschool child from the standpoint of public hygiene and education.* Boston: Houghton Mifflin, 1923.

2. Gesell, A., & Abbott, J. W. *The kindergarten and health education. No. 14.* Department of the Interior Bureau of Education. Washington, D.C., 1923.

3. Gesell, A. The preschool child as a health problem. *American Journal of Nursing,* 1923, p. 8.

4. Gesell, A. Normal growth as a public health concept. *Public Health Nurse.* July 1926, 394–399.

5. Gesell, A. *Infancy and Human Growth.* New York: Macmillan, 1928, xvii + 418.

6. Gesell, A. The mental welfare of normal infants. *Public Health Nursing,* 1934, *5,* 229–232.

7. Gesell, A. et al. *Atlas of infant behavior,* Vol. 2. New Haven, Conn.: Yale University Press, 1934. 525–922.

8. Gesell, A. The psychological factor in infant feeding. *Bulletin Internationale pour la Protection de l'enfance.* August 1937, no. *147,* pp. 22–26.

9. Gesell, A., & Ilg, F. L. *Feeding behavior of infants.* Philadelphia: Lippincott, 1937, ix + 201.

10. Gesell, A. et al. *Biographies of child development.* New York: Hoeber, 1939, xvii + 328.

11. Gesell, A. et al. *The first five years of life.* New York: Harper, 1940, xiii + 396.

12. Gesell, A. & Amatruda, C. S. *Developmental diagnosis.* New York: Hoeber, 1941, xiii + 447.

13. Gesell, A. Pediatrics and the clinical protection of child development. *Journal of Pediatrics,* December 1941, *19,* 6, 753–761.

14. Gesell, A., & Ilg, F. L. *Infant and child in the culture of today.* New York: Harper, 1943, xii + 399.

15. Spock, B. *The common sense book of baby and child care.* New York: Duell, Sloan & Pearce, 1945, 1–527.

16. Spock, B. Monthly article in *Red Book Magazine*, October 1963, p. 124.
17. Spock, B. Monthly article in *Red Book Magazine*, June 1974, p. 29.
18. Gesell, A., & Ilg, F. L. *The child from five to ten*. New York: Harper & Row, 1946, xii + 475.
19. Gesell, A., & Ames, L. B. *Bottle and cup feeding*. Encyclopaedia Britannica silent film, 400 feet, 16 mm., 1947.
20. Gesell, A., & Ames, L. B. *The conquest of the spoon*. Encyclopaedia Britannica silent film, 400 feet, 16 mm., 1947.
21. Gesell, A. Developmental pediatrics: Its tasks and possibilities. *Pediatrics*, March 1949, *1*, 331–336.
22. Spock, B. Monthly column in *Red Book Magazine*. (Date unknown).
23. Gesell, A., Ilg, F. L., & Ames, L. B. *Infant and child in the culture of today*. (rev. ed.) New York: Harper & Row, 1976.
24. Gesell, A., Ilg, L. & Ames, L. B. *Youth: The years from ten to sixteen*. New York: Harper, 1956, xv + 542.

CHAPTER 14

1. Gesell, A. Developmental diagnosis in infancy. *Boston Medical and Surgical Journal*, 1925, *192*, 1058–1064.
2. Gesell, A. Infant behavior in relation to pediatrics. *American Journal of Diseases Children*, 1929, *37*, 1055–1075.
3. Gesell, A. Pediatrics and the supervision of child development. *Journal Pediatrics*, 1932, *1*, 38–45.
4. Gesell, A. Diagnosis and supervision of mental growth in infancy. In Brenneman (Ed.), *Practice of Pediatrics*, (Vol. I). Hagerstown, Md.: W.F. Prior Co., 1936, Chapter IX.
5. Gesell, A. Developmental diagnosis and clinical medicine. *Digest of Treatment*, May 1940, 840–841.
6. Miles, W. R. *Arnold Lucius Gesell: 1880–1961. A biographical memoir*. Reprinted from *Biographical Memoirs*, Vol. *xxxvii*, published for The National Academy of Sciences of the United States. New York: Columbia University Press, 1964, 1–96.
7. Gesell, A., & Amatruda, C. S. *Developmental diagnosis: A manual of clinical methods and applications designed for the use of students and practitioners of medicine*. New York: Paul B. Hoeber, Inc., 1941, xii + 447.
8. Gesell, A. Pediatrics and the clinical protection of child development. *Journal of Pediatrics*, 1941, *19*, 6, pp. 755–761.
9. Gesell, A. et al. Panel discussion on clinical aspects of growth and development. Boston, October 11, 1941. 11th annual meeting of the

American Academy of Pediatrics. *Journal of Pediatrics*, 1942, *20*, 259–278.

10. Gesell, A. Developmental pediatrics: Its task and possibilities. *Pediatrics*, 1948, *1*, pp. 331–335.

11. Gesell, A. Developmental diagnosis and supervision. (Rev.) Brenneman (Ed.), *Practice of pediatrics*, Vol. I. Hagerstown, Md.: W. F. Prior Co., 1942, Chapter IX, 1–29.

12. Gesell, A. Developmental pediatrics. *Journal of Pediatrics*, 1947, *30*, 188–220.

13. Gesell, A. Developmental diagnosis of infant and child: Its role in clinical medicine. *Postgraduate Medicine*, 1947, *1*, 29–35.

14. Gesell, A. The pediatrician and the public. *Pediatrics*, 1951, *8*, 734–737.

Chapter 15

1. Gesell, A. Preschool development and education. *The Annals of the American Academy of Political and Social Science*, 1925, *121*, p. 148–150.

2. Gesell, A. Cinema as an instrument for parent education. *Parent Education*, 1935, *2*, pp. 8, 9.

3. Gesell, A. et al. *An atlas of infant behavior*, Vols. I & II. New Haven, Conn.: Yale University Press, 1934, 1–922.

4. Gesell, A. Infant behavior researches of the Yale Clinic of Child Development. *Proceedings of the International Congress on Education for the Deaf*, 1933, 536–542.

5. Gesell, A., & Halverson, H. M. The development of thumb opposition in the human infant. *Journal Genetic Psychology*, 1936, *48*, 339–361.

6. Gesell, A., & Ames, L. B. Early evidences of individuality in the human infant. *Science Monthly*, 1937, *xlv*, 217–225.

7. Gesell, A., & Ames, L. B. The ontogenetic organization of prone behavior in human infancy. *Journal Genetic Psychology*, 1940, *56*, 247–263.

8. Gesell, A., & Halverson, H. M. The daily maturation of infant behavior. A cinema study of postures, movements and laterality. *Journal Genetic Psychology*, 1942, *61*, 3–32.

9. Gesell, A., & Ames, L. B. Ontogenetic correspondences in the supine and prone postures of the human infant. *Yale Journal Biology and Medicine*, 1943, *15*, 565–573.

10. Gesell, A., & Ames, L. B. The development of handedness. *Journal Genetic Psychology*, 1947, *70*, 155–175.

11. Gesell, A., & Ames, L. B. The infant's reaction to his mirror image. *Journal Genetic Psychology*, 1947, *70*, 141–154.

12. Gesell, A. *The mental growth of the pre-school child.* New York: Macmillan, 1925, x + 447.

13. Gesell, A. Photographic studies in child development: A clinical study of early mental growth. (Reference and reprint lost).

14. Gesell, A. Cinemanalysis: A method of behavior study. *Journal Genetic Psychology*, 1935, *47*, 3-16.

15. Gesell, A. Cinematology and the study of child development. *American Naturalist*, 1946, *lxxx*, 470–475.

16. Gesell, A. The method of co-twin control in conjunction with cinemanalysis. *Acta Geneticae Medicae et Gemellogigiae*, 1952, *1*, 25–28.

17. Gesell, A., & Ames, L. B. *The story of child development in motion pictures. A guide to the study and interpretation of the Yale Films of Child Development.* New York: Encyclopaedia Britannica Films Inc., 1947, 1–40.

18. Gesell, A. *Infancy and human growth.* New York: Macmillan, 1928, xvii + 418.

19. Gesell, A., Thompson, H., & Amatruda, C. S. *Infant behavior: Its genesis and growth.* New York: McGraw Hill, 1934, viii + 343.

20. Gesell, A. The ontogenetic patterning of infant behavior: A psychomorphological approach to the problem of constitution and type. In *The biology of the individual.* Baltimore: Williams & Wilkins, 1933, 68–80.

21. Gesell, A. A comparative method for demonstration of normal development in infancy. *Journal American Medical Association*, 1926, *86*, 1277–1281.

22. Gesell, A., & Gesell, B. C. *The normal child and primary education.* New York: Ginn & Co., 1912, x + 342.

23. Gesell, A. Developmental diagnosis in infancy. *Boston Medical and Surgical Journal*, 1925, *22*, 1058–1064.

24. Gesell, A. *The guidance of mental growth in infant and child.* New York: Macmillan, 1930, xi + 322.

25. Gesell, A., & Ilg, F. L. *The feeding behavior of infants.* Philadelphia: Lippincott, 1937, ix + 201.

26. Gesell, A., & others. *The first five years of life.* New York: Harper, 1940, xiii + 393.

27. Gesell, A. Plan your child's pictures. *Popular Photography*, 1940, September, pp. 30–31, 94–96.

28. Gesell, A. *How a baby grows.* New York: Harper, 1945, vii + 78.

29. Gesell, A., & Amatruda, C. S. *The embryology of behavior.* New York: Harper, 1945, xix + 289.

30. Gesell, A., Ilg, F. L., & Bullis, G. *Vision: Its devlopment in infant and child.* New York: 1949, xvi + 329.
31. Gesell, A. *Infant development: The embryology of early human behavior.* New York: Harper, 1952, xi + 108.
32. Gesell, A. *Arnold Gesell: My contribution to a history of psychology in autobiography.* Worcester, Mass.: Clark University Press, 1952, *4*, 123–142.

CHAPTER 16

1. Gesell, A. *The mental growth of the preschool child.* New York: Macmillan, 1925, x + 447.
2. Gesell, A. *Infancy and human growth.* New York: Macmillan, 1928, xvii + 418.
3. Gesell, A. *Guidance of mental growth in infant and child.* New York: Macmillan, 1930, xi + 322.
4. Gesell, A. The ontogenetic patterning of infant behavior. *The Proceedings of the Association for Research in Nervous and Mental Disease, xiv,* December 1933, 68–80.
5. Gesell, A. The tonic neck reflex in the human infant. *The Journal of Pediatrics,* 1938, *13*, 4, 455–464.
6. Gesell, A. Reciprocal interweaving in neuro-motor development. *Journal Comparative Neurology,* 1939, *70*, 2, 161–180.
7. Gesell, A. et al. *The first five years of life.* New York: Harper, 1940, xiii + 393.
8. Gesell, A., in collaboration with Amatruda, C. S. *Embryology of behavior.* New York: Harper, 1945, xix + 289.
9. Gesell, A. Arnold Gesell—Autobiography. In *A history of psychology in autobiography.* Worcester, Mass.: Clark University Press, 1952, *4*, 123–142.
10. Gesell, A. Ontogenesis of infant behavior. In L. Carmichael (Ed.) *Handbook of Child Psychology.* New York: Wiley, 1946, Chapter 6, 295–331.
11. Gesell, A., & Ames, L. B. Tonic-neck reflex and symmetro-tonic reflex. *The Journal of Pediatrics,* 1950, *36*, 2, 165–176.
12. Gesell, A. et al. A film entitled *Embryology of behavior.* Produced by the Medical Film Institute. Published by the International Film Bureau, Chicago, Ill. ca. 1952.
13. Gesell, A. Behavior patterns of fetal-infant and child. *Proceedings of the Association for Research in Nervous and Mental Diseases,* 1954, *33*, 114–126.

CHAPTER 17

1. Rosenblith, J., & Sims-Knight, J. H. *In the beginning: Development in the first two years*. Monterey, CA: Brooks/Cole, 1985, ix + 565.
2. Gesell, A. *Mental growth of the preschool child*. New York: Macmillan, 1925, x + 447.
3. Gesell, A. *Infancy and human growth*. New York: Macmillan, 1928, xvii + 418.
4. Gesell, A., & Thompson, H. *Infant behavior*. New York: McGraw Hill, 1934, viii + 343.
5. Gesell, A., & Thompson, H. *The psychology of early growth*. New York: Macmillan, 1938, ix + 290.
6. Gesell, A., & Amatruda, C. S. *Developmental diagnosis*. New York: Paul B. Hoeber, 1941, xiii + 447.
7. Slosson, R. L. *Slosson Intelligence Test (SIT) for children and adults*. East Aurora, New York: Slosson Educational Publications, 1963, vii + 26.
8. Wechsler, D. *WISC-R Manual. Wechsler Intelligence Scale for Children*. Revised. New York: The Psychological Corporation, 1974, vii + 191.
9. Ilg, F. L., & Ames, L. B. *School readiness*. New York: Harper & Row, 1964, xxi + 396.
10. Gesell, A. and others. *Biographies of child development*. New York: Paul B. Hoeber, 1939, xvii + 328.
11. Ames, L. B. Predictive value of infant behavior examinations. In *Exceptional infant—The normal infant*. Vol. 1. Seattle Washington: Special Child Publications, 1967, 209–239.

CHAPTER 18

1. Gesell, A. Normal growth as a public health policy. *Public Health Nurse*, 1926, *18*, 394–399.
2. Gesell, A. *Infancy and human growth*. New York: Macmillan, 1928, xvii + 418.
3. Gesell, A. The individual in infancy. In C. Murchison (Ed.), *Foundations of experimental psychology*. Worcester, Mass.: Clark University Press, 1929, 628–660.
4. Gesell, A. The ontogenetic patterning of infant behavior: A psychomorphological approach to the problem of constitution and type. In *Biology of the individual*. Baltimore: Williams & Wilkins, 1933, *14*, 66–80.

5. Gesell, A., & Thompson, H. *Infant behavior: Its genesis and growth.* New York: McGraw-Hill, 1934, viii + 343.

6. Gesell, A. et al. *Biographies of child development.* New York: Hoeber, 1939, xvii + 328.

7. Gesell, A. The stability of mental growth careers. In *National Society for Study of Education,* 39th Yearbook, 1940, *39* (2), 149–160.

8. Gesell, A. The documentation of infant behavior and its relation to cultural anthropology. *Proceedings 8th American Scientific Congress, Anthropological Sciences,* 1942, *2,* 279–291.

9. Gesell, A. What makes for likenesses and differences in children? *Childhood Education,* 1945, *21,* 195–196.

10. Gesell, A. *How a baby grows.* New York: Harper, 1945, vii + 78.

11. Gesell, A. Human infancy and the ontogenesis of behavior. *American Scientist,* 1949, *37,* 529–553.

12. Gesell, A., Ilg, F. L., & Ames, L. B. *Youth: The years from ten to sixteen.* New York: Harper, 1956, xv + 542.

13. Gesell, A. *Wolf child and human child: A narrative interpretation of the life history of Kamala, the wolf girl.* New York: Harper, 1941, xvi + 107.

14. Gesell, A. The biography of a wolf-child. *Harper's Magazine,* January 1941, no. 1088, 189–193.

CHAPTER 19

1. Gesell, A. *Infancy and human growth.* New York: Macmillan, 1928, xvii + 418.

2. Gesell, A. *The guidance of mental growth in infant and child.* New York: Macmillan, 1930, xi + 322.

3. Gesell, A. The influence of prematurity on mental growth. *White House Conference,* Part IV, 1932.

4. Gesell, A. The mental growth of the prematurely born infant. *Journal of Pediatrics,* June 1933, *2,* 6, 676–680.

5. Gesell, A. et al. *Biographies of child development.* New York: Harper, 1939, xvii + 328.

6. Gesell, A. The genesis of behavior form in fetus and infant. *Proceedings of the American Philosophical Society,* 1941, *84,* 471–488.

7. Gesell, A. & Amatruda, C. S. *Developmental diagnosis.* New York: Paul B. Hoeber 1941, + 447.

8. Gesell, A. in collaboration with Amatruda, C. S. *The embryology of behavior.* New York: Harper, 1945, xix + 289.

9. Gesell, A. Behavior aspects of the care of the premature infant. *The Journal of Pediatrics*, August 1946, *29*, 2, 210–212.
10. Gesell, A. Behavior patterns of fetal-infant and child. *Proceedings Association for Research in Nervous and Mental Diseases*, 1954, *33*, 114–126.

CHAPTER 20

1. Gesell, A., et al. *The First Five Years of Life: A Guide to the Study of the Preschool Child.* New York: Harper, 1940, xiii + 393.
2. Gesell, A., & Ilg, F. L. In collaboration with L. B. Ames and J. Learned. *Infant and Child in the Culture of Today.* New York: Harper, 1943, xii + 399.
3. Gesell, A. Reciprocal interweaving in neuro-motor development: A principle of spiral organization shown in the patterning of infant behavior. *Journal of Comparative Neurology*, 1939, *70*, 161–180.
4. Gesell, A. Ontogenesis of infant behavior. *In Handbook of child psychology*, New York: L. Carmichael (Ed.). John Wiley, 1946, Chapter 6, pp. 295–331.
5. Ilg, F. L., Learned, J. Lockwood, A., & Ames, L. B. The three-and-a-half year old. *Journal Genetic Psychology*, 1949, *75*, 21–31.
6. Gesell, A., & Ilg, F. L. In collaboration with L. B. Ames & G. Bullis. *The child from five to ten.* New York: Harper, 1946, xii + 475.
7. Gesell, A. Human infancy and the ontogenesis of behavior. *American Scientist*, 1949, *37*, 529–553.
8. Ames, L. B., & Ilg, F. L. The developmental point of view with special reference to the principle of reciprocal neuromotor interweaving. *Journal of Genetic Psychology*, 1964, *105*, 195–209.
9. Gesell, A., Ilg, F. L., & Ames, L. B. *Youth: The years from ten to sixteen.* New York: Harper, 1956, xv + 542.

CHAPTER 21

1. Gesell, A. Jealousy. Doctoral Dissertation, Clark University. *American Journal of Psychology*, 1906, *17*, 437–496.
2. Gesell, A., Ilg, F. L. In collaboration with L. B. Ames & G. Bullis. *The child from five to ten.* New York: Harper, 1946, xii + 475.
3. Gesell, A. *Guidance of mental growth in infant and child.* New York: Macmillan, 1930, xi + 322.

4. Gesell, A., & Ilg, F. L. *Feeding behavior of infants.* Philadelphia: Lippincott, 1937, x + 201.

5. Gesell, A., & others. *Biographies of child development.* New York: Hoeber, 1939, xvi + 328.

6. Gesell, A., & Amatruda, C. S. *Developmental diagnosis: Normal and abnormal child development.* New York: Hoeber, 1941, xiii + 447.

7. Gesell, A., & Ilg, F. L. In collaboration with L. B. Ames & Janet Learned. *Infant and child in the culture of today.* New York: Harper, 1943, xii + 399.

8. Gesell, A., Ilg, F. L., & Ames, L. B. *Youth: The years from ten to sixteen.* New York: Harper, 1956, xv + 542.

9. Gesell, A. *The mental growth of the preschool child.* New York: Macmillan, 1925, x + 447.

10. Gesell, A., & Thompson, H. *Infant behavior: Its genesis and growth.* New York: McGraw Hill, 1934, viii + 343.

11. Gesell, A., & others. *The first five years of life.* New York: Harper, 1940, xiii + 393.

12. Gesell, A. The fears of children. *Public Health Nursing*, 1938, *30*, 586–589.

13. Gesell, A. *How a baby grows: A story in pictures.* New York: Harper, 1945, vii + 78.

14. Gesell, A. Pediatrics and child psychiatry. *Pediatrics*, 1949, *4*, 670–675.

Chapter 22

1. Gesell, A. The ontogenesis of infant behavior. In *Manual of child psychology.* L. Carmichael (Ed.). New York: John Wiley & Sons, 1946, pp. 295–331.

2. Ames, L. B. The sequential patterning of prone progression in the human infant. *Genetic Psychology Monographs*, Nov. 1957, *19*, 409–460.

3. Gesell, A., & Ames, L. B. The ontogenetic organization of prone behavior in human infancy. *Journal Genetic Psychology*, June, 1940, *56*, 247–263.

4. Gesell, A., & Ilg, F. L. *Infant and child in the culture of today.* New York: Harper, 1940, xii + 399.

5. Gesell, A., & Ilg, F. L. *The child from five to ten.* New York: Harper, 1946, xii + 475.

6. Gesell, A., Ilg, F. L., & Ames, L. B. *Youth: The years from ten to sixteen.* New York: Harper, 1956, xv + 542.

7. Gesell, A., & Ilg, F. L. *Feeding behavior of infants*. Philadelphia: Lippincott, 1937, xii + 201.
8. Salkind, N. J. *Theories of human development*. (2nd. ed.). New York: John Wiley & Sons, 1985, 44–47.
9. Salkind, N. J. *ibid.*, p. 253.

CHAPTER 23

1. Editor, *American Scientist*. Brief biography of Dr. Gesell in relation to his article, Human infancy and the ontogenesis of behavior. *American Scientist*, 1949, *37*, 4, 529–553.
2. Gross, M. Z. Men of Medicine. He made a science of child development. *Postgraduate Medicine*, 1963, *12*, 2, 179–184.
3. Pasamanick, B. Arnold Gesell on his eightieth birthday. Foreword to issue dedicated to Dr. Gesell in honor of his work. *Child Development*, 1960, *31*, 2, 241–242.
4. *Time Magazine*. For Freud, for Society, for Yale. March 6, 1939 (Under "Education").
5. *Pageant Magazine*, July 1952, 5–11.
6. Pollack, J. H. Meet Dr. Gesell—The man who knows children. *Parents Magazine*, March 1954, 43, 66–80.
7. Puner, H. Gesell's children grow up. *Harper's Magazine*, March 1956, 37–43.
8. Brody, S. Theory and research in child development. *The Journal of Nursing Education*, Winter 1959, 3–13.
9. *New Haven Register*, May 30, 1961.
10. Gesell, A., & Ilg, F. L. *Infant and child in the culture of today*. New York: Harper, 1943, xii + 390.
11. Gesell, A., & Ilg F. L. *The child from five to ten*. New York: Harper, 1946, xii + 475.
12. Gesell, A., Ilg, F. L., & Ames, L. B. *Youth: The years from ten to sixteen*. New York: Harper, 1956, xv + 542.
13. Miles, W. R. *Arnold Lucius Gesell, 1880–1961: A biographical memoir. Biographical Memoirs*, xxxvii. New York: Columbia University Press, 1964, 96 pp.
14. Gesell, A. Arnold Gesell (1880–   ) Autobiography. In *A history of psychology in autobiography*, Volume IV. Worcester, Mass.: Clark University Press, 1952, 123–142.
15. Kessen, W. *The child*. New York: John Wiley & Sons, 1965, xii + 301.

16. Crain, W. C. *Theories of development: Concepts and applications.* Englewood Cliffs, New Jersey: Prentice Hall, 1980, xvi + 302.
17. Scarr, S. *Mother care, other care.* New York: Basic Books, 1984, xii + 302.
18. Salkind, N. J. *Theories of human development.* New York: John Wiley & Sons, (2nd ed.), 1985, xiv + 270.
19. Hogan, J. D. & Vahey J. D. Modern classics in child development. *Newsletter APA Division on Developmental Psychology,* Spring, 1983, p. 13.

CHAPTER 24

1. Gesell, A., & Gesell, B. *The normal child and primary education.* New York: Ginn & Company, 1912, x + 342.
2. Gesell, A. *The preschool child from the standpoint of public education.* New York: Houghton Mifflin, 1923, xv + 264.
3. Gesell, A. *The mental growth of the preschool child.* New York: Macmillan, 1925, x + 447.
4. Gesell, A. *Pestalozzi and the parent-child relationship.* Reprinted from *Amerikanische Schweizer Zeitung,* October 9, 1946, p. 4.
5. Gesell, A. Pestalozzi: Statement for Pestalozzi Foundation. In *Pestalozzi Foundation Book,* 1947, pp. 28–29.
6. Gesell, A. *The guidance of mental growth in infant and child.* New York: Macmillan, 1930, xi + 322.
7. Gesell, A. A half century of science and the American child. *Child Study,* 1938, *16,* 35–37.
8. Gesell, A. Charles Darwin and child development. *The Scientific Monthly,* December, 1939, *xlix,* 548–553.
9. Gesell, A. *Studies in child development.* New York: Harper, 1948, x + 224.
10. Gesell, A. Arnold Gesell—Autobiography. In *A history of psychology in autobiography.* Volume IV. Worcester, Mass.: Clark University Press, 1952, 123–142.
11. Gesell, A. Genius, giftedness and intelligence. First published in *March of Medicine,* 1942, pp. 100–140. Later published in Gesell, A. *Studies in child development,* New York: Harper, 1948, 137–162.
12. Gesell, A. Introduction to L. A. Warren. *Lincoln's youth: Indiana years —Seven to twenty-one—1816–1830.* Privately printed by the Indiana Historical Society, Indianapolis, 1959, pp. xv–xxii.

CHAPTER 25

1. Gesell, A. Maturation and the patterning of behavior. In C. Murchison (Ed.), *Handbook of child psychology* (2nd ed. rev.). Worcester, Mass.: 1933, pp. 209–235.
2. Gesell, A., & Thompson, H. *Infant behavior: Its genesis and growth.* New York: McGraw Hill, 1934, pp. viii + 343.
3. Gesell, A. Review, J. Piaget, Language and thought in the child. In *Saturday Review of Literature*, August 25, 1928, *5*, p. 72.
4. Gesell, A. Review of J. Piaget, Judgment and reasoning in the child. *Saturday Review of Literature*, October 13, 1928, *5*, p. 208.
5. Gesell, A. Review J. Piaget, The child's concept of the world. In *Saturday Review of Literature*, April 6, 1929, p. 147. (This ref. not certain.)
6. Gesell, A. Review J. Piaget. The child's concept of physical causality. *Saturday Review of Literature*, August 9, 1930, pp. 150/182. (This ref. not certain).
7. Gesell, A. Review J. Piaget, The moral judgment of the child. In *Saturday Review of Literature*, October 7, 1933, *10*, p. 168.
8. Kagan, J. *The nature of the child.* New York: Basic Books, 1984, pp. xii + 309.
9. Mead, M., & Macgregor, F. C. *Growth and culture.* New York: G. P. Putnam's Sons, 1951, xi + 223.
10. Mead, M. On the implications for anthropology of the Gesell-Ilg approach to maturation. *American Anthropologist*, January–March, 1947, *19*, 1, pp. 69–77.
11. Gesell, A., & Gesell, B. *The normal child and primary education.* New York: Ginn & Co., 1912, pp. x + 342.
12. Gesell, A. *The preschool child from the standpoint of public hygiene and education.* New York: Houghton Mifflin, 1923, pp. xv + 264.
13. Gesell, A. Review, B. Spock, Common sense book of baby and child care. New York: Duell, Sloan & Pearce, 1947. *New Haven Register*, June, 1946.
14. Gesell, A. *The guidance of mental growth in infant and child.* New York: Macmillan, 1930, pp. xi + 322.
15. Gesell, A. A half-century of science and the American child. *Child Study*, 1938, *16*, pp. 35–37.
16. Gesell, A. *Infancy and human growth.* New York: Macmillan, 1928, pp. 360–362.
17. Gesell, A. Scientific approach to the study of the human mind. *Science*, September 9, 1938, pp. *2280*, pp. 225–230.

18. Gesell, A. Reciprocal interweaving in neuro-motor development: a principle of spiral organization shown in the patterning of infant behavior. *Journal Comparative Neurology*, 1933, *70*, 2, 161–180.

19. Gesell, A., & Ames, L. B. The ontogenetic organization of prone behavior. *Journal Genetic Psychology*, 1940, *56*, p. 247–263.

20. Gesell, A. The genesis of form in fetus and infant. *Proceedings of the American Philosophic Society*, 1941, *84*, 4, p. 471–488.

21. Gesell, A., & Amatruda, C. S. *The embryology of behavior*. New York: Harper, 1945, xix + 289.

22. Gesell, A. The ontogenesis of infant behavior, In L. Carmichael (Ed.), *Manual of child psychology*. New York: John Wiley, 1946, Chapter 6, pp. 295–331.

23. Gesell, A. A biological psychology. In *Studies in child development*. New York: Harper, 1948, Chapter 10, x + 224.

24. Gesell, A. Arnold Gesell—Autobiography. In *A history of psychology in autobiography*. Vol. IV. Worcester, Mass.: Clark University Press, 1952, pp. 123–142.

INDEX